2

3.⁰⁰

THREE PHASES OF EVE

3⁰⁰

THREE PHASES OF EVE

EVE ARDEN

AN AUTOBIOGRAPHY

ST. MARTIN'S PRESS | NEW YORK

Design by Victoria Hartman

Library of Congress Cataloging in Publication Data
Arden, Eve, 1912–
  Three phase of Eve.
  1. Arden, Eve, 1912– . 2. Actors—United States—
Biography. I. Title.
PN2287.A684A38 1985   792′.028′0924 [B]   85-1692
ISBN 0-312-80267-6

First Edition

10 9 8 7 6 5 4 3 2 1

Many thanks to the following studios for use of their movie and publicity stills: Warner Bros.,
Paramount, Metro Goldwyn-Mayer, Universal, RKO, and Republic.

To my Darling

FOREWORD

• • •

I started this book a couple of years ago, when my daughter Connie expressed a desire to know more about my life than she could remember from her formative years. I had often wished I knew more about my mother than she'd told me. I looked at the wonderful pictures I had of her and thought, I never knew that she'd ridden a horse bareback! So I began my project, in longhand, wearing a deep depression in one end of my favorite couch, as I sat—and sat!

My memories have always remained vivid, perhaps because I've loved living every minute of my life, and now I've enjoyed writing every word of it myself.

In the albums I'd given to each of my children on the occasion of an eighteenth birthday were hundreds of pictures I'd taken of them and also every funny thing they'd said, written on bits of paper and popped into my pockets, word for word to preserve the flavor. The albums were none too originally entitled:

	Liza
THIS IS YOUR LIFE	Connie
	Duncan or
	Douglas

I hope this book brings them, and you, glimpses of mine.

P.S.: Everything in this book is true. Not everything true is in this book! Not enough room!

PART ONE

Part One

CHAPTER
·1·

Early in my life I realized that I was going to have to strive for longevity to crowd in all the kinds of lives I wanted to live. Acting was the only way I knew of accomplishing this. Spying was tempting, with all those disguises and languages and mysterious locales, but being realistic, I feared I lacked the necessary courage.

Because I was the only child of a divorced mother with her own business to run, and the hours were long between the end of the school day and the time when my mother came home from her shop, I filled them with make-believe and reading. Whenever she could, my mother took me to the theater in San Francisco, and my yearnings focused upon that stage.

My mother had had a brief career as an actress many years before. She was studying what was called elocution with a well-known teacher of the day, Leo Cooper, when a theatrical company starring Miss Blanche Bates came to town. They asked for twenty of Mr. Cooper's "ladies" to appear in a costume-ball scene. My mother, who was extraordinarily lovely, was evidently gifted with talent as well; she was selected out of the twenty to join the company and played second leads (shades of her daughter's film career) in the repertoire of plays that followed. When the company was to move on to Australia, they asked my mother to go with them, but Grandfather put his foot down. Being too young for the independence she later developed, she acquiesced and devoted herself to teaching drama to young children.

When I was two, my mother divorced my father because of his incessant gambling, and then realized she was going to have to support the two of us. Since she had great style and was noted for the hats she loved to design and make for herself, she apprenticed herself to the best-known milliner in San Francisco and learned the business in six months. Then she left, taking a trimmer with her, and opened her own shop.

1

When I was a little girl, Mother would almost weekly take me to the Palm Court of San Francisco's Palace Hotel for tea. It was a favorite setting for both of us, and I still remember the large leghorn hat trimmed with rosebuds and narrow velvet ribbons she had made me for the occasion. How proud I was of my beautiful mother in her favorite veiled hat! Our day out together was a joy to both of us. We had great fun studying the people around us and making up stories about them and what their lives were like. Tea-time also turned out to have beneficial side effects for Mother's business, as many of her wealthiest customers came from among the tea-drinking ladies, who would stop by our table and say to her, "Would you mind telling me where you got your lovely hat?" Or, to me: "I would really like to find a hat like that for my little girl."

Mother's business grew to a point where she had very little time to herself or to devote to me. We lived in my grandmother's three-story house on a San Francisco hill. Mother and I occupied a small apartment on the top floor, adjoining a large attic where the laundry was hung to dry on long wire lines. This became my theater, with curtains made from sheets hung by large safety pins, which parted with a satisfying rattle to reveal the "scene" created with furniture dragged from our apartment beyond. The audience consisted of the neighborhood children, who tiptoed quietly up the long winding stairway, past my grandmother's apartment where she was napping, while my mother was busy in her millinery shop a few blocks away.

My "plays" were drawn from an active imagination, and I played all the parts. Since most of the audience was younger than I, no one objected, and when the curtains rattled closed on my improvised tragedy or comedy, the audience trooped down and out, leaving my grandmother none the wiser. On the wall of the stairway to our apartment hung a picture that I credit with my stubborn rejection of my father. It was of a woman who wore her hair like my mother did, in a James Montgomery Flagg knot on top. Her face was hidden in her arms, outstretched on a round table that had obviously been used for gambling, with cards and poker chips lying on it. I had never seen my mother cry and never did hear her complain. Nevertheless, this *was* my mother, and I was outraged that anyone could make her feel such despair.

Then came the best part of my day, the evening, when my mother, happy to be home, cooked delicious-smelling things in the tiny kitchen while I set the table and we chatted about the day's adventures. After dinner, my mother visited her mother while I devoured my current book. The most blissful time of all came when, ready for bed, Mother would curl up with me and, at my pleading, recite all the "pieces" she had once taught her small pupils, or, with further urging, tell me about her experiences in the theater.

Some nights she would go to the opera with a friend, resplendent in his top hat and tails. He had a prickly mustache that stung as he kissed me good night and then swept my mother, ethereal in chiffon and feather boa, out the door. As she threw me a kiss she suppressed a smile, knowing my feelings about this "stuffed shirt."

As the door closed behind them, loneliness and fear would attack me. One day she might leave me alone like this for good. Then what would I do? I remembered a time when we were on the way to visit friends across the bay and had to change trains at a junction. My mother and I accidentally waited on the wrong side of the train. The conductor, seeing us, got off and lifted me aboard. As he turned to pick up our suitcases and assist my mother, the engineer, seeing no one on the right side, started the train. I stood bewildered, then horrified, as I saw my mother left behind forever (in my mind). Standing on the lowest step, I grasped the metal handbar with one hand and frantically clawed at the redwood fence that covered the lethal third rail. My arm full of redwood splinters, I crouched to jump, in spite of my mother's cries, as the train gained momentum. Fortunately, a man aboard, realizing the situation, had stepped onto the car platform and grasped me by the seat of my pants in midair. By this time, the engineer, alerted, had stopped the train and backed up, and my mother and I were reunited. But the fright of losing her stayed with me until I faced the real nightmare of her loss years later.

I started school at Pacific Heights on the top of those famous San Francisco hills, and there I remember a very humiliating experience. Six years old, I sat in the classroom with my hand raised for permission to leave the room. Neatly dressed in white middy-blouse, navy pleated skirt and bloomers to match, over long white stockings (my mother dreaded colds), I tried in vain to catch the teacher's eye. She was a cold fish of a woman, and I was terrified of her. So when she ordered us up on our feet for exercises and acknowledged my flapping hand with a curt "not now," I meekly joined in the knee bends she indicated. "Down, up, down, up,

. . . one, two, one, two," she barked. Then nature thumbed her nose at one who dared to thwart her, and I stood in dripping mortification as navy-blue stripes made their way down my white-clad legs. The giggles around me rose to a crescendo and stiffened my backbone. I pierced the teacher with a daggered look and strode from the room. Schoolbooks dragging behind me on a leather strap, I half stumbled, half slid down the ultra-steep hills while people on the crowded cable cars were pointing and snicker-ing, I was sure. I burst into the millinery shop past the bewildered eyes of my mother and a customer, sharing tea. I hurtled myself into the bathroom and barricaded it against my mother's coaxing tones. How vivid that memory remains, although the only feeling now is one of amusement.

I loathed cooking class because we were forced to eat the con-coctions we made, which always seemed to be codfish cakes. The reward came after school, when I'd take the wicker suitcase that held my apron and cooking utensils, and dash two blocks out of my way, to one of the steepest hills, sit on the suitcase and slide down at an alarming speed, until the wicker would smoke and almost burst into flame. My thrill for the week!

My mother's business was reaching its zenith, and she worried that I wasn't getting the supervision and discipline I needed, so one evening after she'd closed the shop, we went to see the mother superior of a San Francisco convent. It was a dark night, full of wisps of fog, and I was a frightened seven-year-old as we stood before the huge Gothic church and mother rang a bell at the side door leading to the convent. We followed the nun who answered down a long, shadowed hallway and into the office of the mother superior, who sat at her desk writing. She removed her pince-nez and, after greeting my mother, turned her gaze on me. I'm sure she was a lovely woman, but to me she looked as menacing as the Wicked Witch of the West. The severe black-and-white habit and her serious, stern face were from another world I knew only as "Catholic," and that seemed as far away and mysterious as Mars. As the two women discussed tuition and necessary supplies, I sat twisting my long-stockinged-legs around each other and grew more and more apprehensive.

When the big door clanged behind us, shutting out the dark hallway, I threw my arms around my mother's waist and begged her not to send me away, most of all not to that dismal, dreary place. Mother hugged me comfortingly and said she was sure we'd find a happier place where she could come to see me often.

Soon after that, through one of her customers, she found a Dominican convent in San Rafael. About a month later, uniform and other necessities name-tagged and packed, we arrived at the imposing front door of a quite beautiful convent building set deep in a lovely garden.

In the reception room we had a brief visit with the Mother Superior, whose myopic eyes behind thick, steel-framed lenses made her seem even more awesome than the first. My heart pounded with fright and excitement at the imminent departure of my mother and the unknown life that lay ahead. It was decided I should be assigned to the younger children's dormitory and given the responsibility of the two youngest, who were orphans. Perhaps they thought I might feel less lonely that way.

That was very astute, as my desire for siblings had been demonstrated at the age of four, when I kidnapped a baby parked by its trusting mother outside the Mill Valley post office. My Aunt Elsie, whom I was visiting, had followed the mother out and heard her scream of alarm at finding the buggy and the baby gone. Aunt Elsie understood the situation immediately and led her around the corner. There was her niece pushing the sleeping baby rapidly in the direction of home (Aunt Elsie's home). "Nobody wanted it, Auntie!" I whispered guiltily. "They just left it there."

I was happy enough in the convent in the daytime, as we were kept busy with lessons, games, and walks. But night found many a soaked pillow as I cried out my loneliness in the dark room, lit only flickeringly by a single candle, as Sister Ann prepared for bed in her curtained cubicle. It cast an ominous shadow as she removed the headpiece of her habit. Later, we were to play tricks out of curiosity: Did she or didn't she have hair? As soon as the headpiece was removed, one of us would emit a great groan, then when, throwing a towel over her head, she would run to bend over the afflicted one, the occupant of the next bed would give a slight tug on the towel. We only succeeded once in catching a glimpse of the half-inch stubble that looked something like a bad crew cut.

The nuns were strict taskmasters, but the only one I really feared was the French teacher, who had a special talent for striking knuckles with a ruler. On the credit side were Sister Cecile and Sister Evangeline. Sister Cecile played a heck of a baseball game. With her skirts hiked high, she rounded bases like a whippet, while we scrambled for the ball in the outfield. She must have been a blonde, from her light skin and large blue eyes. She was tall, with a relaxed, bony frame, and she made me laugh a lot.

Sister Evangeline was small and dark and very lovely, with a sweet, understanding nature. When I came down with chicken pox, it was she who brought my doll to the infirmary, gave me peppermints, and stayed to visit a while. She won my undying gratitude and the right to be my "crush," a fad among the older girls that I felt must be the "in thing."

Sister Evangeline certainly qualified for a crush, but I must admit my gratitude wasn't all that undying. In assembly the following week, all the girls with crushes were asked to stand, and as I was proudly preparing to proclaim mine, I heard "penances" being handed out and realized that having a crush must be a heinous crime. Coward that I was, I promptly tossed Sister Evangeline to the wolves and prudently retained my seat.

Mother came every weekend and Aunt Elsie on the Wednesday visiting day, and I was allowed one phone call in between. Mother would bring a delicious picnic lunch and we'd take it into a nearby meadow to eat. I was supremely happy just to hear her talk and to gaze at her beautiful face, which unfortunately I hadn't inherited. Auntie, by contrast, made Wednesday a debauch of banana splits, frowned on by Lucille, my mother, and a foray to a nearby toy shop to select a toy or game. I felt guilty at preferring this to my mother's form of entertainment.

Since I was the focus of my mother's life, she was inclined to be overly protective and fearful for my health and safety. My aunt, however, had a deep sense of security due to an early cure of an illness which she attributed to Christian Science, and her faith embraced me as well. Consequently, when I was with my mother, I wore long wool stockings and a sweater and was told to "be careful, dear." At Aunt Elsie's, I ran barefoot in any weather, climbed tall trees, and was encouraged to "try it if you think you can." It produced a kind of dichotomy in my nature, which alternated between derring-do and "dare I do?"

Both women, though, set me examples of generosity in different ways. My mother had a more practical nature and constantly did thoughtful favors and errands for people. Aunt Elsie was lavish in her giving, prodigal with those in need. I remember one of our convent outings when we came out of a toy shop to find two little girls, around eight or nine, with their noses pressed against the window, in which a beautiful doll stood, posed stiffly in organdy and lace. Through adroit questioning, she found that neither girl had ever owned a doll. Ten minutes later, each had selected and was clutching to her bosom her own prettily dressed "child," and I saw expressions on the faces of those "new mothers" that gave me a strange feeling of happiness and taught me vividly that "it is more blessed to give."

My buddy in the convent was an irreverent, adorable Irish girl named Margaret. She had a mop of super-curly copper hair and sapphire-blue eyes. We plotted weekly to run away to a life full of adventure and devoid of penances, but somehow never got beyond the big iron gates.

On the day Margaret received her First Communion, I sat on the center aisle in the incense-laden chapel, bemused by the flowers, the ritual, and the unearthly beauty of the girls in their white dresses and veils. Margaret was a redheaded vision as she received the Host, then stood and turned up the aisle toward me, head bowed over prayer-clasped hands. Suddenly the sharp blue eyes opened, fixed on me, and turned inward in a hideous cross, and a very pink tongue pointed at my horrified gaze. I felt myself the focus of raised eyebrows all around me. To my surprise and, I'm sure, Maggie's disappointment, the incident passed unnoticed.

Every Sunday morning we rose at six and arrayed ourselves in spotless white serge (in contrast to the daily uniform, which was navy with white collars and cuffs) and, as soon as we were dressed, trooped in lines of two through the long, dark halls, clattering down the wide curved stairways into the chapel. There we sat through a long mass, stomachs rumbling and feeling slightly queasy from the incense. Some girls were less equipped to stand the ordeal than others. I remember a morning when one of the older girls sitting behind me, a tall, anemic-looking teenager, fainted and slid under my chair, turning it and me over on top of her. The nuns were moving two by two up the aisle, eyes closed in prayer, and no one moved a muscle to help. There I lay like an impaled bug, unable to struggle off the pin, and certain that I was breaking every bone in that poor girl's body. I can't really remember how I extricated myself, but I can see her being restored with a glass of water and, eventually, breakfast.

At the beginning of my second year at the convent I was finally to be moved to the cubicled dormitory, but because the convent was crowded, I was temporarily placed in one of the high school dorms. Next to me was a strange girl—no, let me reword that: She was weird! One of a family of five girls in the convent, she was admitted by her own sisters to be a little "off." I spent a few nights of anguish as she went through a routine worthy of a horror movie.

After the first night I knew what to expect, and I'd tense up as I heard her enter the cubicle. Then I'd lie frozen with fear as she got into bed. A few minutes later a white hand would appear between the dividing curtains, clutch one and shove it on its rings to one side. By now there was a lump in my throat the size of a duck's egg. She would lie there staring at me with expressionless eyes in her white face. Then slowly the hand would reach out and grab the iron rail of my bed and inexorably draw it next to hers. Then nothing more, just the stare. When finally my fright demanded action, I would leap from the other side and pull my bed back. In bed once more, I would wait in rigor mortis until the whole process was repeated. Finally, she would weary and close her eyes in sleep; but not until a light snore signified my release would my limbs relax and permit me some exhausted rest and uneasy dreams.

Why I suffered all this in silence I can't imagine, unless the alternative, complaining to the nun in charge, was more frightening than the ordeal. However, I was greatly relieved when I was transferred to my new cubicle. Poor dotty girl!

There are little shafts of memory from my two years in the convent. Roller-skating in the courtyard on summer evenings with the sounds of squeals and laughter hanging in the air. The Grotto, where we buried treasure of coins and jewelry and sneaked away occasionally with delicious stealth to dig it up and make sure no one had pilfered it. My first taste of show business when the convent had a pageant in which I appeared as a jewel-bedecked page, with my hair in tight curls under a gold pillbox. I felt like the star of the show.

CHAPTER
·2·

After my second year in the convent, my aunt persuaded my mother to let me live with her in Mill Valley, which was across the bay from San Francisco. Aunt Elsie was my father's sister, but heartily disapproved of his gambling, and she and my mother remained close friends.

Life in the country was full of freedom, with hills and trees to climb and wildflowers to pick. My aunt permitted me to have animals to my heart's content, and that covered a lot of territory: a puppy, a kitten, a canary, and six baby ducklings—and that was only the beginning. I was completely happy living in Mill Valley, which had once been dubbed the little Switzerland of America by Jack London, with its wooded beauty at that time untouched by real estate developers. School was unpressured and joyful, with recess full of giggling girls in gossip sessions, baseball games, mostly coed, and boys walking atop walls, climbing trees, and flexing muscles, intent on impressing the gigglers.

There were recitation contests twice a year, run by the WCTU (Women's Christian Temperance Union). I won a gold medal with a touching rendition in Italian dialect on the horrors of drink. I recall that the lady who introduced me was six inches shorter than I. She was attired in black, with a shiny straw bonnet under which, as she spoke, a fat braid unwound itself from a cow pat and slithered down her back. I felt very mature as I rose and quietly whispered that fact in her ear. I received a grateful upward glance as she deftly wound it back.

Each weekend mother took the Golden Gate ferry to Sausalito and the train to Mill Valley to be with me. She brought me gifts, and I remember a beautiful bisque doll for which she'd had a wig made from the long blond curls I'd recently had cut. She had also sewn her a coat and bonnet of rose-pink velvet trimmed in fur. What bliss! Mother bought a lot next door to Aunt Elsie, on which

9

she built our first home. She followed this by buying the hillside behind it and gradually added four more houses. By the time I started high school, my grandmother had joined us there. Mother then sold her business and retired to oversee me and the houses she'd built.

Two agonizing experiences remain vivid; one in grammar school, and another when I became a sophomore in high school. In the fifth grade, a boy I remember only as Charlie conceived an infatuation for me. I felt a great revulsion for this poor soul because of his constant gaze and his cowed expression, and one day I thought, I wish he was dead.

A week later I stood rooted at our dining room window, from which I could see the marshy reaches of the upper bay and a rowboat in which some men were using grappling hooks to find Charlie's accidentally drowned body. Oh, the guilts we acquire unbeknownst to our parents!

A repetition, only worse, occurred in high school. Standing at the top of the steps leading to the school, a chum and I stopped a pudgy little freshman on her way down to the train waiting to take the commuting students home (who lived as far away as San Rafael). She had thick hair fastened tightly back with a rubber band, which made her look even younger than thirteen. We delayed her to give her a note for her sister, a friend of ours, already aboard the train.

She clattered clumsily down the steps and over to the station, where the train was beginning to move. Running alongside, she jumped on the steps but slipped and fell, rolling off the platform onto the tracks. As the train gained speed, her heavy hair caught in one of the wheels and dragged her with it.

We stood stunned throughout the awful pantomime that followed—the screeching halt of the train, the disentangling of her inert body—and watched her being carried up the stairs into the dean's office. Frantically we tried to inquire about her, but no one had time to answer us. We parted numbly, and I went home where I was greeted by Aunt Elsie with a huge cake. My birthday!

I went through the pretense of being excited by the huge box of presents, unwrapping each and every one. When urged to eat my cake, however, I pleaded a stomachache and made my escape to my room. Later my friend called to report that Janice (that name I remember!) had died, and we cried quietly together in grief and guilt.

That was only the beginning of a couple of weeks in which I barely ate or slept. Both my aunt and my mother suspected something was wrong, but since I wept silently and alone at night, and dissembled during the day, they were not aware of the intensity of my pain. When I'd lost pounds I couldn't afford, my mother became alarmed and kept at me until the dam overflowed and I cried out the trouble in my heart. From that moment, healing set in, but the memory is indelible.

Fortunately, happy experiences are in the majority. There were Dad McClellan's watermelon parties, which I attended annually. A dear old man living alone in a wooden house on the oak-covered hillside behind us, he each year invited all the children of his acquaintance, and we came prepared to wallow. Dad McClellan stayed busy in the kitchen slicing huge, dark-red rounds as our mouths watered. You'd take your slice outside and join the others on the wide veranda steps, already dotted with shiny black seeds. The best thing was that at Dad McClellan's there was no limit! At home, with others to consider, you were lucky to get a second slice. Here you just ate the heart of the slice and dropped the remains into a huge trash basket and went back as often as you could without bursting. It was gluttony to be sure, but oh, how soul-satisfying!

The only comparable time was an after-school watermelon fight at the Gardner twins' hillside house. With their music-teacher mother on her round of piano students, we would don bathing suits. On the lawn under huge redwood trees, we'd bite into the luscious parts of our ammunition, then pelt each other with the remains. Afterward, covered with sweet, sticky pulp and clinging seeds, we'd hose each other clean, and go home with dripping hair in time to do homework and set the table.

Throughout high school, my urge to perform found outlets. I appeared in every form of entertainment that offered itself—short plays, song-and-dance skits; I even staged and performed in an occasional musical comedy. The climax was the senior play, in which I played the title role of *Dulcy,* the comedy in which Lynn Fontanne had made her debut several years before.

I was madly in love with my leading man, who double-crossed me by inviting the cutest girl in school to attend the senior prom. Unexpectedly, I was asked to be the date of a "real college boy" from Stanford, to whom I almost lost my virginity in a hand-to-hand struggle in a niche outside the gymnasium—nobody told me he drank! A friend and her date delivered me safely home.

CHAPTER
·3·

Not long after graduation and my triumph in the senior play, I was invited to dinner at the San Francisco home of friends of my mother. I thought it strange that she wasn't invited, and I think she was puzzled too. Since I was very fond of them I went, and after dinner they suggested a ride in their car. It seemed odd, but as we drove they discussed my performance in *Dulcy* and how good they thought it was. Then, abruptly, they stopped the car and suggested I get out. The street was dimly lit, and I stood there bewildered, until I heard them slam the door and the husband's voice said, "Go in and get yourself a job." His wife chimed in, "We'll pick you up later," and off they drove.

When the shock receded, I turned and looked at the globe bearing the illuminated words STAGE DOOR. Only then could I place myself. I was around the corner from the marquee of Henry Duffy's theater. The blackness of the street was all that drove me to turn the knob and enter. Inside was utter chaos. It couldn't have been a worse night to catch anyone's attention. There was a stagehand strike on, and they were confusedly playing a three-set comedy in one set.

I stood and waited and finally a woman smiled at me and asked if she could help me. My wavering request for whoever might cast the shows went by relays to the director's office. He must have retreated there in despair, but to my surprise he consented to see me.

What I saw was a cross, elderly man, and I almost lost my nerve, but *Dulcy* came to my rescue, and I related my recent triumph. He seemed rather impressed, and took my name and address.

Outside again, my heart beating a tattoo, I found my friends lurking around the corner. We rode home in high spirits, anticipating my climb to fame in short order.

Days passed, then weeks, and no word came, so I turned my

thoughts toward college. Then THAT letter: "If you will drop into my office on a matinee day, I believe I have a part that may interest you." Would it *ever!*

It was several days before I found exactly the right outfit to wear and waited for a matinee day to roll around. During the long ferry and streetcar ride, I almost fainted with anticipation. I was on my way to being an actress at last.

I got out at the corner and looked at the marquee in front of the theater. ALICE BUCHANAN IN *COBRA,* it read. Good casting, I thought. I had seen Miss Buchanan in several plays, and she was always a villainess. I had read that she had recently had a baby, and I pitied the child. I walked up the side street to the little door under the globe, and took a deep breath.

The activity inside was much less hectic than before. I even got a glimpse of the star in a slithering lamé dress, her dark hair caught in a knot. Her green eyes flickered toward me and she flashed a lovely smile. I returned it politely, but my prejudice had jelled too far. She can't be that nice, I thought, or she couldn't play all those mean parts.

I was shown into the director's office again. He was pleasant but very vague about why I was there. I told him about the part he'd mentioned, and he said that he remembered me, but there was no part in the next show. I took the tattered note from my purse and handed it to him. His brow unknitted and he smiled. "Oh yes, I was going to do another play and sent this off. But I've decided on this one, and there is nothing in it for you." He looked at my frozen smile and his eyes narrowed. "I don't suppose you want to do a walk-on in a scene; then perhaps in our next play . . ." His voice hung in midair.

I returned to Mill Valley an actress with a job paying $35 a week, even though it was only a walk-on.

From that moment, life seemed very simple. You got a job and you made a salary and you went to rehearsals every day and worked with real actors and actresses, and college was somewhere in the future—maybe. I can't remember what the play was about, except that at one point I ran onstage with some other actors and got very excited about something or other, but I loved every minute of it. I even managed to interject a few lines, at which the director nodded approvingly. I was befriended by a character actress who diplomatically taught me how to apply the unfamiliar theatrical makeup.

Henry Duffy's company played on the basis of what was called superstock. It was an ideal setup for learning your craft, since each play ran at least four to eight weeks, and a real hit could last for months. Also, in one play you could have the leading part, but in the next you might play a comic maid or a "bit." So we all worked like a team and felt like an exceptionally close-knit family.

There is a camaraderie among theater people unlike in any other group I know. Occasionally there is a "miserable company," but its misery generally springs from insecurity in high places—producers, director, or star—which infects the whole.

In my second appearance, to my own great surprise, I had the ingenue lead—unusual, because in those days to be five feet eight was a distinct disadvantage. Since it was a comedy, they didn't seem to worry about my topping the comedian-star by an inch or so.

During that second show I learned a lesson about losing concentration. I came offstage, removed my makeup, donned my suit and galoshes, and walked out the stage door and downhill to the streetcar. As I was raising a foot to board it, I heard a tremendous yell from the stage door. The stage manager was standing there, eyeballs distended, in the drizzling rain.

"THE SECOND ACT!" he was shouting.

My foot dropped off the streetcar as it was starting, and I raced up the hill, through the door, and down the ramp to the stage. I could hear the cast ad-libbing lines like "I saw her in the garden, I think" and "She'll probably be here any minute."

In hat, suit, galoshes, and no makeup, I dashed into the group in evening attire on stage and came to a screeching halt in front of the leading man. There was a moment of silence as I gasped for air—then we both burst into laughter and the audience joined us.

Somehow we finished our lines. But ever since, I make sure the play has ended before I leave the theater.

CHAPTER
·4·

In the next play, I was to have a very special and sympathetic part with the stars, Henry Duffy and his lovely wife Dale Winters. The woman who was to play the villainess and win me the audience's sympathy was none other than the "Cobra Lady." I worried about working with her and not feeling antagonistic, but there was another cloud on my horizon. I went to see the man who was to direct the show. He was a short, pudgy man, and it was rumored that he was the stepfather of John Gilbert, who was in love with Greta Garbo, which made him pretty prestigious. I approached him in the darkened theater one day as he talked to the set designer. I introduced myself and mentioned the part I was set to play. He fixed me with a pair of translucent blue eyes and just stared. A little nervous by now, I asked if he had seen the present production. He nodded. Then, to my shocked surprise, he said, "You were not my choice for this, you know, but whatever Terry [Mr. Duffy] wants is it."

Now thoroughly shaken, I asked what he found wrong with me. He enlightened me. "Watched you at rehearsal. Having too much fun. You'll never be a success in this business. Don't take your work seriously enough." And with that, he left.

It was the first intimation I had that not everybody was going to like me or what I did. I went home sobered and thought about it, but for the life of me couldn't understand why you shouldn't enjoy your work as long as you did your best and the audiences and critics seemed to like you.

Nonetheless, what with his watchful eyes and the anxiety of working with my boss and his wife *and* Alice Buchanan, I stayed solemn until well into rehearsals. Then the Duffys were so sweet that I fell madly in love with *him,* but decided I couldn't take him away from *her,* since I adored her too.

Alice Buchanan still awed and frightened me a little, until one day she asked where I had lunch. I mentioned a nearby "greasy spoon." She said, "Why don't you have lunch at my house?" And without waiting for an answer, she walked back into the scene.

By the time I got my mouth shut and thought of a good excuse, my curiosity about her baby and her life trapped me. At lunch break I found myself walking up a steep San Francisco hill and into her apartment.

It was my initial visit to an actress's home, and I must say I was let down by the rather dreary rented apartment she lived in. Where were all those satin couches and pillows and things befitting the Cobra Lady?

Her baby was plump and adorable, and it was obvious Alice was a devoted mother. I played with the baby while the nurse ate her lunch, and Alice tied on a ruffled apron and whipped up a corn chowder of which I have never since tasted the equal. For the first time I realized that actresses are not always what they seem beyond the footlights.

Incidentally, footlights have almost entirely disappeared from theaters, and I for one resent it. They were a part of the illusion of acting, and created that barrier that separated the commonplace from the magical.

We ate our soup with one eye on the clock and talked like buzz saws. A deep friendship developed between us from that day on. For all her aloof beauty, she had a kooky sense of nonsense that blended nicely with mine. She helped me with my part, and thanks to her playing of the nasty sister, my role got great sympathy and very nice notices.

Alice was very much in love with her husband, a redheaded reporter named Rex Smith on the *San Francisco Examiner*. She was content with her lot and had no great ambitions, but she drew from me all the dreams I hadn't yet admitted to myself: to be a big stage star in New York, first, and then to fall in love with some wonderful man and have lots of children. Alice, twenty-seven or so, obviously enjoyed my anticipations. She nibbled on a cracker and inquired what sort of man I had in mind.

"Oh, someone like Clark Gable," I said.

A couple of weeks later I was following Clark Gable across the backstage of a Chinese theater! Rex Smith, as a top reporter, met almost every celebrity who came to San Francisco, and Clark had asked him to take his party through Chinatown. My new friend Alice had included me in the group.

Several years later I did a picture with Clark called *Comrade X*, in which I played a reporter, and his girlfriend. We became friends, but by that time, alas, he was married and so was I. However, life is full of little miracles like that!

In the spring, when we had been doing the show for several months, I was disturbed one evening to hear that Alice hadn't arrived at the theater. The fifteen-minute call had already been given.

Both of us liked to get to the theater early, apply our makeup leisurely, and gossip and chat until "five minutes" was called. There was no answer at her apartment, and Mr. Duffy, who could get pretty tense, especially when he was appearing in the show, had ordered the stage manager to call all the hospitals and was preparing to call the police himself, when suddenly the sound of singing electrified us and we bolted down the hall.

Alice appeared, regally swaying toward us. "G'd evening everybody, wasn't it a gorgeous day?" she caroled. And before anyone could recover, she swayed into her dressing room and slammed the door. We heard the lock click.

Terry Duffy sprang to the door and pounded on it.

"Alice, open the door," he commanded. "Immediately! Do you hear me?"

Evidently, she only heard her own singing.

Just then the stage manager announced, "It's five minutes, Mr. Duffy. What shall I do?"

Mr. Duffy's face went even paler under his makeup as his pounding and commands went unheeded. I was terrified, sure that my friend would lose her job. I was also bewildered, as I'd never seen her drunk.

Meanwhile, the poor stage manager was flipping through the script, preparing to make his entrance reading Alice's part. Everyone looked distraught and disheveled when suddenly the door clicked open and out stepped Alice in her First Act evening gown, makeup on and every hair in place. She smiled pleasantly. "April Fool," she said, and calmly walked past us onstage, just in time for her opening line.

I'm sure if he could have gotten to her, our boss would have fired her then and there, but every time he made his exit she managed to disappear, and by the time the final curtain came down, his sense of humor had returned and he was grinning at the idea of the elegant Alice putting him on.

My mother was very fond of Alice, and so allowed me to go along when the company moved to Los Angeles. Alice promised to watch over me, and I was thrilled to have a one-room apartment as an actress on my own. My salary was now $50 a week, a munificent sum when you could actually get a small butterfly steak to cook for 15 cents!

The play ran for several months. Late one afternoon, I was having dinner with Alice and Rex when they broke into a terrific argument. I was embarrassed, and more than a little afraid of Rex's temper, which I'd seen in action before. Like Terry Duffy, he was a redhead with pale-blue eyes and a goodly spate of freckles. In anger his skin went milky-white and every freckle stood out as his eyes flashed blue lightning.

At one point in the midst of his shouting he became aware of my presence and ordered me out of the house. At Rex's bark I was out and walking down the street. Their apartment house was a brand-new one, off alone in a newly developed tract. My imagination, never inert, began to overwork. Suppose he lost his head and murdered Alice! There had been such a murder in the paper just yesterday. I couldn't let that happen to my friend, but what could I do about it?

I began to run, and as I ran I sobbed. I hit their front door, left unlocked, and ran into the dining room where Rex was still bellowing, and startled them both into immobility. I gasped out a dramatic story of a man with strange mad eyes who had followed me down the street and, when I attempted to pass him and return, grabbed me. I gave a brilliant account of the struggle that ended in my escape—so brilliant that Rex grabbed a carving knife from the remains of the roast and started for the door, ordering Alice to leave for the theater as she was late. He said he would bring me after our report to the police. Alice left with some comforting words for me, and I could see she was eager to relay to the cast the story of my horrible experience.

Unhappy at this turn of events, I went to work convincing Rex that the man had immediately fled the scene. I insisted that I would be mortified to tell my story to the police, and that my mother would be alarmed enough to order me home if it reached the papers. Some of my best acting went into those fifteen minutes.

Very late when I reached the theater, I had time only to dress and make my entrance. For the whole second act I was the recipient of compassionate looks, hand squeezes, and murmurs of sympathy from the cast. I don't think I ever could have convinced them or Alice that my act had been a fraud.

CHAPTER
·5·

When the show closed, after Mother had paid an investigatory visit and approved of my cheerful, Woolworth-embellished apartment, she agreed to let me stay in Los Angeles and to send me a limited allowance until my next job.

One reason for my desire to stay was that I had met a *man!* Older than the boys I had known, and an urbane New Yorker, he was fun to be with and a "gentleman" to boot. I was beginning to think I might be in love with Cubby Parker. The only trouble with the world at the moment was that it was deep in the depression, and my friend suddenly lost his good job. I too was "in between" and hadn't found an agent yet. To top everything, we had made two new friends who were also unemployed, a young and witty Englishman trying to break into pictures and an ex-army colonel who was looking for any civilian job he could find. Each day the three males went hunting for work and I for an agent, a dreary process.

My mother had presented me with an ultimatum. She had limited my allowance to the rent, hoping I would give in and come home in time for Christmas.

It was the only time in my career I ever went hungry, but the memories are some of the most lighthearted of my life. Since my apartment had the only full kitchen, we'd pool our resources and cook dinner there. Occasionally one of the fellas would get a part-time job or would work a few days in pictures. Then we would live high off the hog. There were many evenings when we would sit down to cards instead of dinner, and the best I could produce was a plate of fudge from chocolate, sugar, and tinned milk. But I made marvelous fudge, the stories of our job hunting were hilarious, and the card games so ferocious that we hardly noticed the grumbling of our stomachs. Then the next day I'd get a letter from my mother into which she couldn't resist slipping a bill or two, and that night the card game was preceded by a feast.

20

In the fall, before things had gotten so bad for all of us, I had done my Christmas shopping for my family, Alice, and the card-playing group. By Christmas Eve morning, things had reached a desperate state and we convened in my kitchen for watered-down coffee and toast from the last loaf of bread, while the gentlemen, really worried about what kind of Christmas "the kid" would have, passed a resolution that somehow one of them had to find work to provide us with Christmas dinner.

They went off with determination, if not much hope, and I set about cleaning the apartment. My constant faith in miracles proved sound, however. In midmorning a recent acquaintance of ours, one profitably employed by an advertising agency, dropped by to wish me a Merry Christmas and leave a small tree. I thanked him, we chatted awhile, and he left, unaware of our predicament and the fact that I promptly burst into tears when he'd gone. I dried my eyes, arranged the bare tree in the corner, and brought out the presents I'd hidden weeks before. As I finished doing this, the mailman arrived at my door with several large packages to be signed for and two letters, from my mother and Aunt Elsie.

Excitedly, I opened the packages. From my aunt, tree decorations and a cake she'd made, trimmed with the tiny Cecil Brunner roses that grew in a mass on her wall. There were presents for me, and she'd remembered each of my card players with a gift. My mother, having met them on her visit, had also included gifts for all. I trimmed the tree, placed the gifts under it, and sat down to read my letters. In each one was a sizable check.

I rushed out, after drying my eyes once more, and purchased groceries to stock the kitchen, and a chicken, which I figured I'd be more successful with than a turkey.

Weary after their fruitless search for work, my friends convened again outside my door to decide how to break their sad news. Hearing them, I threw open the door and wished them a "Merry Christmas, gentlemen."

Their faces as they saw the lighted tree with presents heaped beneath, and smelled the cooking chicken are another indelible memory. I'm not sure how good my cooking was, but I've never had higher praise for any accomplishment—truly a Christmas to remember.

Within the week, the pendulum had swung back for all of us. For myself it was an offer to join a newly formed repertory company, which gave me a year of the intensive training and practical experience I needed right then. The Bandbox Repertory Company was comprised of only four actors and a girl manager with social connections who booked us into exclusive resorts like Palm Springs, the Santa Barbara Biltmore, El Encanto Hotel, and several private mansions in Pasadena and Palm Springs. We were provided with gorgeous rooms, exquisite food, and carte blanche of the hotel's furniture to create our sets; in a lounge, at the bottom of a stairway, or in a patio or garden. We carried with us only costumes, hand-props, and our lights, which we distributed for the best effect. We just predated theater-in-the-round, and I occasionally made my entrance to find an ancient Pasadenan occupying the chair I was heading for, or sitting at the table our stage dinner was set on. This led to much improvisation and ad-libbing, and we were certainly a unique group.

At the end of our Bandbox season someone suggested my name to Leonard Sillman, who was about to open a revue at the Pasadena Playhouse. One of their featured girls had quit in a fit of temperament, and since I was what's known as a fast study, I was able to open with them a few days later. *Lo and Behold* went very well, and it was decided to move it into Hollywood at the Music Box Theater. This area was in its respectable period, and we drew good audiences. We played for several months, and as several of the girls left the show, I stepped into their numbers as well.

About that time, Lee Shubert came to Los Angeles looking for performers. He was about to cast his version of the *Ziegfeld Follies*, to be done in New York under the banner of Ziegfeld's widow, the actress Billie Burke. I was shortly the stunned recipient of an offer to be featured in that show at the sum of $100 a week.

In shock, I called my mother, and she said joyfully that it seemed like a wonderful opportunity and of course I must go. I'd been anxious about her health, which hadn't been too good, and the subliminal fear of losing her was always there. She dismissed my anxieties and said she was fine. She assured me that I had plenty of courage and self-reliance to see me through.

I'd been told by the Shubert office to report to them in New York on August 15, 1934, so I closed my apartment and said good-bye to my boyfriend and card-playing associates, with the sad recognition that the profession I'd entered was not a static one, that I'd be constantly meeting new friends, growing fond of them, and saying good-bye again, as long as I remained an actress.

I went home to stay with my mother, aunt, and grandmother until it was time to leave for New York. Mother indeed did seem better, and happy about my adventure, though I suspected she dreaded our parting as much as I did.

Now, for a change, I was worried about Aunt Elsie. She was full of good spirits, but Mother told me she had occasional attacks of severe head pains, during which she seemed to become incoherent and her limbs would suddenly collapse under her. But Auntie laughed off my concern, said she was fine and that she couldn't wait to get my letters from New York, where she'd never been.

Mother and I went shopping for a winter wardrobe and, since she still worried about my catching cold, she insisted on buying me a black Persian lamb coat collared in another fur, suspect in origin but handsome to look at. It was a very expensive coat and unnecessary, from my point of view, but it made her so happy to give it to me that I cheerfully wore it aboard the train when she and Auntie saw me off that hot August day.

My emotions were a confused mixture of elation at being on my way at last, terror that I might not be able to live up to what everyone expected of me, and a deep sadness at leaving the two dearest people in my world and with them any lingering trace of my childhood. There were no tears, only tight embraces, hands reluctant to let go, and assurances of letter writing and telephone calls.

Yet even in the midst of this I was aware of an attractive young man regarding the tableau of parting with an amused smile. I felt guilty at finding my anguish diluted by an acute interest in his appearance.

As the train pulled out, the anguish was pure again and tears forced their way, but my mouth kept smiling as the figures on the platform diminished and finally disappeared around a curve in the track. I dug for a handkerchief and made my way inside.

Later the young man spoke to me—a few innocuous words about the difficulty of leaving home for the first time. I stiffened suspiciously, but it took only a moment to place him among the "good guys." I couldn't have been more perceptive. He was a nice young lawyer or doctor—I can't remember which—and his pleasant conversation and dinner invitations bolstered my flagging spirits.

But on the morning we reached Chicago I was so depressed by the tenement slums I saw on the way into the city that I vowed that if New York looked like that, I'd tear up my contract and go back

to the redwoods and oaks of Mill Valley. The nice young man
assured me that Chicago had better scenery to offer than I was
looking at at the moment, and since the New York train didn't
leave till later that afternoon, he took me up Michigan Avenue in
a cab for lunch at a lovely restaurant before saying good-bye and
going off to his business appointment. I window-shopped at Marshall Fields and then transferred my baggage to the *Twentieth Century.*

I slept badly, between the rattling of the train over bumpy tracks
and fitful nightmares in which I cried, "I can't stand it!" and tore
up my contract under Mr. Shubert's astonished nose.

At eight o'clock I woke from my first deep sleep to a berth filled
with sunshine. Along the tracks lay the Hudson River under a
bright bare sky, and on it was a slew of tiny sailboats. Their bellying
white sails reminded me of high school weekends when the boat-
owning boys who lived in Sausalito sailed us around San Francisco
Bay, cutting across the wakes of the ferryboats, skimming past
Alcatraz Island, and tying up at Belvedere or Tiburon for lunch.

My heart lifted several inches at least, and I went to breakfast in
a happy frame of mind. Even the tenements we passed seemed less
depressing and more full of life than Chicago's had been. From the
cab I took, the skyscrapers and Madison Avenue shops gleamed
with chrome and glass. Windows were full of chic clothes, arrangements of the newest books, or exquisite table settings of china and
crystal. The size and magnificence of the city amazed the girl from
Mill Valley. It seemed the most exciting city in the world, and in
its heart lay the Broadway theater, the pinnacle of an actress's
dream.

The cab reached the Times Square area and drew up at the hotel
where the Shuberts had arranged for me to stay. It was one of their
many properties, and actors were given a special rate there.

It was well run, the rooms were pleasant, and from my window
I had a great view of the Astor Hotel and the Paramount clock. The
place had its quota of prosperous underworld characters, but in my
naïveté I didn't recognize this fact for the entire two years I spent
there, and traveled confidently up and down in its elevators with
never a word or incident to mar my joy in discovering New York.

I spent days wandering up and down Fifth Avenue and Park
Avenue and treading the side streets with small hotels, shops and
the many theaters—which were not on Broadway, where I ex-

pected to find them, but on cross streets like Forty-fifth and Forty-sixth.

When several weeks had passed with no call from the Shubert office, I decided to beard them in their den, if I could locate it. So one morning I walked down the famed Shubert Alley and found the elevator to Mr. Lee's office. Timidity stayed my hand at the door, but righteous anger pushed it open. To my dismay, I discovered that Mr. Lee was out of town and not due back until the following week, and I was referred to Mr. Harry Kaufman.

Mr. Kaufman, a corpulent dandy with cold marble eyes and a paradoxically benevolent smile, informed me that rehearsals were not due to start for another month. Then why had they brought me to New York six weeks early? I asked.

Mr. Kaufman's smile grew more benign as he assured me that my credit at the hotel was good until I started work. Then, having disposed of me and my problems to his satisfaction, he bowed his way into the inner office.

I was in shock as I rang for the elevator. The money I'd brought would never last that long. It offended my sense of independence to have to ask my mother's help, but I had nowhere else to turn.

When Mr. Lee came back to town he listened to my complaints of having had to come to New York too early. I told him I was determined to repay my mother and that therefore my salary would be inadequate to live on in New York, and suggested that he give me a raise. Mr. Lee's beady eyes twinkled in his deeply tanned immobile face that had earned him the nickname of the Sphinx.

He said it would be very unusual to give someone a raise before she even started to work, but that he appreciated my position and had a solution. He would put a maid's salary of twenty-five dollars on the payroll and then it would be up to me to decide whether I needed a maid or not.

I was delighted, and went off in a daze of gratitude and a layer of perspiration. The latter was not so much from nervousness as from the fact that New York was in the throes of an Indian summer and the temperature was in the nineties. I was wearing my fur (and only) coat and a wool knit dress. Totally unprepared for eastern humidity, and in the damp fog of San Francisco, I had discarded my summer clothes. The fur coat I could and did remove, but for the next three weeks I lived in the happy chill of air-conditioned movie theaters.

Finally, I was summoned to the studio of a well-known photographer and cajoled into a series of shots of "the new Ziegfeld Girl" —embarrassing to one who considered herself an actress—and shortly after that, rehearsals began.

I was especially thrilled to meet Fanny Brice, whom I'd gone to see every time she'd played the San Francisco Orpheum. When Fanny learned that I'd done imitations of her, she insisted I do "Mrs. Cohen at the Beach," and said, "You've got a good accent for a goy!" She asked for another, but stopped me after a few sentences.

"I never did that number," she stated flatly.

I was disconcerted, but managed to insist it was the only way I could have learned it. I finished the number and she said, "My God, you're right. I tried that one out for a couple of weeks in San Francisco!"

The comedians Willie and Eugene Howard and the singers Jane Froman and Everett Marshall were also in the show. George Balanchine staged the marvelous ballets. There was a wonderful brother-and-sister dance team named Buddy and Vilma Ebsen. Buddy, tall and loose-limbed, and Vilma, tiny and vivacious, had a style of dancing that was original and happy-making. I loved to watch them from the wings.

It was a joy to do sketches with Fanny and the Howards, and I had my own musical number, "The Economic Situation," complete with a group of lovely showgirls behind me. In my gorgeous gown, wearing beaded eyelashes, I came my closest to feeling beautiful. All this, *and* a new name on the marquee!

One day Mr. Shubert called me and said that the names were to go up on the marquee in two days, and that Quedens (my real name—pronounced Q*wadenz*) was a name impossible to pronounce, and combined with Eunice it was too long to fit—would I please select a shorter, less difficult name.

I sat in the office of my new manager (the famous Louis Shurr, suggested to me by the Shubert office, which covered all bases) and pondered the question of names. On my lap rested the current book I was reading, whose heroine has now become a part of my life. You guessed it: Eve.

Next to it lay a package of the products of Elizabeth Arden, a lady of such accomplishment that I recognized the name as a symbol of quality and aspiration. *Voilà!* Eve Arden!

Also, there was no other Arden in show business, I thought.

Only later did I learn, by seeing it emblazoned in lights on a burlesque house outside of Boston, that not only was there an Arden, but an Eve Arden, who appeared nightly adorned in a single white fox fur. However, by then the die was cast.

After four weeks of rehearsal and two weeks tryout in Boston, the *Billie Burke Ziegfeld Follies* opened at New York's Winter Garden to the eternally deadpan first-nighters of New York. We went home depressed at the failure of our efforts, only to read in the next day's papers that we were a definite hit and launched on a long run!

Somewhere in a moldering trunk lie a few notices I have treasured because of who wrote them. Among them is a very kindly word from the dean of New York critics, Percy Hammond, even then preparing to retire. Another is from a man I had worshipped in high school and whose books I had read aloud to anyone who would tolerate me. I was later to count him a good friend. At the time, though, Robert Benchley's praise of my beauty and talent on the pages of the *New Yorker* magazine was a "treasured report" indeed!

The only words that matched those were ones he handed me on his card as I marched to the ladies room in Romanoff's famous restaurant during the time I knew him in Hollywood. He was sitting in a booth with an eagle-eyed Dorothy Parker and some others, and he merely passed it to me with a brusque "Read this later."

Mystified, I continued to the ladies room, where I read, "Why don't you give all this up and marry me?" A jest, to be sure, but I cherished the affection it expressed from this shy and very dear man.

Meanwhile, back at the *Follies*, I floated on air at this nod from someone I'd admired for so long.

CHAPTER ·6·

During the show one evening, Fanny asked me if I'd go shopping with her the next day at Klein's.

I said, "What is Klein's?"

Fanny was astonished. "You've never heard of Klein's?" I hadn't. Fanny explained that it was a famous store where you found marvelous clothes "cheap."

When we arrived "downtown" somewhere and entered what I remember as a large building, I was horrified to find that there were no dressing rooms, only open cubicles. Women were snatching dresses from racks, two and three at a time, and rushing to find a cubicle, out of most of which protruded bare bottoms (it was hot that day), as arms and heads struggled into garments. To my surprise, Fanny—always slim and elegant—joined in the frenzied action. Coolly, she selected four or five dresses, swept them into an available cubicle, and stripped.

"Hey, kid, why don't you pick out something and try it on?"

She didn't realize that she was talking to Miss Modesty of 1934, not long out of Mill Valley, California.

"I'd better not, Fanny. I wasn't expecting to buy anything, so I didn't bring any money," I stammered.

"I'll lend you some, kid," Fanny countered. She tried on another garment. "Come on," she urged.

"Thanks, Fanny, but I really don't feel so well," I said, looking down the row of bare bosoms and rears and flailing arms.

Fanny bought several things that day, and on her they looked terrific. How I regretted my cowardice!

Fanny's good friend Bea Lillie, the wonderful, pixie comedienne, would often sit in the front row and watch our show. Then she would come backstage to wait for Fanny to dress, and they'd go off to join a party, sometimes at Elsa Maxwell's new club, which opened, briefly, on top of the Winter Garden.

Bea was funny on- and offstage as well. She told me that she envied a piece of business I did in a Major Bowes sketch—and it really was a Bea Lillie "bit."

After Fanny appeared as a girl from the Bronx, and Judy Canova as a hillbilly, I stepped before the microphone in a blue satin evening gown, wearing a beautifully coiffed white wig.

"And what do you do, Lady De Vere?" asked Major Bowes.

"I am a kazooist, and I accompany myself with two cymbals." And so saying, I hummed the first strains of "Sweet Sue" on the kazoo, ending with a terrific crash on two large cymbals fastened between my knees, hidden beneath my skirt. It was a complete surprise, and the audience howled. It was the same kind of surprise Bea had given them in a previous show when, having sung a charming song, leaning against the proscenium, she lifted her long satin skirt and gaily roller-skated across the stage.

My life in New York settled into a pattern of six nightly shows and two matinees a week. In between I saw the shows that had a Thursday matinee instead of our Wednesday one. Alice Buchanan, now divorced from Rex, and living in Virginia with her child and family, was in town doing a play.

Since her curtain went down earlier than ours, she'd come by the theater for me a couple of nights a week and we'd embark on our favorite expedition. First to a nearby delicatessen, where they wrought wondrous sandwiches of corned beef, turkey, and ham. We'd take these, carefully wrapped, along with kosher pickles (an acquired taste) and two luscious chocolate éclairs in cardboard boxes, and we were off to a midnight movie on Broadway. The thought of those fun evenings makes me yearn for the days when we felt completely invulnerable to danger. Only occasionally would some sick soul move nearer, aisle by aisle. But when he forayed into our row, Alice would stand up and, in her best Cobra voice, warn him that we were about to send for the usher. Then we would giggle nervously as he backed away. Today we would hesitate to walk the block to the delicatessen without a bodyguard. As for going to a movie at that hour without a black belt in karate —forget it!

What has happened to that lovely world where a drunk sleeping in a doorway was regarded with compassion and perhaps left a quarter for food? Now he is given a wide berth as a possible mugger. I'm glad I knew Broadway then, as it gives me hope that someday the pendulum will swing back again.

It was still possible then to go to Harlem to hear Cab Calloway, or perhaps Hazel Scott with her fingers flying over the keys, and then take a hansom cab back through Central Park with one of my more prosperous admirers, and finish the evening dancing at the St. Regis Roof. I'd met several attractive men, and one was threatening to become a serious romance, so life was rosy.

The only cloud on my horizon was a letter from my mother saying she had had a "small operation" but hadn't wanted to worry me. Now it was over and she was fine. I worried anyway, but I was still grateful I could send her my maid's salary. Mr. Lee had kept his word to me, as he did about any problem I could take directly to him. I suspected that anything he couldn't or didn't want to solve took him "out of town," and those problems were turned over to Harry Kaufman of the marble eyes and shark's teeth hidden behind his closed smile.

One day, as I was disagreeing with Mr. Lee over a clause in my contract, I was aware that he was smiling at me in amusement and not hearing a word I said. I couldn't believe my ears when I heard, "How would you like to have my limousine pick you up after the theater every night and take you to a nice apartment that you could pick out?"

I stood in shock at the only proposition of my career. Then he said, a little wistfully, "We could have lots of good times together."

I still couldn't speak. I liked Mr. Lee and didn't want to hurt his feelings. Then the picture taking shape in my mind of little Mr. Lee ushering me, swathed in furs, into that big black limousine, tickled my funny bone. In spite of myself I laughed. Mr. Lee didn't take it amiss, though. He merely sighed and said, "I would have to like someone like you!" and went back to the clause in our contract.

The subject was never mentioned again, and somehow I think we respected and liked each other more than ever.

The man I was daily becoming more attracted to was an advertising man who had arranged radio shows for various members of the cast. After rehearsal one day he invited me to have lunch with him to discuss doing another show. On the way to the restaurant in the cab he asked me if I enjoyed dancing. I said, "Very much," so he suggested that we have dinner and mentioned a delightful place to dance. My suspicious nature led me to ask, "But aren't you married?"

His answer was, "Oh, I thought you understood." He went on to say that he and his wife were actually separated but that his new and very important job depended on his boss, whose wife was the best friend of his wife; therefore, as far as the business relationship went, the time the foursome spent together was presumably as two happy couples. Since he seemed to have plenty of time for lunches and dinners with me, I accepted this explanation, and when he told me with tears in his eyes that he was madly in love with me, how could I doubt him?

Through Alice I met Ann and Stanley Amster, who were to become such close friends in the years ahead. I went to their beautiful little farm in Connecticut on the weekends, and the joys of pink and white dogwood and birch trees in the spring, along with the adjoining forest of trees that turned vermilion and yellow in the fall, were to be, many years later, my children's joys as well.

When the *Follies* closed after a year's run on Broadway, my contract called for a tour with the show.

With several weeks before the *Follies* was to leave on tour, I found myself seeing more of my still married love. In spite of my desire to keep our relationship platonic until he was free, I now admitted to myself that I was as deeply in love with him as he seemed to be with me. I fought my own urges, and he didn't pressure me; but tragedy was my undoing.

As I was dressing for our dinner date one night, Mother called from California to tell me that my wonderful Aunt Elsie had died suddenly from one of her mysterious attacks. "She didn't suffer," Mother said, "and we must be grateful for that." Mother said that I should be brave and go on with my life as Elsie would want.

In shock, I went to the restaurant where I was to meet the only one who could comfort me now. My belief in the world Aunt Elsie had taught me about, where everything was perfect and people lived "happily ever after," was shattered. But he was late, and after waiting awhile I went back to my hotel room. Mixed with my grief were anger and bitterness. On this night of my life when I desperately needed him, why wasn't he there?

The phone rang, and he was in the lobby apologizing for being so late. He sensed the tension in my voice and insisted on coming up. His sincere sympathy and love when I told him of my aunt's death, and my own need to obliterate my anguish, crumbled my feeble defenses, and we became lovers.

The following days made it much more difficult to leave him when the tour began, but in the weeks that followed his phone calls and flying visits to nearby cities helped make our parting easier.

Being on the road was exciting but strenuous, with split-weeks and one-night stands. I can still remember Miss Brice, all in black, a Chihuahua dog peering from her muff, preparing to disembark the train after an all-night poker session with the crew, and stating in her inimitable way, "It took the Shuberts to invent a new way to kill the Jews!"

I think she really loved touring. It was a lonely life, though, away from her children, and she often asked me to have dinner with her in her dressing room between performances.

In those moments she would tell me of her life with Nicky Arnstein and her final disillusionment when, now married to a wealthy Pasadena woman, he invited her to have dinner at their home. Still unsure of her feelings, she was impelled to go, but his constant bragging attempts to impress her with his new life freed her from her obsession with him.

Later she was to tell me of the collapse of her marriage to Billy Rose when he left her for Eleanor Holm. The loss of his companionship and the fun they had shared she was finding especially painful at that stage of her life. It was her talent and the love of her children, as well as a great interest in art and decoration, that helped her to rise above it. She had a certain toughness and was capable of occasional small cruelties, but in those moments of confiding in me I felt great empathy with her.

When our spirits flagged from the weariness of constant travel, there was always Fanny's court jester to make us laugh. Roger Davis was blessed with a tremendous sense of nonsense that constantly bubbled. He was a spare little man with an egg-shaped head, bald except for a fringe of pale-red hair. On formal occasions he would paste on a delicate matching toupee. One evening when we were the mayor's guests in some large midwestern city, Roger was keeping us in hysterics with an improvised monologue when in the middle of a sentence he spied two matrons obviously interested in whether his toupee *was* or *wasn't*. Without dropping a stitch in his discourse, he whipped it off, then, with his own homosexual flourish, waved it merrily at them. Their faces were something to behold. He was so funny that he was always in Fanny's shows, and on the road he had his own room, courtesy of the Shuberts, in her hotel suite.

Unlike many comedians who are extremely unfunny offstage, Roger, who constantly kept us amused during rehearsals, became a "dull thud" the moment the curtain rose. The only clue to this phenomenon was a story Fanny told me when I found her giggling into her makeup before the performance one night.

That afternoon, as Fanny was quietly sewing in her bedroom, Roger was reading the paper in the living room, unaware that Fanny was in the suite. The radio on the table beside him was broadcasting a children's story by "Uncle Don." At its finish, Fanny heard Uncle Don say, "And now, boys and girls, I have a big surprise! To the first little boy or girl who calls, Uncle Don will send a little white kitten with two pink ears and a long pink tongue and a long white tail." He gave a telephone number, and then Fanny was relieved to hear Roger turn off the radio, but surprised to hear him dialing the phone. Then she heard him ask in a high, childish voice, "Iss diss Uncle Don?" The answer was appropriate and Roger went on, "Do you have the kitty wit de looong white tail?" Uncle Don did. "And duss it have two little pink ears and a looong pink tongue?" It did. Then Roger, with a voice two octaves lower, boomed, "And duss it have two big black balls?" And, hanging up, he went happily back to his newspaper.

Fanny never let him know she'd heard him, but we concluded that Roger's comedy had to be spontaneous, and solely for his own amusement.

We were getting closer to San Francisco, and I was excited at the thought of being with Mother again. When we had played Milwaukee, I'd committed the extravagance of buying her a five-skin scarf of kit fox. I'd thought it the most luxuriously beautiful gift I could give her. Later in San Francisco I wondered why she wasn't wearing it. She admitted apologetically that, while she adored it, every time she shook it to put it on, it seemed to disintegrate in clouds of fur before her eyes. I'd been royally skunked! I was heartbroken, but the absurdity of it struck us both at the same moment, and we laughed—albeit a bit ruefully on my part.

My first sight of Mother had shocked me, as she was very pale and seemed to have aged suddenly, but in a few days her skin had regained its color, and she sparkled with happiness at seeing her girl in a show. I took a suite at the Clift Hotel so that we could spend every day together. I made a trip to Mill Valley to see my grandmother and walked through Aunt Elsie's sadly empty house.

From San Francisco, we went to Los Angeles, and I took Mother with me for the weeks we spent playing the Biltmore. Via the telephone, I introduced her to the young New York executive, and he told her how much he loved me and wanted to marry me. I had an uneasy feeling that she was too happy over this news, as if she wanted to know I was taken care of before she left me.

I told myself this was only my imagination, but the night my former Los Angeles boyfriend came to drive me to the train and I looked back at her, sitting up in bed smiling, I felt with a sudden sharpness that I would never see her again. By the time I got to the train I'd talked myself out of it, and once back in New York, her cheerful letters allayed my fears.

I was now out of a job, although still under contract to the Shuberts. This was unfortunate, because they didn't have to pay me, yet they turned down plays I wanted to do, because the producers couldn't meet my growing salary as a featured musical-comedy performer.

Enforced idleness was depleting my savings. Happily, I was offered a revue the Theater Guild was producing, called *Parade* and starring Jimmy Savo, a wistful pixie of a comedian.

The show poked fun at all the shibboleths of conservatism. Since most of the Theater Guild subscribers were Republicans, it was somewhat like tossing insults into the teeth of our patrons.

They had some funny material written for me: a Vassar graduate who made a terrible Macy's salesgirl, a take-off on *Tobacco Road,* and a lecture on "My Escape from the Soviets" by a Russian princess who went from Minsk to Pinsk to another insk I can't remember. I was given an avant-garde song by Mark Blitzstein, called "Send for the Militia," for which I wore an elegant evening gown and a beautifully coiffed wig as a society woman who considered herself very liberal. However, at the first sign of anything irregular, she cried out, "Send for the Militia, the Army, the Navy. Quick, bring out the Boy Scouts, every Captain, every Ace. The country's on the brink of disaster—we'd better have the troops around us—in case."

The night before we opened I stood on stage after doing my number and listened to the Theater Guild hierarchy discuss whether or not the number should be cut. The reluctant consensus was that it was needed to allow time for a scene change.

On opening night I was surprised to hear warm applause as I rushed to make the next change, pulling off my wig as I went. Half undressed, I was horrified to be told that the number had stopped the show cold. In a dressing gown, with my wig over one ear, I faced the gratifying applause. At the next performance I was given an encore to do. Such are the fortunes of war and show business.

During the run of *Parade,* I met Russel Crouse and Howard Lindsay, who were enthusiastic about writing me into a new musical they were doing, but the Shuberts were demanding my services for the second *Billie Burke Ziegfeld Follies,* again with Fanny Brice. This time Bob Hope co-starred, and we two were to introduce a new Ira Gershwin song, "I Can't Get Started with You," in which he sang to a glamorous showgirl, me, while I exhibited signs of boredom—powdering my nose, inspecting my teeth, and snapping my girdle.

I was beginning to think I might not be the ugly duckling I had always supposed, when as a child I'd heard people say, "Too bad she doesn't look like her mother."

Vincente Minnelli directed this *Follies,* and Ira Gershwin and Vernon Duke wrote the wonderful score and lyrics. I had offered to understudy Fanny for this *Follies* as well as the previous one, and the Shuberts accepted with alacrity but no salary. So, after a month or so of understudy rehearsal two days a week, I decided my time could be put to better advantage, since Fanny had never been known to miss a performance. I began to work on Shakespeare with an actress coach.

Some months later, mentally fogged after a coaching session followed by a large spaghetti dinner, I arrived at the theater to be greeted by a frantic stage manager. "Where have you been?" he hissed. "I have been trying to reach you all day! Fanny's sick and you'll have to go on in her place." Disbelief and terror struggled for possession of my tired brain. He pushed me through the door impatiently. "You'll have to do Fanny's sketches as well as your own, and her big dance number and Baby Snooks. We've got Milton Berle to take over most of the last act and close the show. Hurry and put your makeup on so you can rehearse the big lift with the chorus boys."

When strength returned to my limbs it was too late to run. Numbly I dabbed makeup on my rigid cheeks and muttered a few remembered lines to myself. In the wings I tried to keep my knees stiff as four chorus boys grabbed me by my thighs and I flew high in the air. "Just don't bend anything and you'll be okay," they advised.

Bob Hope came from somewhere and patted me encouragingly. "You'll be great." Did I sense insecurity in his voice?

"But I don't remember all the lines in Baby Snooks," I gasped.

Bob played a Hollywood director driven mad by the ineptitudes of his child star. "Look," he said, "when Fanny forgets a line, she grabs me around the waist and we wrestle around the floor till she gets it."

And that's what we did as I grabbed Bob and steered him to the wings in search of a line. The audience may have been puzzled by our gyrations, but they laughed and I was grateful.

By the time the dance number came along, I was relaxed and enjoying it, except that I kept my knees stiff in anticipation of the big lift. Up in the air I went and came down to a nice burst of applause, and I could finally collapse at the end of one of the longer days of my life.

CHAPTER
·7·

Toward the end of the second *Follies,* I had to face my nightmare's reality. Unsuspectingly, I had opened a letter and read the words written there by an acquaintance of my mother.

If I hoped to see my mother alive again, I'd better do something immediately, it said. I stared into space as the old fears flooded back. I looked again at this frightening message. My mother, it said, had had two operations, the second of which she hadn't told me about. Now she seemed to be failing rapidly. "Hurry!" the letter said.

Gradually, I gained control and picked up the phone. When I reached my number, the voice at the other end sounded so delighted that I thought, Why, she's fine! Evelyn must be imagining things.

"How'd you like to come to New York and stay with your daughter for the run of the show?"

A hesitation at the other end, then: "Oh, darling, how wonderful it would be to see you, and I've never been to New York, you know." Another pause. "But are you sure you could afford it, sweetheart? Of course, I could pay for our food and keep house for you . . ."

"Sure," I broke in, "I'll find an apartment. We'll have such fun! You'll love New York and you can see all the shows."

In our excitement we topped each other. "How soon could you get ready?"

The voice considered. "I'll have to arrange for someone to look after Grandma. I hate to leave her, but I'm sure she'll insist that I go." She brightened. "It shouldn't take more than a couple of weeks."

I hung up, busy with plans. Stanley Amster, who was in real estate, could help me find an apartment, and Alice would help me with Mother if she had to stay in bed or anything.

37

Four days later, my world broke into pieces with a phone call from her brother. "Your mother is in the hospital," he said. "She was so anxious to leave for New York, then she collapsed." Then: "I hate to tell you this, dear, but your mother has cancer."

How strange, I thought numbly, her one great fear.

My uncle continued: "The doctor wants to speak to you."

A calm voice expressed sympathy and then said, "I understand you were planning to bring your mother east to stay with you."

My voice shook a little. "Yes." I didn't dare ask the question.

"I really wouldn't advise it at this time. Your mother has some very loyal friends here. Two of them have divided up the day, and one is with her each morning, the other in the afternoon, and she has a nurse at night." His voice softened. "I understand it's necessary for you to work, and I don't think you could continue to do so and care for your mother, too."

I interrupted. "I'll give my notice and be there as soon as I can."

He spoke sharply. "My dear, don't do anything immediately. As it is, you will have to contribute, I imagine, to her hospital expenses as well as support yourself. For the moment you can serve her best by keeping busy. She's very proud of you, you know, and if you wish, you can call and talk to her often."

The flood burst through. "Doctor, isn't my mother going to live?"

"No, my dear," he said.

The next three months were my purgatory. Ann Amster and Alice did what they could, and eventually Fanny found out and helped by being brusque when I needed it most. During the daytime I wandered the streets in a daze and sat in endless movie houses, with tears I wasn't even aware of dripping off my chin and spilling on my clenched hands.

In between, I pulled myself together for my calls to Mother and told her stories about Roger Davis that made her laugh. I invented parties I'd gone to and she responded, sounding weaker all the time.

When I questioned the doctor about coming back, he would reply, "Oh, not yet, not quite yet."

I had broken off my romance months earlier—too many complications—and now a boy I'd met in the Theater Guild show became my greatest help, by his realistic attitude and refusing to allow me self-pity. When I'd dissolve into tears over dinner in the Automat, which was all we could afford, he'd sting me with contemptuous words intended to make me mad. Sundays, when I had no performance to force myself to face, he'd take me to visit his family outside of New York and encourage his friends to tease me and inveigle me into games. Bless him!

One day, a telegram came. My heart stopped, but it was my grandmother who had slipped peacefully away in her sleep. I cried in gratitude that she had not outlived my mother and would never have to know when Mother went.

Three weeks later, Fanny invited me to dinner. "I can't come, Fanny. I have to call my mother tonight."

"You can call from my place after dinner."

I phoned and reached the nurse. "She's in a coma, dear," she said gently.

"Let me try to speak to her," I begged.

All the endearments in the world couldn't reach her. With the click of the receiver, one nightmare was over, and when, three days later, the news of her death came, it was almost an anticlimax.

In the months that followed, I worked through a new nightmare, of guilt and remorse that I hadn't gone to her sooner.

I had no feeling about the funeral. She was no longer there, and her request had always been for cremation and no ceremony. I had no doubt that her command to me would have been to stay where I was and go on working. Indeed, without work I would have ceased to function.

Not long after, there was a reencounter with my ex-love. His honest sympathy and protestations of his need for me ended in plans for marriage in Los Angeles when I'd settled my mother's affairs. I stifled my misgivings.

By the time the show had closed and I'd finished going through the empty houses where, in such a short time, I'd lost three of the dearest people in my world, I knew the complications were too many, so I ended it. It wasn't easy, as my loneliness was so acute, but once again work came to my aid.

In the spring of 1937 I had a call from my agent. He said I'd been offered a part in a motion picture at Universal Studios. It was called *Oh Doctor!* and its title was an apt description of the final result. However, it gave me a chance to play a villainess, and, more than that, I formed a friendship with Edward Everett Horton, a wonderful man as well as a great comedian.

He invited me almost weekly to the champagne breakfasts he

gave at Belly Acres, his estate in Encino. The place was like Tara, and filled with antiques that he bought by the houseful. He was continually building guest houses to hold all the antiques and visitors.

His mother, in her eighties then, made biscuits and luscious breads for his many guests. Eddie's breakfasts, and the more elaborate dinner parties he gave often, made up most of my social life, and in a very grand manner indeed. His dining room was a baronial hall where musicians played on a balcony high above. After dinner the guests would take coffee in an enormous living room with two great fireplaces facing each other and, at one end, twin grand pianos, on which famous musician guests would play.

These guests were the famous from the worlds of theater, films, ballet, and opera. Offhand, I can name three who impressed me for different reasons: charming Herbert Marshall, for his delicious sense of humor; Merle Oberon, for her beauty (I was later to make a movie with her); and Ronald Colman, a man who personified romance.

How could I have known that someday I would be living in Colman's former hideaway on the acres in Hidden Valley, where my husband and I and our four children would spend nineteen years? How mysterious life can be.

I decided not to return to New York right then—too many memories. So when Universal wanted to do a screen test of me for a contract, I agreed. Meanwhile, I rented a charming apartment on a hill on Vine Street and bought a small convertible and arranged for driving lessons, as I hadn't driven since high school. I took three of them, and, having acquired great confidence, backed out of the garage, tearing off a fender and the garage door in the process. Not at all dismayed, I became the scourge of the highways. I was so elated at the freedom it gave me, that I remember a male friend saying in an exasperated voice, "Do you realize you are now doing *seventy-five miles an hour through a town!*"

The test at Universal I thought a disaster. A scene that featured two girls doing dishes was assigned to a neophyte director on the lot. He promptly cast a lovely starlet, a close friend, as the dishwasher. He stationed her at a corner of the sink facing the camera, bathed in an ambience of light. Then he told her to keep her chin high and her lashes lowered.

When I saw the test, I hardly recognized the girl who stalked the background in a gray area, drying and putting away the dishes as she spoke the funny lines. I thought my movie career was over before it had begun, and the studio evidently agreed with me.

But Fate, ever a pixie, arranged that Gregory La Cava, a fine director, send for the test to see the beauteous starlet as a prospect for his upcoming RKO picture. Instead, he became intrigued with the gloomy figure in the background, and sent for me.

The picture, he said, was to be called *Stage Door.* I had seen the play in New York and loved it. It was to star Katharine Hepburn and Ginger Rogers and feature Gail Patrick and Andrea Leeds, and, among the studio contract players, Lucille Ball and Ann Miller. The men were Adolphe Menjou and Jack Carson.

Mr. La Cava said, "I work differently from many directors, and my writer and I write most of our scenes as we go, so I can't offer you a specific part, but I like certain qualities I see in you and want very much to use you in the picture." I was flattered by these words from an eminent director, but couldn't see much room for me in that galaxy of names. Also, my agent was asking an impressive salary for his "stage star."

I had a sudden inspiration. "Look, Mr. La Cava," I said boldly. "Suppose I work for you for a couple of weeks. By that time you should know if a character is developing satisfactorily for you, and I will know whether I want to continue. If not, no hard feelings on either side. Okay?"

He smiled and we shook hands on it, and a week or so later I turned up for a reading. All the girls in the group were assembled, and sheets containing lines were handed around. Lines one, two, three, et cetera, were tossed to us like bones to puppies. I had immediately spotted two lines I was drooling over, but alas, they were not to be mine.

When the reading started, however, the first of the juicy lines was greeted by complete silence. Finally, I could stand it no longer. "If no one wants this, I'll take it," I said bravely, read it, and was rewarded with a laugh. Katharine Hepburn hooted from her perch on a ladder overlooking us. "She's the one to watch out for, girls." She laughed. No more than a minute later, the second line came due. I couldn't believe it when again no one read it. This time I didn't wait so long. "Well, if you gals don't know a good line when you see it!" I read it. Everyone laughed again, and the reading was over.

The next day Mr. La Cava called me in. "I've been trying to think how we could give this character something different than the others. Got any ideas?"

I didn't have, but finally said, "I just got a couple of cats from the pound and have had a few funny experiences; maybe I could be the girl with a cat. Maybe I call it Henry, but it turns out to be a pregnant Henrietta." I looked none too hopefully at my director, but he grinned and said, "Not bad."

So when shooting commenced there was Henry, incarnate in a white shorthair who earned more money than most of the contract girls.

When we shot the first day, I was to be cracking peanuts as I walked around talking to the girls. A little stymied with only two hands, I draped Henry around my neck and he hung there peacefully. Greg yelled, "Hey, that's great. Will he stay?"

In my first scene in the picture I appeared to be wearing a fur scarf over my blouse until the fur scarf's tail switched angrily into the air.

It was an enjoyable picture, and several of the women from it weave through my life now and then. Ginger and I constantly crossed paths doing theater in Chicago. When she was appearing in *Hello, Dolly!* in New York, I had taken over from Carol Channing to do *Dolly* in Chicago, and dancers from the two shows occasionally changed places and brought us messages from each other.

Lucy and I filmed "I Love Lucy" and "Our Miss Brooks" on adjoining stages, and at one time Lucy and Desi gave a weekly square dance, which I attended and loved.

After *Stage Door,* Gail Patrick had a yearly Christmas party, which I rarely missed.

Andrea Leeds and I are still good friends. She lives in Palm Springs and has a beautiful shop there called Andrea's. I don't get to see her often, but she has always remembered my girls at Christmas, starting with dolls complete with wardrobe, and on to lovely necklaces or bracelets. I write and say, "Enough already! Do you *know* how old Connie is?" Andrea has had much sadness in her life, having lost a husband and a lovely young daughter, and it gives her joy, I guess, to remember my girls, lovely lady that she is.

Ann Miller was a very young gal from Texas, and I remember her always for an episode that was funny, even in the context of tragedy.

The sudden death of Jean Harlow had shocked all of us on the set that morning. Ginger and I were reading the black headlines: JEAN HARLOW DEAD AT 27. The other girls clustered around the sofa where we sat, shaking their heads in disbelief.

I suddenly became aware of Annie behind me. Dressed in a short pleated skirt and jacket, with a beret on her curly head, she looked all of thirteen. She was chewing gum ferociously and murmuring sympathetically as she tapped a time step: "Oh my gawd, poor Jean Harlow. Oh my gawd, poor Jean Harlow!"

I began to entertain a little in my attractive apartment. Discovering that a large party Eddie Horton invited me to was a celebration for his birthday, but that the actual date was two weeks later, I invited him for dinner on that night and said I would have his favorite dishes for him. I was chagrined when he suggested beef stew and ice cream. How can you make a big to-do about beef stew?

I rallied cheerfully, and made plans. I had discovered a priceless couple who came by the day and made entertaining a joy. For the sum of $25, Gertrude, the German wife-cook, and Robert, the English butler-husband, arrived in the morning and took over. They raised an eyebrow at the order of beef stew and ice cream, but banished me from the kitchen and went to work.

The rested hostess, feeling glamorous, greeted Eddie and a few other guests and the evening went merrily. The beef stew was a triumph. Robert the Magnificent brought it to the table piping hot. On a huge yellow platter, the meat, carrots, potatoes, string beans, and onions were arranged in checkerboard squares like a modern painting, gravy boat on the side. Eddie was delighted and poured the wine he brought.

At that moment Robert's soft voice penetrated my ear. "Madam," he said, "I can't seem to locate the ice cream. Can you tell me where it is?" The expression of horror on my face explained that I'd forgotten it. About to blurt out an apology, I was deterred by Robert's warning finger.

Some uncomfortable moments later, he served a delicate dessert from a can of nectarines he'd found and combined with thinly sliced oranges.

"What a beautiful finish for a delicious dinner," Eddie declared. I beamed at Robert as he set before me a finger bowl (my cereal dish) floating some pink rose petals.

Where, oh where are Robert and Gertrude now, when I need them?

I did pictures at Paramount, Universal, and RKO. *Having a Wonderful Time,* in which I played a Brooklyn wallflower in horn-rims and hideously ruffled organdy, was a reunion with Ginger, Lucille, and Ann Miller.

I remember a funny moment in a Paramount picture when Fred McMurray, the leading man, still terribly nervous, kept blowing his lines. He was a big favorite of mine and I cringed each time the sound man would identify the beginning of the scene with "Take 64," then, "Take 65," as poor Fred muffed it again.

Finally, some perceptive soul got to the sound man and warned him that he was making Fred more nervous with his bellow. So, on the next take, the contrite sound man hissed softly, "Take 66," and the tense set erupted in laughter, in which Fred joined heartily— and the next take was perfect.

The days were fine now, but the nights, when I read myself to sleep only to wake from the nightmare that told me my mother was gone for good, were still bad. It made it difficult when those phone calls from my New York love still came, less frequently now, and I yearned to say, "You're right, it will still work out," when any compromise seemed preferable to loneliness. I refrained, and gradually things improved.

CHAPTER
·8·

Around that time, Alice Buchanan came to town in the Clare Booth Luce play *The Women.* She was playing the juicy comedy part of Sylvia the bitch. She spent her Sundays with me, and during the third week she said, "A young friend of someone in the cast has been backstage several nights. He's on vacation from New York and kind of lonely, I think. He's very attractive and really nice. I'd like you to meet him. Could I bring him out next Sunday?"

So on Sunday I met the highly touted—Edward Bergen, and immediately dismissed him as too handsome and not my type at all. But there was my need for companionship, and I began to accept his persistent invitations to "dinner and a movie," and before I realized it, the relationship had jelled into a pleasant habit. Ned and I enjoyed each other's company and laughed a lot together. Then followed a short period of arguments as he began to press for marriage.

Feeling the net closing around me, I fought back and didn't see him, while I asked myself all those questions. Did I love him enough? Did he love me enough? Was it career versus marriage?

Tired of the mental conflict, I remembered my mother saying, "I think you have the talent to become whatever you want as an actress, but knowing you and your love for children, I think you'd be happier with a husband and family."

I gave up the struggle and became a June bride, in Reno of all places, and life was satisfying. Ned got a job in the insurance business in Hollywood instead of New York. I made picture after picture and had a husband to come home to at night. I seemed to have it all.

Persuaded by friends that we should build instead of paying rent, my homemaking instincts came alive. We bought a hillside lot and I drew my own plans on brown paper. Then I sat daily with the architect and he translated them to beautiful blueprints. And

45

then came the joy of climbing through the framework of our first home. In the midst of my preoccupation with building I began a picture with Loretta Young and darling old C. Aubrey Smith. Travis Banton made me lovely clothes. It was hard to comprehend the threat of war that was hanging over Europe, even when David Niven, Loretta's co-star, told us he was leaving to join up in England. He amused us with hilarious routines as a British officer, urging his troops on out of the trenches, but never quite making it himself. It was long before Pearl Harbor, though, and had little reality for us.

Between pictures I haunted the antique shops and began a collection of Early American furniture, with its soft glowing pines and maples. The furniture was a direct antithesis of the kind of modern woman with a cool, fashionable exterior and a sharp, witty mind for which I was beginning to be known in my films.

I was drawn to American Primitives of children, and collected them, along with pewter occupational shaving mugs and a group of early clocks called Wag-on-the-Wall. A lovely pine grandmother clock was a prize. Later I had the clocks all put into working order, and one night I happily wound them all and went to sleep to their ticking, only to be brought bolt upright in my bed every fifteen minutes all night long by a cacophony of gongs and tintinnabulations of bells. This became unbearable, of course, and required a bolt of absorbent cotton tucked into various clock crannies to stop.

When our house was finished I experienced the joy a bird must feel when she tucks the last twig in place and flies a little way off to get the full effect of her creation. My work in pictures had never given me the same kind of reward. Having learned from the few premieres I'd attended that I was totally unable to be objective about myself, I simply stayed away. But this lovely white house with its green shutters and its fireplaces had reality for me. My favorable opinion of it was reinforced when *House Beautiful* photographed it and later made it the cover of a yearly issue called "How to Be Your Own Decorator." The letters I received asking "Where can I get . . ." or "How should I do . . ." were as flattering to me as any fan mail ever was.

We had barely moved into our house and were spending our nights gazing at the sea of lights below us when I had a call asking me to meet with Oscar Hammerstein II and Jerome Kern at the latter's Beverly Hills home.

It was about a musical to be called *Very Warm for May*, to be produced for Broadway almost immediately. If I'd had precognition at that moment, and had known that it was really to be "Very Cold for October," I'd have said no. But Jerome Kern played the beautiful "All the Things You Are," and other songs from the score, and I went home, bemused, to discuss the offer with Ned. He thought it was a great chance for me, and since his job was as easily done in New York, we called a friend's mother, who was delighted to care for our new house, and we were off.

The experience of working with Oscar and Jerome Kern was one I treasured. Oscar, a shy, kindly bear of a man, startled me on the fourth day of rehearsal by asking me if I would mark on my script any scenes or lines I felt could be improved upon. Encouraged by his interest, I did as he requested and underlined what I felt were the weak spots, and hoped he wouldn't be insulted by the number of them I had marked. A few days later, he shyly handed me a sheaf of papers in which every point I'd mentioned was vastly improved. If only I'd had Mary Martin's voice, I'd have fought like a tiger to work in any of his subsequent hits.

Strangely enough, on opening night we were greeted with laughter, applause, and even bravos, and dear Max Gordon, our producer, was ecstatic. I had a chilling feeling that he was being premature, knowing the unpredictability of critics, and I was right. We did, however, run eight weeks.

Fortunately, I had some good personal notices and had been seen by the producer of a revue to be called *Two for the Show,* and I went to work even before we closed our musical. The revue offered me very good material: a take-off on Gertrude Lawrence, my idol at the moment, and some other satirical numbers and sketches. It was a strenuous show for me, and after several months it began to play havoc with my voice.

Only an actor who has experienced it can know the terror when night after night your voice leaves you high and dry in the middle of a sketch or number. I realized I was running the risk of losing my voice permanently, so I gave my notice. Weeks dragged on as the management claimed they couldn't find a replacement who could do the varied material.

So on the night I opened my mouth to emit not so much as a faint croak, I became hysterical, and they agreed to parcel out the less important numbers among the company and get an immediate replacement for the part. I bade a sad farewell to my second company that year. Ned and I drove dejectedly across the country, taking our time to allow me to recover my voice. It took three months before a whole octave of my vocal chords returned to normal.

We were thrilled to be home again in our barely lived-in house, and now began to plan the garden, a never-ending process, since we eventually bought the lot below and added a pool. With that in view, I blithely hired a man to start building stone terraces. He agreed to stay a few weeks until we could "see where he was going." Where he was going was into five years of stonework and paths and rose beds and trees and more terraces.

In 1939, I was called to do a picture at MGM with the Marx Brothers. They were at their zenith then, and the fair-haired boys of the lot. The picture was *A Day at the Circus,* and my part was a zany one. I was to be the lady who walked on the ceiling. I couldn't imagine how they were going to shoot it, but the day I reported for a fitting of my spangled velvet bodice and black tights, I got my information from the wardrobe woman, familiarly known as "the horse's mouth." They had already fitted the stunt girl who was to double for me, and she was busy practicing walking upside-down with plumber's helpers on her shoes. She was to do the stunt on a platform fastened to the top of the big circus tent.

In a day or so, I arrived, letter-perfect, to do a scene with Groucho. As I slipped on my leotard and spangles in the set dressing room, I could hear Margaret Dumont, the grande dame of the Marx Brothers pictures, complaining in her most elegant voice that her dressing room had no top on it. "They wouldn't *dare* do this to Greta Garbo," she boomed.

I was summoned to the set and introduced to Groucho, and the director explained the action. I may have been provided with a stunt girl, but they also saved a stunt or two for little Eve!

I was to climb up on a sort of pipe grid and lie flat on it—being careful to keep my fanny above the camera lens (not too difficult, since by now my rear was much smaller than it had been in *Stage Door*). Groucho was to enter, looking for me, and as he called I was to swing, head down, hanging by my knees, and read several lines of dialogue with him. Then I was to pull myself and my fanny out of sight. No hands, please!

Well, I thought, good thing I still have those strong stomach muscles from my tree-climbing childhood. Several rehearsals later they were wearing down a little, and I was looking with a slightly jaundiced eye at Mr. Marx, who seemed more inclined to play than work that day. Seven spoiled takes later, I couldn't have cared less what his reasons were for muffing his lines. I was furious.

I requested permission to descend from my "rack" and stalked past Mr. G. to a makeup table off the set. I shook the angry tears from my eyes, gave my nose a defiant blow, and stalked back again. Fixing Groucho with a steely eye, I said, "Let's get it now, shall we?" And we did. And became good friends.

I enjoyed the rest of the picture, particularly knowing Harpo, a charming, gentle man. The line from the picture that most people remember happened when Groucho, knowing the money was hidden in my bosom, leered at my décolletage, then at the camera, and said, "There has to be a way of getting that without getting into trouble with the Hays Office" (censor, to you). I'm afraid in these days he'd have unzipped my bodice and wrestled me to the floor.

Next, I made *Women in the Wind* with the lovely "Kay Fwancis," who couldn't pronounce her *r*'s. Directed by John Farrow, Mia's father, it concerned the first Powder Puff Derby, and I was the girl who crashed. I had a very dramatic scene in the plane, struggling with the controls, oil spurting in my face, and then the plane crashed. Finally, I was carried on a stretcher past Kay Francis and urged her to "go on and win for me!"

It was one of the few premieres I was "requested" to attend and, to my horror, after the oil-in-the-face scene, I saw them cut to a plane in a completely vertical dive, flames shooting from every angle, ending in a crash to forecast the atom bomb. A little fanciful work by the special-effects man who had not watched the rest of the scene! As they carried me on a litter across the screen, virtually untouched and every hair in place, the audience howled!

Almost immediately Warner Bros. cast me in *A Child Is Born.* Among the featured players was Gladys George, who had been one of the most beautiful and talented of the Henry Duffy leading ladies while I was still in high school. It saddened me to see her playing little more than a bit part in the hospital maternity ward. I had heard she was now addicted to alcohol, and I could see her hand shaking as I approached.

Playing a nurse in the background of the scene being shot, I studied her chart, then smoothed her bedclothes and fluffed her pillows.

"Hello, Miss George," I whispered. She looked at me, startled. "My name is Eve Arden," I went on, "and I'm a longtime fan of yours." She smiled faintly, but with a distracted air.

"Say, do you know this guy?" she asked in her throaty voice. I looked where she was nodding. Lloyd Bacon sat there in his director's chair. His usual porkpie hat was tipped over his glasses. His chin rested on his hands atop the cane that was his constant companion.

"Not very well," I confessed. "Why?"

"Well, that guy's driving me nuts," she complained. Her eyes flickered from side to side as if looking for the cigarette or drink she couldn't have to calm her.

I plumped her pillow again and asked out of the corner of my mouth, "What's he doing?"

"That's it," she moaned slightly. "He doesn't tell me anything! I don't know what he wants from me. When I finish my lines he just stares at me through those goggles and then he says, 'Do it again.' He's driving me nuts."

Between takes of the scene up front I tried to soothe her and tell her that she'd done her scene beautifully, but she was too distraught. "Why doesn't he tell me what he wants and I could do it?" Her voice was becoming a bit shrill, and I hoped it wouldn't attract Mr. Bacon.

I moved between them. "Listen," I commanded, and got her attention. "It's just the sort of director he is," I explained. "Some know exactly what they want and can give you explicit directions, but others like to leave it to the actors and see what comes out of the scene. He does it over and over in the hope that maybe, because you're tense, he'll get something even better."

Her eyes pleaded with mine. "Honest?" she said.

I smiled reassuringly. "I know if he didn't like what you did you'd have heard. Now why don't you lie back and relax and think about your next scene." I patted her hand and walked quickly away from the gratitude in those eyes. Damn, I thought, damn, damn! Why were actors always so vulnerable?

I had made about six pictures in a row now, and my marriage was beginning to feel the strain. The long hours left me ready for bed, but Ned, with nine-to-five hours, was wanting to party or go to a movie or have friends in. Nothing drastic yet, just tension and a tendency to argue.

I usually left the house before six, and I remember one morning noticing a police car peeking around the corner a block away. Curious, I got in my car and prepared to turn the key. The police car glided alongside.

"Goin' somewhere, lady?" the driver asked.

"Why, yes. I'm on my way to the studio to work," I replied, wondering just what else they suspected I might be doing at that hour.

"Not in that car, lady," he said. "Take a look."

There stood my car, on three sets of blocks and one wheel. I couldn't believe my eyes.

"There's been a lot of car stripping lately," the officer said. "But this is a new one on us." On me, too!

CHAPTER
·9·

Where pictures were concerned, I was now on what is called in Las Vegas a hot roll. I went over to Metro-Goldwyn-Mayer for two pictures. The first was *Comrade X*, with Hedy Lamarr as the Russian, and—joy, oh joy!—I played Clark Gable's girlfriend in it.

We worked on the same newspaper in Moscow. Of course I lost him to the flawless beauty of Hedy Lamarr. But off screen we struck up an immediate rapport, and I was invited to have "tea" with him in his dressing room on the stage every day. We shared lots of laughs because Clark loved to tell stories and so did I.

As I left the studio one evening, I stopped at the gas station across the street from MGM, and in a minute or two Clark drove up as well. As the gas was pumping, he stood by my car to chat. He suddenly asked if he could drive me home. I looked into those Gable eyes and felt as if we were in the middle of a familiar scene. Befuddled, I almost asked, "Where will I leave my car?" Coward that I was, I refused, and smiling sweetly, stepped on the gas while I still had the strength. *Remember,* this was a longtime crush!

Clark was known by his crew as the King. I knew why when I reported for work the next morning and he immediately put me at my ease with the offer of a cup of coffee and was his usual jovial self. We met at a couple of parties after that and exchanged our latest jokes with warm affection.

I stayed to do *Ziegfeld Girl* with Lana Turner, Hedy Lamarr, and Judy Garland. Judy used to read me the poetry she'd written when we met in the makeup department each morning. She was in love with David Rose, the composer, so the poetry was on the sentimental side. She seemed like such a baby to me, and so vulnerable. During the years that followed, I was to see her in many different places and circumstances.

When she was married to Vincente Minnelli and happily pregnant, I showed them photos of my newly adopted baby girl named Liza, and they told me they'd already picked that name if their child was a girl, which of course it was. In a few years the two Lizas attended ballet school together.

Much later, when Judy, now married to Sid Luft, had added Lorna and Joey to her brood, and I was living in Hidden Valley with three more of my own, I heard that my vulnerable little friend was staying at a nearby guest farm, trying to break the hold that liquor or pills had gotten on her. The nurse brought the children over to play with ours, and I hoped I'd see Judy, but she never ventured out of her cottage. Years later, in 1963–4 in London, I saw a picture taken of her on board ship announcing her marriage to someone named Herron. I was so shocked at her appearance. Oh God, I thought, she's dying! But less than a week or so later we attended a costume party given by Zsa Zsa Gabor. As we left, across the huge crowd I spotted Judy, surrounded by people and looking radiant. I couldn't brave the mob but I was happy to see her looking so well. Two days later, we were invited to a cocktail party given by an American singer who lived almost next door to our London mews house. I was greeting one of the few people I knew there when I saw Judy standing by the window. She came toward me with a bright, welcoming smile, but when her cold, tense little hands clutched mine, my heart sank and I knew she was neither well nor happy. When we returned from Europe I saw her once more at the theater one night, and she told me with such pride that she was now known as Liza Minelli's mother. What a loss of talent and spirit!

After *Ziegfeld Girl* I did six pictures one after the other, all at different studios. They included *She Knew All the Answers,* with Joan Bennett and Franchot Tone, and *Manpower,* with Marlene Dietrich, in which I played a B-girl. In *Last of the Duanes*, a Western, I was the saloon owner and took a bullet in my back as I threw myself in front of George Montgomery. I wondered if it had really been worth it, as I tried to play a death scene in his arms while he giggled in my ear and a bored crew chomped hamburgers and waited for the last shot in the picture to end so they could go home to their families.

The three other movies restored some self-esteem. *Obliging Young Lady* meant working with the able Eddie O'Brien and playing a chic southern belle. *Bedtime Story* meant a reunion with Loretta Young and meeting Fredric March and, finally, a man I had always felt I knew through his books, who became a real friend at last, Robert Benchley.

That year I met the director who made the biggest impression on me of any I ever worked with, Ernst Lubitsch. A swarthy, short man, lips constantly mouthing a large cigar, he was an inventive director with a great mind for comedy. He was wonderful to work with, and he made you feel free to offer a line or a bit of business, without offending you in the least if he turned it down.

The picture was *That Uncertain Feeling,* with Melvyn Douglas and lovely Merle Oberon. I was amused and impressed watching Ernst, who, without removing his cigar, demonstrated to Merle how to be seductive—and he really was, stogie and all. I was thrilled when he spoke of our working together in the future, but his sudden death several years later, which shocked and saddened me, made that impossible.

I was beginning to yearn for the theater again and, sure enough, an unexpected offer came to do a new musical called *Let's Face It,* with a book by Dorothy Fields and her brother Herb and music by Cole Porter. It was based on the old play *The Cradle Snatchers.*

Ned and I agreed it was something I should do, so we found a friend to stay in our house and oversee our busy gardener. We took an attractive sublet on West Fifty-fourth Street in the same building with the fabulous Gertie Lawrence and her husband Richard Aldrich.

When we started rehearsals, we had an immediate feeling of success. Danny Kaye, a new young comedian from the "Borscht Circuit," had incredible energy and talent. The rest of the cast, including Vivian Vance and Nanette Fabray, were very good and we were all excited about the show.

After we rehearsed the numbers for a week or so, we were summoned to Cole Porter's suite in the Waldorf Towers to sing for the great man. I was intrigued at the thought of meeting one of the musical geniuses of our day.

Mr. Porter sat in a chair and acknowledged each of our introductions with a curt nod. After we'd sung our way through several numbers to an impassive face, Mr. Porter stood abruptly and said, "That's all." We sat stunned for a second, then found ourselves hustled out into the hall by our musical conductor. Not a good-bye, thank you, or any indication of whether we were good or just plain lousy.

I was indignant. "How rude can you be?" I asked. It was then

1. My mother Lucille, the actress, second lead to Blanche Bates, the star.

2. My mother, the beauty.

3. My mother's mother, Louisa Frank, in her wedding gown, also a beauty.

4. Lucille—even on a houseboat rail she wore a hat and large buttons with style.

5. I never knew that my mother rode a horse, bareback too!

6. The Ladies Auxiliary?
My waist was never
that small!

7. Lucille is on the left in the leg-of-mutton sleeves
and the boater hat. Her best friend is in the tree
above her, and her brother, Arthur, in the
rear with the derby.

8. I *was* cute, if not
a raving beauty!

9. Pre–convent,
but obviously worried
about leaving mother.

10. Knitting is a
serious business.

11. The Shubert's idea
of a Ziegfeld Girl.

12. On the road, in Chicago,
I changed to *my* idea
of a Ziegfeld Girl.

13. In Chicago everybody who was
anybody was photographed by Bloom.

14. *Two For The Show*
in New York at
the Booth Theater.
I play Dietrich in
Destry Rides Again.

16. Peerless Pauline, the girl
who walks on the ceiling,
in *At the Circus* with
playful Groucho!

15. *Two For The Show* leader of the
girls' band, Booth Theater.

17. My life's dream! I got to play Clark Gable's girlfriend in *Comrade X*. Hedy Lamarr took him away from me, darn it!

18. Clark Gable restrains me from telling off Hedy Lamarr in *Comrade X*.

19. This is not a session with my psychiatrist. I was taking dictation in Ernst Lubitsch's film *That Uncertain Feeling*.

20. Bob Hope and I did a Broadway show and this film, *Let's Face It,* and got along famously. "Thanks for the Memory," Bob!

21. *Covergirl* is the only film I did with Gene Kelly and Rita Hayworth, and I loved them both.

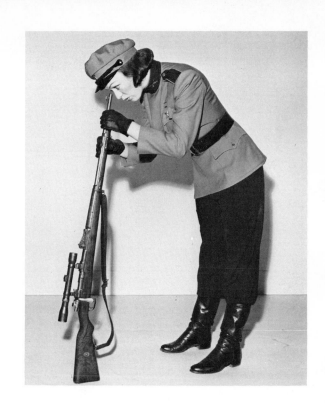

22. A stupid publicity still!
But this is the role in
Doughgirls that got me
my Warner contract.

23. From left to right, my buddy Bob Benchley, Phil Terry, and Eve,
the milliner's daughter. In *Pan-Americana* at RKO.

24. Audrey Long and I calm Benchley's nerves as we welcome him to the set. Audrey married Leslie Charteris, author of the "Saint" series.

25. I'm passing the buck to Joan Crawford while Ann Blythe watches in *Mildred Pierce.*

I learned of the agonies Cole suffered as a result of legs broken years before in a fall from a horse. Badly set, they had healed and then had to be rebroken and reset twice. Later, gangrene had set in and maggots were applied to eat away the infection. He refused to let the legs be amputated, which would have saved him considerable suffering and maybe his life.

We became used to seeing him sitting in his aisle seat during rehearsal or performance and suddenly rising and, with the help of his cane, leaving the theater. We were all distressed by his ordeal.

The publicist for *Let's Face It* had asked me to do an article for a Boston paper while we were appearing there, and I think I did a "humorous piece" on gardening, prompted by the endless terraces at home. It evidently appealed to a number of readers, and he extracted a promise from me to do another article when the show had opened on Broadway. I had good intentions but no inspirations, until he had one, and awoke me one morning with the news that my "article" would be picked up by a messenger from the *New York Herald Tribune* in half an hour.

I now understand writers who claim they can work only under pressure. At any rate, I had it ready in short order. When I found that the paper was sending Mr. Hirschfeld, the noted cartoonist, to do no less than two cartoons to illustrate it, I was thrilled.

He arrived, and I sat almost paralyzed until he'd finished. Then he rose, looked at me (for the first time), and spoke! He said, "Have you ever thought of doing a book of these?"

I cleared my throat and said, brilliantly. "No, ah well, yes—not really."

He cut me short. "Well, I think you should. I just finished illustrating the critic John Mason Brown's book. and I think this is as funny as anything in it."

So saying, he gathered up his accoutrements and left me speechless, but with his words engraved on my brain. I'll let the readers judge for themselves:

AN ACTRESS IS GUEST
OF A WOMEN'S MATINEE CLUB

By Eve Arden

On a sunny day not so long ago as *Let's Face It!* completed its 100th performance at the Imperial Theater I was asked to be the luncheon guest of a women's matinee club. One always

accepts these invitations because apart from the fact that the hostesses are charming, an actor owes it to his profession to encourage mass theatergoing.

From the moment of consent on I believe the routine is the same with every actor. Your smile of acceptance changes to a look of mild trepidation and you ask, "Will I be expected to say anything?" The charming woman's face plainly says that all actors are insane but necessary evils if there are to be shows for matinee clubs to attend.

However, her voice says reassuringly, "Not at all, my dear. Just be there, just be there, and we shall be ever so happy!"

So the actress (in this case me) relaxes in her fool's paradise until the fatal hour is only sixty minutes away. Then suddenly an insidious thought strikes swiftly and treacherously, "What if they do call on you? You can't stand there like a dope, you dope." Suddenly you are panic-stricken and conjure up a picture of miles of women with forks suspended in midair, waiting breathlessly for you to speak. With your hat and coat on and ready to leave for the luncheon, you seat yourself at the desk to jot down a few notes.

Every one of those screamingly funny stage anecdotes you tell at parties has fled your mind. What about those jokes you tell with such devastating effect? You soon realize that the funny ones are not suitable and the suitable ones aren't funny!

Time is of the essence, and you can't sit there chewing a pencil. So you button on your gloves and gird your loins with the thought that after all you are an actress and will be inspired, as you were the time when three actors failed to enter on cue and you brilliantly ad-libbed a four-way scene. Any doubt as to your ability to handle the situation is crushed by the memory of that impressive feat, and you set forth for the luncheon gayly.

The moment you enter you are drowned in a sea of women's faces and hats (you rarely, if ever, see the bodies) and you bob around in a corner wave, hoping someone will recognize you and throw you a life preserver—or a cocktail! No one does. And just as you are going down for the third time, the name of the "boss lady" pops into your consciousness and you grasp at the nearest arm and inquire where she can be found. No one has the faintest idea! The overpowering loneliness of the next few moments can have been experienced only by big-game hunters when they have strayed too far from their party and realize that they probably will never see Broadway again.

Suddenly, however, you spy a fellow actor, and though you never have met socially, this soul-testing experience has forged a bond between you which draws you into a firm little knot of mutual appreciation. Things improve in the next few minutes. The "boss lady" appears, profuse with apologies, and you are introduced to forty-five women, all of whom "loved you" in your last show. A libation soothes you, and a large orchid is pinned on your shoulder.

But you are gnawed by new doubts and fears. First, the women show no signs of drifting lunchward, and, this being matinee day, time, tide and half hours wait for no actor. Also, unless your hair is pinned up for its customary twenty minutes, it becomes more uncooperative through each costume change until your lovely finale gown appears to be topped by a tired bird's nest.

Now, too, you eye your actor comrade-at-arms furtively and wonder what he will say when called upon. To your prejudiced eyes he looks smugly calm and is really enjoying the food that you are toying with. It would be bad enough to disgrace yourself before these hundreds of women, but defeat before a fellow-craftsman, never!

On the last occasion of this sort I discovered accidentally the solution, which I herewith present to all actors for what it is worth. Being strictly a one-cocktail girl myself, I nervously and unconsciously picked up the second drink proffered to me and drank it quickly, thinking to clear my throat. What it did was to clear my thinking, if not my eyesight. And I realized immediately that I was a superior actress with a fund of information and anecdotes at my command—probably charming to see, if not beautiful, with undisputed wit and intelligence. And bestowing a look of sympathy from my one wide-open eye upon my less fortunate "friend-in-Equity," I arose, hiccupped slightly, and gently staggered to the rostrum, where I lived happily ever after —until the matinee!

Let's Face It was a big hit, Danny Kaye the toast of New York, and my notices almost as good. I found myself being photographed for *Harper's Bazaar* (on a tiger-skin rug, though fully clothed) and being interviewed by national magazines. It was all very exciting, except that each night as I made up, I listened to the radio reports from Europe and the war, by H. V. Kaltenborn and Edward R. Murrow. The Germans were marching through all the countries I was hoping to travel to someday. Each night became more depressing. Frightening as it was, one had to listen.

On stage we were able to forget and enjoy our own play world. Blessed with keen eyesight and a talent to dissemble, I was able, during the ingenue's number, to locate the celebrities out front, at the urging of more nearsighted cohorts. From night to night I would report, "The Duke and Duchess of Windsor are on the right aisle, fourth row," or, "Cary Grant's out front, seventh row center."

The night Greta Garbo was rumored to be there I was besieged by the cast and, abandoning subtlety, frankly stared. But it must have been Harriet Brown or one of her other aliases that night, as I never did find her.

One night I said to Danny, "I have a surprise for you. Tallulah Bankhead's in the front row, disguised in a long black wig with a diamond tiara, black gown, and diamond harlequin glasses. The man with her is wearing white tie and tails and has a wide red ribbon across his chest. I don't know what they're planning, but for heaven's sake, let's not let them break us up."

"It" happened in the middle of a dimly lit garden scene as I was proposing a long toast. Across the distinguished gentleman's chest the red ribbon lit up in white lights with "Call for Phillip Morris," Tallulah's radio sponsor at the time.

To my everlasting credit, with hardly a crack in my voice I finished the toast. Forewarned, everyone refrained from laughing at Tallulah's elaborate joke. Later, backstage, she complained, "How in the world did you recognize me, dahling?" Somehow, Tallulah was Tallulah, even if disguised as Shirley Temple.

One Sunday afternoon I was running a vacuum over our sublet carpet and could catch only an occasional phrase from the radio I had on. "Attacking in waves," I heard. "Battleships already sunk," and the words "Pearl Harbor" and "Japanese planes."

Well, I thought, Orson's done it again. A moment later, vacuum silent, I realized that indeed they were bombing Pearl Harbor. I sat numbed, trying to accept the fact that we were now at war.

Monday after dinner, we joined a dazed group backstage at the Imperial Theater. Unexpectedly, we found an audience waiting. I guess they figured they might as well go to the theater as anywhere.

We experienced our first blackout, which was terrifying but didn't last long, and after the shock wore off we settled down to a steady diet of bad news on two fronts, and tried to give our audiences a couple of hours of release from tension.

Bob Benchley cheered me up when he dropped backstage with his son Nat and Liz Whitney, whom I knew only as a socialite and thoroughbred horse breeder. They'd been dining well at "21" and, I suspected, drinking even better. My dressing room was the closest to the stage, so I got more and more nervous as the laughter grew more hilarious. The stage manager began hissing at me from the wings because Danny was doing his "scat" number. I did my best to shush them, but they were very happy! When Danny came off he was delighted to meet Bob. Shortly after we were both due on stage, so I gave a sigh of relief when the visiting threesome continued on their merry way.

I had refused to extend my year's contract, so when it was up we returned home to await Ned's army summons. Shortly after that, he left for training in Texas. Again, I was alone.

Fortunately I stayed busy. Paramount signed me for the movie version of *Let's Face It*, with Bob Hope, since Danny Kaye had signed a contract at Goldwyn.

ZaSu Pitts, a great lady, was in the picture and, with my husband in camp and hers a professional tennis player, we spent a lot of time together, mostly in her fantastic kitchen, making date-nut cookies for the cast and crew.

CHAPTER
· 10 ·

My longing for children began to fill my thoughts more and more. I'd often considered adoption and felt that anyone who loved them as I did should adopt. In spite of certain fears about childbirth I had never done anything to prevent conception and assumed I was not to have my own. Now, with the war promising to last for years, I didn't want to wait any longer. On Ned's next visit home I discussed the idea of adoption with him and he agreed we should investigate the way to proceed.

A month or so later I was beginning a picture called *Pan-Americana* at RKO. Phil Terry was playing the lead, and one day I got up the nerve to ask if he could give me some advice about adoption. He was married to Joan Crawford then, and I knew they had two adopted children. Phil said, "Well, I could tell you a little, but Joan's the one to speak to. I'll have her call you." I thanked him but thought I won't wait for *that!* At six forty-five the next morning my phone rang and That Voice said, "This is Joan Crawford, Eve. I have a baby for you!" I was almost too stunned to answer, but we made a date for lunch two days later and although that baby was not to become mine, Joan did initiate action that was to lead in six months or so to the first of my brood.

When I went in for my second fitting on the gorgeous clothes for *Pan-Americana* I was happy to discover that Bob Benchley was also in the picture and working that day. Bob was very nervous when he acted, and his first day on a picture was agony for him. So when the wardrobe girl reported from the set that he was blowing one line after the other, I grabbed the ingenue who was there and we ran into the prop department. She took an armful of fake calla lilies and I chose some huge purple thistles. Thus armed, we approached a back door to the set in time to hear Bob miss another line. Bursting into the tense atmosphere, we sang to the tune of "Happy Birthday," "Welcome to RKO, welcome to

Check us out
on the Web at
www.bhg.com
AOL Keyword: bhg

BUSINESS REPLY MAIL

FIRST-CLASS MAIL   PERMIT NO. 120   BOONE, IA

POSTAGE WILL BE PAID BY ADDRESSEE

BETTER HOMES AND GARDENS® Magazine

PO BOX 37428
BOONE IA 50037- 2428

RKO, welcome to RKO, Robert Benchley," et cetera. The tension broke. Bob laughed and hugged us, and the scene went well after that.

At Columbia Studios the picture that followed for me was *Cover Girl,* a tremendous musical largely because of the radiant though still shy Rita Hayworth and Gene Kelly's vibrant dancing. A bevy of glamorous "real" cover girls fleshed out the spectacular show.

Orson Welles was an occasional visitor on the set, as he and Rita were soon to be married. In this film I was Otto Kruger's consultant in charge of hiring the girls.

Harry Cohn was the shrewd producer and head of the studio. He was not noted for his charm or tact. A well-known woman designer from New York had done most of the clothes, which were chic but a trifle conservative. After lunch one day, we were summoned onto the set in costume along with the designer. Then Mr. Cohn appeared and beginning with "You call these rags designing?" he proceeded to take the poor woman apart outfit by outfit. It was a shameful exhibition, and although we finally wound up with more theatrical clothes, it was unnecessarily cruel.

A few weeks after this, I was doing a scene in which I walked through my boss's study containing a billiard table. As a piece of "business" I suggested I pick up a cue and attempt a shot, but since I'd obviously never played before, my cue would catch in a soft spot and, to my horror, I'd rip the green cover right down the middle. Then I'd look around, quietly put down the cue, and leave. Our director, a sort of sour Hungarian, surprisingly liked the gag, and the prop room, always ready, came up with a false green top as we prepared to do the shot.

Harry Cohn, who'd been out of town for several days, picked this moment to appear on the set, in time to see me destroy what appeared to be his expensive billiard table. He gave a roar like a wounded bull elephant, and was only restrained from mayhem by a rapid explanation in a nervous Hungarian accent.

In spite of Harry's interference, *Cover Girl* was one of the biggest hits of the year, and shortly after, Warner Bros. offered me a chance to work with Barbara Stanwyck in *My Reputation.* I'd always admired Barbara, and working with her only increased my admiration. She was adored by cast and crew alike.

Incidentally, in this picture the rules were bent for the first time, when my screen husband and I were filmed in bed together, without observing the Hays Office dictum of keeping one foot on the floor. A breakthrough indeed, but I refuse to take the blame for where things have gone from there.

Around the lot or in the commissary during the filming of *My Reputation,* I noticed a striking Russian military uniform walking around, each day with a different female body in it. Curious, I inquired and found that they were testing for the part of the Russian guerrilla in the film to be made from the Broadway play *Doughgirls.* Knowing that Annie Sheridan was to play the wise-cracking girl that I often portrayed, I thought the Russian part might be fun to do. I knew Mark Hellinger, the producer, and asked him if I could test for it. Mark liked the idea, but said, "I don't think Jack Warner would give that part to anyone who isn't under contract."

He did get me the test, however, and my love of dialects and the off-beat character resulted in a test the crew found hilarious. Evidently, so did Jack Warner, because the afternoon he screened it, my agent was summoned immediately to discuss a contract. So I joined Annie, Jane Wyman, and Alexis Smith in what was a romp to make, but due to the first effort of an inexperienced director, it didn't make much "dough" for Warner Bros., and I regretted that they hadn't released my test instead! It did, however, get me the only kind of contract I wanted to sign: two pictures a year, an option for a third, and the right to do Broadway shows and radio. I signed with Warner Bros. for seven years.

During the making of *Doughgirls* everyone on the set had been excited about my adopting a baby. Hairdressers, wardrobe women, and script girls knitted booties, sweaters, and blankets. And, strangely enough, most of them were pink. Jane Wyman gave me a baby shower at the Riviera Country Club.

I had made two dear friends in Connie Raffetto and her husband Mike. He was a writer-director-actor in motion pictures and radio, and had created the part of Paul in *One Man's Family.* Connie, beautiful and talented, did unusual ceramic figures of people and animals, and had a growing reputation as an artist. She had become my closest friend in Hollywood.

Connie was expecting a baby very soon. Being close friends, we hoped that our babies would be the same sex and not too far apart in age so that they too could be friends.

It was not long after I finished *Doughgirls* that Mike called one morning to tell me that Connie had just given birth to a baby girl named Pamela. Coincidentally, an hour and a half later, the little girl I was to call Liza was born.

Only days after that, I opened my front door to see a smiling woman who looked to me like a messenger from heaven. She was holding in her arms one of the cherubim, and the most adorable baby I'd ever seen, my own daughter, Liza.

For days I hung over her crib, hardly daring to breathe for fear she might vanish. This was fulfillment beyond anything I'd felt before. To know that this incredibly small being was dependent on me for her welfare made me suddenly feel inadequate. But I knew I couldn't fail at something I wanted so much.

I'd been preparing for months for her arrival, and had interviewed several recommended nurses. I'd easily settled on a sweet-faced white-haired woman with soft brown eyes. She became "Nanny" to Liza and gave me such peace of mind when I had to work that I am forever grateful. To come home and find Nanny, who insisted that we didn't need a housekeeper, cooking my dinner, the house in order, and a baby who was starting to recognize me and smile, was giving my life a focus, and a sense of purpose for my work.

I was getting help in another area now. For a year or more I'd been seeing a psychoanalyst to help me with the lingering traumas of loss. But something else was disturbing me. From time to time I had found myself strongly attracted to several men, always married ones, and I worried that this was becoming a pattern in my life. Perhaps I felt safe because they were "taken." Once I had started with analysis, it was like hiring the gardener "to see where we were going," and it lasted five years. I suppose analysis is like eating popcorn—it's difficult to know when to stop. I finally wrote this poem to my analyst and shortly thereafter "resigned."

PLEA TO A
PSYCHIATRIST
CHRISTMAS 1951

Save this patient's battered ego
help express her shy libido
guide her faltering feet, lest she go
    berserk and hog-wild

Teach her to "let out" aggression
turn away despair, depression
make unpleasant nightmares "lesshion"
    for mothers' little child

Lest she deem her fault a virtue
make her dig up all the dirt you
know must lie beneath the hurt (you
    big sadistic bum!)

Now her dreams with symbols filling
as "unconscious" does her willing
no more feels she need for killing
    adjustment day will come

So, out the window with her humor
"generous girl," it's just a rumor
but she'll never get a tumor
    suppressing thoughts so bad

So, hurrah for couch and notebook
what becomes of all the notes "took"
can't we print them like a cookbook
    they would sell like *mad!*

Before I go into a coma
or become a real "dip*s*oma"
Can't I please get my diploma?
    Joyeux Noel, doctor dear

Turn me out so well adjusted
libido free, and hot as mustard
but do it *quick,* before I'm "busted"
    and a *Very* Happy New Year
            ——*Eve*

When Liza arrived in my life, I also took my first Foster Parents child, a little French boy named Daniel, whose father had died of the wounds he received from the Allied bombings as they landed in Saint-Lô. As I watched my baby grow plump and rosy, it made me happy to think of another child, a few years older, living a little better than he would otherwise.

CHAPTER
· 11 ·

While I was grateful for the picture offers that kept coming my way, it was still the theater that excited me. Sometime before, I had met Gregory Peck and his wife Greta and been part of a group that met now and then to play charades, which all actors love. Greg, Mel Ferrer, and Dorothy McGuire had started a theater in La Jolla for the summer months, and they had asked me to do a play. We decided on *Biography* by Sam Behrman, and we did a production with a wonderful cast: Barry Sullivan, Sig Ruman, a great character actor and a lovely man, Patricia Medina, a real English beauty, and John Hoyt, with whom I had worked in New York. We got splendid notices and decided to take it to Hollywood, where the Las Palmas Theater had just been refurbished. We played there for eight weeks, and I could spend my days at home.

Warners assigned me to a picture called *Mildred Pierce* with Joan Crawford, to be directed by Michael Curtiz. It seemed a fairly interesting script, but I would never have guessed that it would bring Crawford her only Oscar and me a nomination in the supporting category, and become a classic that still plays on TV after all these years.

Joan and I got along well together, and I always enjoyed working with Curtiz, who was one of the few directors who knew what he wanted and was able to express himself exactly, even in his amusing Hungarian accent. Jack Carson, Zachary Scott, and Ann Blythe completed the cast.

On the night of the Academy Awards Joan was terrified that she wouldn't win and terrified that she would. She promptly got a psychosomatic cold and laryngitis, and was photographed by a news cameraman in bed, with a lacy handkerchief around her neck, receiving her Oscar from Michael Curtiz. I sympathized with Joan, but was "requested" by the studio to attend the Academy Awards, and watched Anne Revere sweep the Oscar from under my nose

65

for her marvelous performance as Liz Taylor's mother in *National Velvet*. But it was great being nominated.

Several weeks later at a surprise birthday party I was given, the Gregory Pecks, Danny Kaye, and others admired the baby, but by the time Crawford arrived, Liza had been asleep for a while. Joan insisted on seeing her, and I couldn't refuse her since I felt so grateful for her help. I warned her that Liza had had trouble getting to sleep with all the excitement.

Joan bent over the crib and said, "Oh, how adorable," and then, to my horror, picked up the baby and clutched her close, cooing and laughing in her ear. Poor Liza, waking from a sound sleep to find herself in the tight embrace of a stranger, screamed bloody murder. It didn't seem to affect Joan. I could hardly pry the baby away. I attributed Joan's excessive reaction to a few martinis before she arrived.

When Joan adopted her twins, who she refused to acknowledge were twins, Liza was about two. I called Joan on a Sunday and said that, if she was free, we'd like to come out and bring a gift for the babies. Joan replied, "Oh, darling, we're not doing a thing, and the children and I would love to see you both." Joan made it sound as if she were just scrubbing the bathrooms, which she often did, and that we would be a welcome diversion. So Liza and I—neat but far from dressy—arrived at Joan's Brentwood door. Before we could ring the bell, the door opened and there stood Joan in a white organdy-and-lace pinafore dress, Christina, slightly behind, in matching organdy, and Christopher in an Eton suit with a tight white collar. We were embraced and led inside, where the adorable curly-headed twins, dressed in blue organdy, sat on the floor and stared at us.

When we had finished admiring the new additions we chatted awhile, and I began to notice little Christopher, who got no response from a much younger Liza, pulling at his Eton collar and shuffling with boredom. Suddenly he said, "Mommy, can I go outdoors and play?" As I was opening my mouth to encourage him, Joan shut my mouth with an indignant "Christopher, how dare you ask to go out and play when we have company! You stay right where you are!" I made our excuses and we left shortly after.

My friendship with Joan, such as it was, sprang from her help with the adoption of Liza, and probably from the fact that she didn't consider me a threat, neither as an actress nor as a rival with men. When she was making *Flamingo Road,* she heard me say how attractive I thought David Brian was. He was her leading man, and to my surprise she brought him to a set I was working on to meet me, and even arranged a date for us after work at a place in the Valley. Meanwhile, I had learned that he was married. I did go to meet him, but my fear of getting involved in another dead-end situation helped me fight off his magnificent blond handsomeness. At the first sign of heavy breathing on his part, I told him that I knew he was married, and at the end of our drink I left—but don't think it was easy.

Universal offered me a part in *One Touch of Venus,* starring Ava Gardner and Robert Walker. In this production I played the secretary to Tom Conway (George Sanders's brother), who owned the department store where the statue of Venus came to life as the gorgeous Ava.

When she first stepped on the set, I thought she was certainly one of the most beautiful girls I'd ever seen. Those catlike green eyes looked me over, and then she smiled. Draped all in white, with her dark curls piled on her head, she shamed the statue from which she turned to flesh. I could understand the rumors floating around the set that Robert Walker was already madly in love with her. He seemed to have his problems with drink, even then. His wife, Jennifer Jones, had left him, and indeed she married David Selznick not long after.

Since most of my scenes were with Tom Conway, I didn't see much of Ava during the picture, but felt she was very much down to earth and likable. One evening about a month after the picture was finished, I ran into her with Howard Duff in the neighborhood drugstore near my home. After a brief chat, Ava said, "Eve, you have a swimming pool, don't you?" I had had one put in during the picture so that Liza could learn to swim. It was a very hot night, so I promptly invited them up for a dip. I dug out one of my bathing suits, which Ava draped over her much smaller figure, and we tied it on with knots. Bikinis were unknown then.

Venus on my diving board was sensational in a suit of knots. What Howard Duff wore I happily can't remember. Later, we sat around my living room talking. I made some coffee because they'd been drinking something called Pernod, which sounded dangerous to me. Ava looked at my pictures of Liza, and I realized how much she must want a child.

Many years later, when my husband and I were in Rome, I heard that Ava had left Spain and was now living in Rome. I remember thinking that I was glad Ava had given up bullfighters, and hoping that she would marry one of those nice warm Italians and have some babies. I'd forgotton that she'd already divorced a singing Italian known as Old Blue Eyes.

After the success of *Mildred Pierce,* Warner Bros. kept me busy. If they didn't have a picture for me, I did one on loan-out, and Warners got the extra salary. That was one little gimmick that many actors were to find tucked away in their contracts, along with the one that said if he or she refused to do a film, the time they held out was simply added to the length of their contract. Olivia de Havilland and Bette Davis were constantly embroiled in fights over clauses like that. I think it was Olivia who managed to put an end to that last one.

I was loaned to Sam Goldwyn for *The Kid from Brooklyn,* with Danny Kaye. It was a routine girlfriend-of-the-villian role, enhanced by lovely clothes made for me by Jean Louis.

Goldwyn ran a tight ship, but I crossed swords with him once, and that had to do with a costume. I had chosen a perfect hat for the suit I was wearing. I arrived in my dressing room to find a completely different hat waiting for me, one I hated on sight. I was told that Mrs. Goldwyn had chosen it and that Mr. Goldwyn had sent word I was to wear it.

I was definitely annoyed. As we sat at lunch the day before with the writers and Danny, Mr. Goldwyn had complimented me on a certain piece of business I'd done and my playing of the part in general. Now I felt betrayed. For the daughter of a milliner, noted for her own taste in hats, to be commanded to wear one that I was sure looked charming on Mrs. Goldwyn and was doubtless destined for her own wardrobe later—well, enough was enough!

I sent word that I had already chosen my hat, and *that* was the one I would wear in the scene, or else. The wardrobe gal tremblingly delivered the ultimatum, and everyone waited, along with me, for Vesuvius to blow.

In fifteen minutes the word came down from on high. Miss Arden was to wear her own hat. The relief on the set was palpable. And while there were other occasional blow-ups, none of them, thankfully, involved me. Sam Goldwyn was one of the few really colorful characters in the business, and his Goldwynisms were genuine and cherished. Above all, he really cared about his pictures.

It was during the making of this picture that I saw Bob Benchley for the last time. He came to visit me on the set, wearing an admiral's uniform, and brought me, unsolicited, a picture of himself in it. I was touched, because Bob never assumed that someone wanted his picture, and I was so delighted that he beamed. When I said I wanted it suitably inscribed, he bore it off saying he'd bring it back in a day or so.

As it happens in show business, I didn't work for the next several days, and when I returned I was told that his short subject was finished and he was off the lot. Ah well, I thought, next time I see him I'll get it. Next time never came. He died shortly after that, and the world, including me, was a lot poorer.

Back to Warners I went to for *Night and Day,* a fictionalized story of Cole Porter that even the magnetic Cary Grant couldn't raise much above a pedestrian script. However, I adored playing a French music-hall performer who was persuaded by her friend (Alexis Smith), in love with the hero, to introduce one of his songs.

Fortunately for me, the song was not supposed to be a hit, but I enjoyed singing "I'm Unlucky at Gambling, I'm Unlucky in Love" and my own brief scene with Cary. I'd admired him as the finest light comedian on the screen, and it was unbelievable to me that he'd never won an Oscar, and until, in the seventies, the Academy voted him an honorary one, he never did.

I did four more pictures the following year, including *The Unfaithful,* with Ann Sheridan and Zachary Scott. The script was confusing, with the writers barely staying ahead of us. I found myself playing three different parts as we went along. When I complained to producer-writer Jerry Wald, he assured me that the rushes looked great, and it would all come together in the final cut.

There was nothing for any of us to do but call on a sense of humor. This we did, to the point where one day we were unable to look each other in the eye without laughing. It became painful both to us and the director, but there was no help. If I gained enough control to read a line, Annie's lip would begin to quiver and her eyelashes would bat. Then Zach's voice would break and the director would yell, "Cut!" As we struggled for composure, someone made the mistake of threatening to call Jack Warner down to the set. That did it. Tears of laughter ruined three makeups and we took a break to recover and repair. Only the fact that we were three of the studio's most professional actors saved our combined necks.

Fortunately for my self-respect, I followed that picture with *Voice of the Turtle,* in which I gave one of the few performances that I was able to watch and enjoy. Our ex-governor and now president, Ronald Reagan, and the lovely Eleanor Parker were the stars. Oddly enough, I have yet to see it on TV, perhaps because for some strange reason it was later retitled *One for the Book.* Why? Who knows! Outside of the money they paid me and some of the people I worked with and the time they allowed me for my child, making pictures was pretty much just a job for me.

So I went back to La Jolla to play *The Road to Rome,* by Robert Sherwood with Wendell Corey playing Hannibal. In the play, as the wife of an elderly Roman senator made captive by Hannibal, I pleaded with him not to sack Rome. Even though pregnant with Hannibal's child, I refused to leave with him, as I wanted him to make his decision for the sake of his own soul, not for love of me. Wendell was marvelous as Hannibal, his only drawbacks being a pair of knobby knees under a short tunic and a tendency to think faster than he could speak. One evening in the last scene, he was making a speech to my elderly husband that was really directed at me, as I stood draped against a column looking pensive. His line was, ". . . and I hope your son inherits the greatness of his father" (meaning himself). What he said was, ". . . and I hope your son inhor . . . , inhor . . . , inhor . . . goddamnit!" And he strode offstage followed by his minions, leaving me to bring down the curtain as best I could.

Liza came down to La Jolla with Nanny to see *The Road to Rome.* She was then two years old. In the scene when Hannibal's soldiers roughly dragged me before him, I heard a piping little voice in the audience: "What are those men doing to my mommy?"

CHAPTER
· 12 ·

On Ned's infrequent visits home from camp we found ourselves little more than strangers, and on his release from the service agreed to a divorce. It was an amicable one. In fact, since I was
in the middle of a long picture schedule, Ned offered to establish
residence in Reno and sue for divorce. Then I would come up and
countersue. So when I arrived in Reno with Liza, Ned met us at the
train and took us to dinner that night.

The next morning, before going to court, my lawyer was telling
me what to expect, when Ned called and suggested we have breakfast with him. The lawyer, who got the gist of the conversation, had
a fit. That could be construed as collusion, he said.

Ned and I remained on friendly terms, but I felt a great sense
of release and more ability to concentrate on my work and, during
my time off, to enjoy my child. Liza was three when she got a baby
sister, which I found—as a single parent—I could adopt in another
state. I named the baby Connie, for my friend Connie Raffetto.
Liza was as delighted as I was with this adorable addition to our
family. The next summer at La Jolla I did a less complicated play,
Here Today, with Bob Alda, whose young son, a pudgy little boy,
showed no signs that he would someday be a triple-threat young
genius known as Alan Alda.

Occasionally the studio gave me a trip to New York to do publicity, and on one of these I took my little girl Liza and my friend
Connie Raffetto. It was my first trip by plane, and I remember Liza
looking out of the window and suddenly asking, "Momma, could
this plane fall down there?" I tried to give a reassuring answer but
I think my lip was quivering.

On the return trip we stopped over in Chicago and had dinner
that night in the famous pump room of Ambassador East. There
I met Bill Paley of CBS Network fame. He was a marvelous dancer

and seemed to think I was, too. It was a pleasant evening, and may have led to my being asked to make a recording test for a radio show to be called "Our Miss Brooks."

A few weeks later I met with Harry Ackerman and Hubbell Robinson at the Beverly Hills Hotel to read the script. When they sensed that I wasn't too interested in the script or in doing radio, they said that two very good new writers, Al Lewis and Joe Quillan, had been given the script and would have a new one for me to read soon. A week later, Harry took me to dinner at Chasen's and the script was so vastly improved that I laughed out loud and I read it between courses. The only problem was that I'd planned to spend the summer in Connecticut with my kids, at the Amsters' farm. I said if they could tape the thirteen scripts before I left, it would be fine. "Miss Brooks" went on the air as a summer replacement, and one day Frank Stanton, then president of CBS, called me at the Amsters' farm and said, "Congratulations!"

"For what?" I asked.

" 'Miss Brooks' is the number 1 program on the air," he answered.

By that time I was completely enamored of my cast and the show, so I was delighted. We were already a family. The unbeatable Gale Gordon, whom I'd known since Henry Duffy days, played Mr. Conklin, the crochety principal. There was Richard Crenna, whose adolescent voice created the hilarious Walter Denton, Miss Brooks's favorite incorrigible student. Jane Morgan was the delightfully daffy Mrs. Davis, my landlady, and Jeff Chandler became our original Mr. Boynton, whose armor Miss Brooks seemed unable to dent. There were other wonderful characters: Harriet Conklin, the principal's daughter, was played by Gloria McMillan; and Miss Enright, my rival for Mr. Boynton, was the talented Mary Jane Croft. There was Len Smith as Stretch Snodgrass, the not-so-bright athlete, and Maurice Marsac played the attractive French teacher with whom Miss Brooks tried to prod Mr. Boynton into a modicum of jealousy.

Meanwhile, still under my Warner contract, I did two pictures with Doris Day, *My Dream Is Yours,* and *Tea for Two,* and another, *The Lady Takes a Sailor,* with Jane Wyman and Dennis Morgan.

I remember Doris Day advising me to "look for a man who will be your friend as well as a lover." She was happily married to Marty Melcher then, and it seemed good advice. I was still trying to find out why I fell madly in love with men who were eager but ineligible, and from whom I would have run like a mouse from a tomcat if they had been completely free.

I began to realize the strain my work could put on me and my children when it led to my doing several pictures in a row with many late hours.

A problem was developing at home, in which Liza's latent jealousy of the newly active Connie led to her clobbering her younger sister a few times. I had warned her severely, when I came home from work one evening and heard a sudden wail coming from the girls' room. Hearing Nanny comforting Connie, I called Liza and asked her to please come to my bedroom. I was undressed and in bed by the time she reluctantly appeared. I drew a deep breath and said, "Liza, what am I going to do with you? I've told you over and over about not hitting Connie and—"

Liza interrupted dramatically. "I know, and you're tired, and you work so hard, and you've got a headache!"

She took the wind out of my sails that night. Later, I gave her a balloon clown as a punching bag with the suggestion that she transfer her anger to him. She gave it a good try, but burst into tears, saying, "I don't want to hurt poor Bozo. I'm not mad at him. I'm mad at Connie!"

And that let the air out of poor Bozo.

CHAPTER
· 13 ·

Life is made up of so many memorable moments, and while I'm not one to live in the past, there are "jewels" I enjoy dribbling through my fingers. Among them are some people I admired but never expected to meet.

I had followed the course of the war with all the great broadcasters, but Edward R. Murrow's reports from London shone above them all, so when some friends of mine had what seemed like a bright idea of doing records of interviews with famous people, and asked me to see if I could contact him on my publicity trip to New York, I was delighted. I asked Mr. Paley if he could arrange a meeting at CBS. He did better than that. Mr. Murrow called to invite me to lunch with him that day. I agreed, of course, and he said he'd pick me up in forty-five minutes.

When he hung up I got hysterical, as I'd just washed my hair. It was soaking wet, and I had no hair dryer. I was still frantically trying to towel-dry it when he called from the lobby of the Hampshire House. I begged for ten more minutes, and he said he would wait in the bar. Finally, I dragged out a hat and plunked it on my head, not wanting to keep my hero waiting any longer.

Having seen Mr. Murrow only on film in black and white, I was totally unprepared for the much taller, very tanned, dark-haired version who rose from the bar to greet me. He was so gorgeous that I was hard put to recover my poise and make some kind of sense. He asked me if I'd like to have lunch in the garden of the Ritz.

What an ideal spot that was, to sit opposite those hypnotic brown eyes and listen to that memorable voice, surrounded by a Japanese garden, as water burbled under the Japanese bridge near our table. I had never been there before, and never went again. It was a moment I wanted to preserve.

We disposed of business in the first five minutes. He had already

74

signed to make recordings. I can't recall what we talked about, but he was charming and flirtatious and made me feel attractive and desirable, in spite of a strand of dank hair that occasionally slipped from under my hat. I went back to California with a delightful memory, and when I heard of his death in 1965, I was as saddened as if I'd known him well.

When I was making my last pictures for Warner Bros., someone talked me into hiring a top press agent, Russell Birdwell. My life was pretty quiet at the moment, so he attempted to spice it up with an imaginary Canadian millionaire who was seriously in love with me, and who sent Liza extravagant presents to persuade me to marry him. The problem was that Birdwell never consulted me before these things appeared in print, so when my friends would call to hear more, I would laugh and say, "Never believe what you read in those columns."

But when my suitor presumably presented Liza with a pony and filled my pool with gardenias, and Hedda Hopper called to check, I denied everything, as I knew she wasn't above coming up to get some pictures. Birdwell and I called the whole thing off.

The happy result of this whole mishap, though, was that I found a new PR man who could stick to the truth and make that interesting. Glenn Rose became my publicist first, then my friend and my manager. In over thirty years we've never signed a contract. He is also the reason that I've always had work when I wanted or needed it, and I can depend on him to tell me the truth. He has been a good friend to my husband and me, and a very stable factor in my life.

I'd always worked for scale in La Jolla, just to do theater again, but I spent so much on costumes, particularly for *Road to Rome,* that it became an expensive hobby. Then some bright soul suggested that I do summer stock in the East, where I could make a great deal of money. So I called Barry Sullivan to see if he'd tour with me. Barry said he'd just signed a contract with Metro, which precluded that. I asked him if he knew a good actor back east. He thought a moment, and then made a remark that changed my life.

"Yeah, a guy named Brooks West that I worked with in Mount Kisco."

So my agent contacted the aforementioned Brooks West and two other actors, and when I arrived in New York I met them at my agent's office. Though I felt the name didn't influence me, his reading of the part did, and off we went to Olney, Maryland, to rehearse *Over Twenty-One*. My girls were at the Amsters' farm with Nanny, and Brooks and I spent Sundays with them, driving long distances after the show on Saturday night, then on to our next destination on Monday.

Olney, Maryland, was an ideal place to begin my new venture in summer stock. The area was woodsy and green. The theater was a large barn with great charm, and an enormous sycamore was growing from the center of the auditorium through the roof.

Daily, after rehearsal, Brooks and I would walk down leafy Bachelor Forest Road, running through our lines, and I got to know more about my good-looking leading man.

He was a graduate of Texas University, where he'd been a member of the Curtain Club. During that time, he'd been introduced to Lynn Fontanne and Alfred Lunt, who were appearing in Austin on tour. He'd been invited to "look them up" when he would come to New York in pursuit of an acting career.

When he arrived in New York, he heard that they were casting *The Taming of the Shrew*. Turning up at a "cattle call" of over a hundred actors, Brooks was recognized by Miss Lynnie, as she was affectionately called.

"Alfred, look who's here. It's Tex," she called to Mr. Lunt, and the lucky young actor found himself with a job on his fifth day in New York. He went on a national tour with that show.

Then Robert Sherwood and Alfred Lunt offered Brooks a part in *There Shall Be No Night,* as the radio operator, and as understudy to Montgomery Clift. After playing Boston, New Haven, and seven months in New York, Brooks left the company to enlist in the Air Force before Pearl Harbor.

Four and a half years later, Brooks found that jobs in the theater were not so easy to get. He was fortunate enough to be cast with Ingrid Bergman in *Joan of Lorraine,* but it was a limited run of only several months in New York.

Since that time, Brooks had faced the fact that television must be a part of every working actor's future. He was working in a TV show that Yul Brynner was directing when he got a call for a summer tour with Eve Arden, whoever she was. Brooks hadn't seen many movies in the army.

Incidentally, we spent a weekend in New York later that season, and Brooks took me backstage to meet the Lunts after a performance of *The Great Sebastian.* To the girl from Mill Valley, it was like being presented to royalty. The Lunts had been my inspiration ever since I'd played *Dulcy*, which Miss Fontanne had created on Broadway.

After *Over Twenty-One*, Brooks offered to drive my new station wagon back to California while I took the train with Nanny and the girls. Although neither of us was thinking of marriage (he had just received his divorce during the tour, and I wasn't all that far away from mine), I think we had an inkling of what the future held. At any rate, neither of us wanted the other to drift away.

So Brooks found a few TV things to do, and I did a picture called *Three Husbands*, with a favorite English actor of mine, Emlyn Williams. It was an independent production and never got off the ground, but I liked my part, a beer-drinking wife who bet on horses and went barefoot a lot. The only bit that was typecasting was going barefoot, since, when not working, I'm usually shoeless.

I did my second picture with Crawford, *Goodbye My Fancy*. The part was the usual secretary-friend of the heroine but with great lines. It was miscasting for Joan, as an intellectual returning to a college reunion with an unrequited love for a professor, Robert Young.

CHAPTER
· 14 ·

During the next year, we prepared to translate "Miss Brooks" to television. This was comparatively simple, since we had a backlog of radio scripts that could be made visual. We were faced with changing our Mr. Boynton. Jeff Chandler was fast becoming a big movie star, and though he was sentimental and hated to leave the show, when Mr. Boynton had to be seen, Jeff was too macho in appearance and attitude.

One day after a radio taping of "Miss Brooks," Jeff Chandler took my hand and pulled me back into the studio as the others left. I looked at him questioningly, as Brooks was outside waiting for me. Jeff had been seeing Annie Sheridan since he'd broken up with his wife. I was fond of both of them, and with my matchmaking tendencies, I'd been very happy for them.

Only in pictures am I prepared for the unexpected, and when Jeff kept holding my hand and said that he had to tell me that he was very much in love with me, I'm sure that I stood there with my mouth open. Maybe that's why I was always the girlfriend of the heroine. I'm sure that heroines, even if they're married, have hormones that quicken and react properly when told that someone is "in love" with them. Not Evie the one-man-on-her-mind-at-a-time girl. I think I mumbled something about "not knowing what to say" and left poor Jeff feeling foolish, but somehow we parted friends—why was it only in the movies that I said all those clever things?

However, we did find the perfect Mr. Boynton in Robert Rockwell, who, while handsome and manly enough, could play the diffidence and shyness of the character, while now and then displaying a spark of interest that kept Miss Brooks's hopes alive.

The TV show became even more successful than the radio show. We'd been on TV only a few weeks when I was being deluged with fan mail from teachers and asked to address teachers' meetings.

Finally I was made a member of the NEA (National Education Association), and honored at a very grand dinner. It seemed that teachers had taken Connie Brooks to their bosoms, and the public was not far behind.

And I'll never forget my landlady, Mrs. Davis, of the deep gravelly voice, who could always make me laugh. One night we did a scene where the two of us were locked up together in the "pokey" and she picked up a tin cup and ran it across the cell bars, then, in her inimitable voice, called for the guard. She bellowed, "Screw" as I fell apart and couldn't finish the scene the next five times.

Gale Gordon, the ferocious Mr. Conklin, was a pussycat—a really shy but loving man. He was also very relaxed. Once we were about to shoot a scene in which Walter Denton brought Mr. Conklin's daughter Harriet home very late one night, while he was waiting, furious, on a porch swing in the shadows. The cameras checked the lights and moved in to photograph. They followed Dick Crenna and Gloria up the path to where Gale was waiting. As Dick prepared himself for the irascible Conklin's bark, a gentle snore rose from the sound-asleep, thoroughly relaxed Gale.

As we rehearsed one day and Mrs. Davis, my darling, daffy little landlady, was giving Miss Brooks some good advice, I noticed that her voice was slurring and she seemed to be disoriented. I stopped rehearsal and asked if we could take a break. I could see that she really wasn't aware of what was happening to her. I took her to my dressing room and told her I was going to call for a car and someone to drive her home. My spunky little friend struggled to stand straight and said, "Oh, nonsense, I can drive myself home!" I sat her down firmly and said, "Now you wait here until I come back," and charged out to call the nurse and ask her to get someone to drive Jane Morgan home. When I got back she was gone. She'd staggered out to the parking lot and driven off in her little Model T.

When the studio car arrived, I sent the driver buzzing after her, and he found her driving in a zigzag pattern down the middle of the street. A doctor was called and reported to us that Janie had had a stroke but that she was stable, and worrying about getting back to "her job." Knowing her background as a leading woman in stock in the Seattle/Portland area for most of her career, and where she'd never missed a performance, we all bet that she'd be back with us again. For six weeks we managed to shoot around her, and sure enough, she came back, feisty as ever. For the next several weeks I was photographed on my wrong side, as the only sign of Janie's stroke was a drooping cheek that couldn't be photographed, so we changed places. But would you believe—within a few more weeks her cheek had sprung back into place.

PART TWO

CHAPTER
· 15 ·

On our next hiatus Brooks drove the station wagon east. It was loaded with some quilted chairs and other furniture I wanted the Amsters to have for the farm, only partially furnished then. The girls, and their new nurse Dobbs and I, were waiting for him at the Warwick Hotel. Nanny had broken an arm that spring and decided it was time to retire.

Brooks came to have breakfast with us, and we were all happy to see him safe and sound. During a lull in the conversation, Liza sat, brown eyes studying him. Suddenly she spoke.

"Brooks, you're a handsome man, and you're a good man too. I'd like you for my father. Mother, could you arrange that?"

Brooks had a little trouble with his coffee, and I can't remember my reply, but two weeks later Brooks proposed. He said, "Why don't we get married?"

I said, "Oh?"

He told me later that he thought, What kind of an answer is that? "Yes," "No," "Maybe," I could understand, but "Oh?" The subject was dropped.

Two weeks later we were at the Amster farm and Brooks and Stanley were discussing the merits of various tires. I was standing by Ann's flower bed as she planted violets. Suddenly, I heard myself say, "How would you like to have a wedding here this summer?"

Sentimental Ann, eyes filled with tears, said, "Oh, darling, how wonderful!"

We made our way over to the car where the boys were kicking tires. Ann stood it as long as she could, then interrupted. "How can you talk about tires when we're going to have a wedding soon?"

Brooks looked up politely as if to say, "Anyone I know?" Then he looked at me and realized he'd gotten his answer.

The following week we left Somerset, Massachusetts, after the Saturday night performance and drove through the most horrendous electrical storm either of us had ever experienced. To make it worse, we were surrounded by huge trees, not the ideal situation with lightning flashing on every side. Nothing frightens me more, but Brooks drove calmly and between thunderclaps quoted statistics to prove that my chances of being struck by lightning or a falling tree were nil. I'm not sure I believed him, but it did the trick, and we arrived at the farm safe but exhausted at 3 A.M.

The girls woke us at seven and, thanks to Stanley's arrangements, the doctor arrived while we were having breakfast to draw the blood for our tests. We each returned, looking ashen, for a second cup of coffee.

That afternoon the minister Stanley had found to marry us came to call. Although the wedding was two weeks away, he felt he should meet us, but he gave us no warning. Brooks had just explained that we wanted to be married by the names "we were using now" when I came up from the pond as muddy as the two urchins I'd hauled away from their frog-catching to bathe. All three of us were bedraggled and barefoot. I'm sure the minister couldn't decide whether we had Mafia connections with our aliases, or if Brooks was marrying his Indian sweetheart for the sake of her illegitimate children. His look of mistrust didn't change until he'd married us two weeks later. The wedding party was composed of the Amsters, Alice Buchanan, our friend Dorothy Howe, who'd flown in from California, Vi Roache, the epitome of English elegance, and four little girls, the Amsters' and ours, in party dresses holding tiny bouquets. Only then did he seem reassured that it was a normal wedding.

Maybe what gave him the feeling it was a good omen was the fact that, as he pronounced us man and wife, a ray of sunshine broke through the overcast and shone on the bridal couple. It really did happen.

We'd tried to keep the wedding our private affair. I'd even gone so far as to put my hair up in rollers, wear no makeup, and, at the last moment, put on the nurse's bifocals when we applied for our license. But the media is all-pervasive, and the night before the wedding they called Stanley to find out if and when we were being married there. Poor Stanley, not a good liar, just said he didn't have the right to give out any information. But the farm was so secluded that we were sure they couldn't find us. While we were toasting in champagne and enjoying the wonderful luncheon Ann had prepared, however, a little Model A Ford chugged through the woods and up to the door. Out stepped the woman who took the census for the area and also did features for the local paper; she alone had figured out how to find us. We laughed and invited her to join us.

When we reached the theater in Ivoryton, where we were playing that night, our dressing room was filled with flowers and lots of telegrams, and the cast whipped up a party for Mr. and Mrs. Brooks West. We spent our wedding night at the Riversea Inn in the quaint town of Old Lyme, Connecticut.

Brooks and I found that one of the theaters where we were to play *Here Today* was near the small town of Eagle Bridge, New York, made famous by Anna Mary Moses. She had started to paint at the age of seventy-eight, and now, at the age of ninety-one, was famous far and wide as the artist Grandma Moses.

Through the publicity man of the theater, we arranged to visit her where she lived with her daughter, and found her working on three paintings at once. She was happy to show us her new stone house and her flower garden, although I'm sure she wondered who these two strangers were. She took us into the garage, where she and her daughter were raising chinchillas. I had always wanted to hold a baby chinchilla, and Grandma Moses had the same childlike love of animals, so, as we talked, we each cuddled one of the softest creatures in the world.

Back in the living room, a tiny girl was brought to say hello to her great-great-great-grandmother, and Grandma Moses patted her gently as her daughter explained how the child fitted into Anna Mary's many descendants.

We had our picture taken with her in the flower garden. I told her I had owned one of her paintings for several years. It is called "They're Having Company at the Jobs'," and is a Christmas scene with sleighs full of people, and with horses taking them through the snow to the Jobs' house at the top of the hill. She had painted far too many since then to remember one.

I had wanted to bring a little gift, but all I could find was a white hobnailed lamp. A couple of weeks later a letter was forwarded from her daughter. She said how much Grandma Moses had enjoyed our visit, and that "Mother loves your lamp. She reads her *New Yorker* by it at night."

Grandma Moses lived ten years longer and painted around forty more pictures before she died at the age of 101.

I intend to start painting seriously when I'm the age at which she began.

Brooks's indoctrination as a father began immediately, with both girls calling him Daddy as often as they could think of a reason. He was very proud, but a week later as we drove cross-country on our way home from the Amsters I think he had his doubts. We spent the first night of the trip in a hotel, with the girls in an adjoining room. I decided to take a bath in their room while Brooks used ours. Liza asked if she could speak with me while I bathed and, not wanting to seem prudish, I said okay. Connie demanded to come too. They sat side by side on a hamper while I soaped myself.

Then Liza stated, "When I grow up, I don't mind having bosoms, but I'm not going to have those little round things on the front." I gulped slightly, but hesitated to explain that she was stuck with them whether she wanted them or not. Then she said, "I wanted to talk to you, Mother, because I'm getting very curious to see a man's penis. Do you think Daddy would show us his?"

I thought of my unsuspecting bridegroom being faced with this question, and I headed off disaster. "Well," I said. "I'm sure Daddy would be glad to show you sometime, but I think I could find a book with some pictures that you could see first." That seemed to satisfy her, and Connie nodded too.

Dinner took their minds off the subject for then. We drove a long distance the next day, and when we reached a pleasant motel I threw myself across the bed while Brooks headed for the shower. Suddenly, Liza was saying eagerly, "Mother, when Daddy finishes his shower, do you think he'd show us his penis now?"

As I searched for an answer, Brooks stepped out of the bathroom with a towel around him. Before I could say anything, Connie, the lisper, was jumping up and down in front of him, saying, "I wanna thee your penith, Daddy. I wanna thee your penith!"

Brooks, in shock, could think of nothing but "Oh, you do! Well —ah—er, that will cost you a nickel!"

Connie quickly pantomimed picking a coin from her palm and said, "Here'th your nickel, Daddy." Poor Brooks was on the spot, and I left him there. So while Liza and Connie watched with saucer eyes, he swept the towel off and back on again and said, "That's all you get for a nickel."

The girls squealed and bounced on the bed, and as Brooks turned hopefully to find his pants, Connie bounced off the bed and, standing before him, said, "Here'th another nickel, Daddy!"

This ended the episode except for one night after we got home when Connie was lying on her tummy writing what she said was a letter, and suddenly looked up and asked, "How do you thpell 'penith'?"

But Brooks adjusted remarkably well and in November told me he had decided to build the girls a playhouse. The only help he had was from George, our gardener, in building the framework. The girls were told it was going to be a workshop for Daddy, and since it was in a corner of the patio below the house, screened from above by trees, the girls were kept busy with projects of their own until Christmas morning. Then they were led to a two-room house with shuttered windows. It was painted yellow with white trim and had window boxes filled with geraniums. Brooks had made a wooden bench and chair with their names on it for the living room, and in the kitchen were a real stove and an honest-to-goodness phone, connected to another by the laundry-room door above. There also was a picket fence and gate and a pathway edged in flowers. It was a child's dream come true. For several months we didn't have to ask where Connie and Liza were. They were on the phone.

The key to our relationship seemed to be the sense of humor we shared and the affection we expressed constantly to the girls and to each other. Even that had its detractors, as we found when we took the girls out to dinner one night, and Brooks spontaneously leaned over to kiss me.

Connie spoke up in disgust. "Mithter and Mithus Gooey Muthy," she said.

Over the years, that's how we've thought of ourselves. Oh, our arguments are fierce and not infrequent, but love is plentiful.

The next season Brooks started a series with Marie Wilson and Cathy Lewis called "My Friend Irma." Since we would both have at least six weeks free in the summer, we planned our first trip to Europe, just the two of us, something I'd looked forward to since I first pored over my mother's hundreds of copies of *National Geographic*. We started bringing home maps and brochures and I felt my life couldn't be any more exciting than it was right then, until I got a call from the agency that had brought me Liza. They had a baby with a background close to ours, which was expected in a couple of months. Brooks and I had discussed adding another child to complete the family, but hadn't thought about one this soon. We were torn between the baby we wanted and the trip we'd looked forward to, neither one too easy to arrange.

Finally I said, "Look, he'll be born a month before we leave, so we'll feel he's really ours, and the six weeks we'll be away he'll be sleeping most of the time. We have a good nurse now, and since the girls are staying at the Amsters' farm, we'll just add the baby. Ann will be thrilled."

So a month before we were leaving, we got a call telling us that we had a redheaded baby boy. In honor of our trip we named him Duncan *Paris* West. His nurse wrote us a letter every day and told us he was thriving.

We sailed on the *Queen Mary* and the girls saw us off. We had a lovely stateroom, and on the *Mary* everyone had a steward and a stewardess. Ours brought us breakfast in bed every morning. I was unusually tired after doing thirty-nine "Miss Brooks" episodes, so, while Brooks investigated the ship, I had a massage from Hawkes, an English masseuse with iron fingers. I admit I reveled in such luxury.

Our first trip to Europe made me realize how much I'd longed to see more of the world. From the moment we picked up the Hillman-Minx we'd ordered delivered in Paris, we were living in a dream. There is so much to see that is strange and wonderful that travel has become our third life. The experiences on our trips I've kept in a book that I've called "That Travel Itch," so I'll just tell you that in those six weeks of adventure we went from Paris and the Loire Valley to Rouen, where we visited my Foster Parents child Daniel, by then twelve years old, and added his brother Jean-Ives as another foster child, on to Lucerne in Switzerland, back into France and over the Alps into Italy. There we saw Torino, Portofino, Florence, Rome, and Venice. Then we left for Innsbruck, Austria, Liechtenstein, and London, and finally boarded the *Ile de France* for home.

CHAPTER
· 16 ·

When we returned on what was to be the final trip of the *Ile de France,* we headed the Hillman-Minx toward the Amster farm. There we were greeted with squeals of joy from Liza and Connie and bland indifference by the pudgy little redhead who was our new son.

We spent the next couple of days getting acquainted with him and exploring the farm with the girls. On the fourth evening I discovered why I'd felt so strange on the first weeks of the trip. I suddenly lost a baby I hadn't been aware I was carrying. Our nurse said that the fact that I hadn't had any of the regular symptoms of pregnancy usually meant that nature had aborted an imperfect child, and it was probably just as well. That was my only consolation.

I went back to work in September, and the following spring I was nominated for the second time for an Emmy for "Our Miss Brooks." But since I was feeling tired and was sure I wouldn't win this time either, I decided not to attend the awards. Glenn was upset with me and said, "Now if you win . . ." I laughed and he said with annoyance, "There's a good chance you will, and the photographers will come to your house right away to take pictures for the morning papers."

We watched the ceremony on TV as I worked on a hooked rug and Brooks paced nervously around the room.

"Darling, sit down and relax," I said. "I'm not going to win!" And, as I spoke, they announced my name.

All I could think of was those photographers coming and that I had a dirty face. I rushed to the bathroom and slathered on cleansing cream. Then the phone started to ring with congratulations. Finally, with a clean face and suitable dress, the pictures were taken. The next morning Brooks and I were looking at them on the front pages of both papers.

MISS BROOKS WINS HER EMMY.

Nice pictures and nice feeling. My phone rang and it was my doctor, Oscar Auerbach, who said, "Congratulations."

"Thank you, Oscar. I really didn't expect to win or I'd have been there."

"No!" said Oscar. "I mean, CONGRATULATIONS!"

Unbelieving, I said, "You mean I can expect *another* little Emmy?"

"Yes," he said, "or an Oscar!"

And that's how I learned I was pregnant.

The previous Christmas Liza had put at the top of her Christmas list, "Some flat ground." When I asked what she meant, she said, "I know you built this house, Mother, and you filled it full of antiques and you'll never leave it, but you won't let me ride my bicycle on a hillside, so I want some flat ground."

It seemed like a reasonable request, and now that we were going to have a fourth child, we felt they should have a weekend place for bicycles and climbing trees and maybe an animal or two. So we began to look for a couple of acres or so out in the country. The places we saw were either complete with everything from stables to sheep pens and chicken coops, or raw acreage with nothing on it. We hoped for at least a livable house and enough land with which we could be creative.

Bill McCann, our real estate man, kept talking about a place called Hidden Valley that he claimed was the perfect spot for us, but nothing was available so far. He drove us through it one day, and I fell in love with the long valley surrounded by low hills and, on one side, a mountain known as Old Boney. I kept hoping that Bill would find something.

When he did call weeks later to say that something just right for us had gone on the market, I was less than enthusiastic, as it was raining, I had a cold, and Hidden Valley was forty miles out of town. Brooks was even less enthusiastic when we were told that it was thirty-eight acres. However, that "small voice" that seems to tell me when to pay attention spoke up, so I coaxed Brooks into driving out.

Even in the gray drizzle the valley was very beautiful, with miles of white fences, open fields, and huge sycamores and oaks everywhere. At the end of the valley we met Bill at a huge double gate and followed his car down, across a bridge over a creek, then up past some white-fenced fields on our left. On the right was a barranca where the water flowed and from which a long line of oaks reached gracefully toward the road.

We came to a stable and workshop on our right, and across from them was a barn at the end of the pasture. The buildings were badly in need of paint. Ahead under more huge oaks, we could see a low house, and on a higher elevation to the right was a small guest house.

The owners, a charming older couple whose children were grown, showed us the house, originally owned by Ronald Colman. I mentally knocked out walls and visualized our paintings everywhere.

Brooks said, sotto voce, "Couldn't you manage to look a little less interested? It might help to keep the price down."

I managed to contain myself until we drove away and stopped to talk to Bill. He said, "I know this is more than you want and I can sell it tomorrow, but he just put it back on the market and I had to show it to you first."

Brooks, the practical one, said, "I can tell you how Eve feels without asking, but I really think we should have our business manager see it before we go off the deep end."

"Do you think we can get him out here tomorrow?" I asked.

Brooks and Bill smiled at each other. "We can try," Brooks said.

Two days later our business representative came, looking very much out of place in his business suit, tie, and hat. He looked it over thoroughly as I tried to point out its advantages.

"Did you see the tennis court?" I asked. "And did you notice the windmill over the well pump, back up that draw?"

Then came his verdict: "It would be a very bad investment, you'd never be able to get your money back."

Since I used to accuse myself occasionally of being willful about what I wanted, I thought maybe he's right, and tried to dismiss the idea from my mind. I did know that I felt so strongly about the place that I wanted someone I liked to have it if I couldn't, so at our next "Miss Brooks" rehearsal I mentioned it to Gale Gordon, who'd also been looking for a place. He saw it and was very enthusiastic, but his business manager agreed with ours.

Then my ex-manager and friend, George Ward, who'd become a Christian Science practitioner, said to me, "It's not necessary to regard everything as an investment, and since you feel that strongly about it and are doing it for your children, I think you should have it."

By now Brooks, with several more visits to the farm, had grown as enchanted as I had, and we decided to take the plunge. So we acquired thirty-eight and a half acres that gave us twenty years of healthful living and provided us with adventures we'd never have had any other way. To top it off, it proved to be the only investment we have ever made that increased tenfold!

After I discovered I was pregnant, we decided to spend the summer out there and moved out—bag, baggage, housekeeper, nurse, two small girls, baby boy, and someone on the way.

We dubbed it Westhaven, and Brooks cut a huge oak leaf out of wood, painted the name on it, and hung it down by the gate. After dinner on our first night in residence, Brooks sat on the front steps fondling the ears of Gertrude, our new basset hound puppy, and puffing contentedly on his pipe, every inch the country squire. I sighed happily, thinking of our redheaded boy, asleep in one of the bedrooms with his nurse. Since the housekeeper required the other bedroom, Brooks and I were installed in the master bedroom of the guest house above, where Brooks had already laid a fire in the fireplace for our first night there. The girls had been sent up to bed in the other guest room.

Almost too good to be true, I thought, and as if reading my mind, Brooks said, "Peaceful out here, isn't it?"

Before I could reply, a door slammed upstairs and two sets of slippered feet pattered down the steps toward us. Connie's treble rose in the air: "Daddy, Daddy, we can't bruth our teeth. There'th no water!"

The faintest suspicion crossed my mind that Eden might hold a few flaws, but I dismissed the thought as heresy. Brooks, ever practical, sent the girls back to bed with instructions to "forget the teeth tonight." Daddy would take care of everything.

In the lower house there was still a trickle of water from some faucets, but the kitchen ones were coughing and gasping, which spelled trouble. The two of us started up the path left of the tennis court, which led to the well. Gertrude followed us, but slowly, as she stepped on her ears a lot. She began to sneeze, gently at first, then more and more violently. I picked her up to see what was wrong. I could find nothing, but Brooks discovered a little blood coming from her nose, and could see the disappearing end of a foxtail, a mean little weed that, if not removed, can work its way even into the brain of an animal.

Afraid of doing more damage, as she was bleeding freely by now, there was nothing for it but to look up the nearest veterinarian—fourteen miles away at that time, in Oxnard. So off we went, Brooks driving madly around unfamiliar mountain roads while I tried to comfort an unhappy struggling Gertrude.

A couple of hours and one nose operation later, two weary pioneers fell into bed, too tired even to light the fire.

The next morning Brooks took charge and located Mr. Dykes, who was to be our mainstay in "well problems" for many years, and who told us that the "shaft needed replacing," a mystery that remained just that to me.

Since it would take approximately ten days to accomplish, and since we'd need much more than clean teeth for that period, Brooks arranged for a tankerful of water, which now sat on the terrace below the guest house, and reassured us with its size.

Our troubles seemed nipped in the bud, and Brooks was happily sloshing paint on the barn, when Connie, the courier of disaster, came on the run. "Daddy, Daddy," she cried, "if you ever had any bulleths, you better bring 'em now! There'th a big thnake at the back door and it almotht bit me!"

Brooks retrieved the .38 pistol he'd gotten a permit for, and ran down the path to the back door. Standing on the wall above it, he took aim, and drilled a hole between the eyes of an eight-rattle rattlesnake. I felt like the wife of a wagon master of the Old West, confident that, come what may, even Apaches, my man could cope.

That summer was full of discoveries in the animal kingdom. One evening we walked outside to find that instead of a plumcot tree (from a graft of plum and apricot) by the front door, we had a "fur tree." After a gasp or two from us, it unwound itself into eight beautiful raccoons who ambled unconcernedly down the path, leaving our favorite fruit tree devastated. Strangely enough, we never saw them again; I guess they were just passing through.

We'd had early visits from quail and, of all things, three peacocks which belonged to our neighbors. There were nightly visits from two foxes, and we could hear their kits squealing and quarreling in their den on the hill above.

One night we heard a bloodcurdling scream from Liza on her way to bed in the guest house. Expecting nothing less than a cobra, we dashed to the rescue. Following her horrified gaze to her feet, we saw a tiny black-and-white skunk, all of two inches long, gnawing on the desiccated skeleton of a frog. She was obviously starving, so I gave her a saucer of milk and, after I put a drop on her nose, she followed my finger to the source and lapped it up eagerly. I picked her up and she snuggled down in my palm and promptly went to sleep. A small box stuffed with Kleenex became Petunia's home near the woodbox for a couple of weeks. Unfortunately, to keep the peace with the new housekeeper, who was the same species as Petunia but entirely lacking her charm, I agreed to see if a veterinarian could remove the scent gland from her body, sure that he'd refuse because she was so small (she was much too young to smell, but the housekeeper insisted that she did). The young vet, however, said he could remove it. He did remove something, but obviously the wrong thing. For the next week I played nurse to a slowly expiring Petunia. Then, in a desperate effort to ease her pain, I immersed her in a warm bath, my own remedy for chills, and unwittingly did her in. She closed her beady little eyes and I wept. Then, before the girls came home from school, I buried her under the oak tree where I'd found her.

We started our own collection of domestic animals that summer with a flock of chickens and three rabbits, who rapidly learned multiplication and ran us out of cages and patience the following year when their number hit forty-seven.

Then Brooks, determined to shirk nothing in learning to run the farm, became part of a team with Buck, our caretaker, and George, our Danish gardener from town, for the disposition of forty-seven wriggling rabbits.

This was one of the bitter lessons we learned on the farm, that occasionally the population explosion calls for drastic control. Buck did the actual dirty deed, which he assured us was quick and painless. George then skinned the furry little fellows. Brooks, with clenched teeth, carried several at a time to what we called the milkhouse. He had to hold the naked bodies under warm water and wrap each one in butcher paper to store in the freezer. He admitted to me later that each one felt like the fetus of an unborn child. Eve, the coward, stayed indoors.

When the girls, home from school, found the empty cages, they realized what had happened and fled in tears. They refused to come in until after dark. Daddy felt like Jack the Ripper for days, while I did my best to explain the darker side of farm living. Then the constant distractions of our new life came to our rescue. Nevertheless, Brooks and I waited months before we introduced "chicken" casseroles into occasional dinners.

Projects for the farm kept us busy. Brooks built a three-car carport on a slope near the stable. Then one day he decided to plow up the largest field, which we'd dubbed the lower forty. He had driven the tractor down to the bridge several times to get used to it, so it was with a certain amount of confidence that I watched him take off around the edge of the big field. He rode triumphantly the entire length and turned toward the caretaker house, where the deep arroyo with its oak trees ran. I must have blinked, because suddenly my husband, tractor and all, had disappeared.

As I ran down the field, all the warnings we'd heard about the dangers of tractors ran through my head, along with a few prayers. I could hardly bear to look over the edge, but when I did there sat my husband, still in the saddle, the tractor neatly lodged in the V formed by two oak trunks. Talk about heavenly intervention!

That first summer was an instructive one for the girls in the facts-of-life department too. We were getting lovely brown eggs from our chickens, and when Brooks and I went to collect them one day, Liza went with us. We went through the nests and came back with our hands full of eggs, to find Liza staring in fascination at one of our roosters, intent on his courtship of a hen. When we attempted to persuade her to leave with us, she protested, "Just a minute, Mommy." It took less. As the rooster jumped down with a triumphant shake of his feathers, Liza spoke. "Well, now she's fertilized," she said firmly, and we went back to the house for lunch.

We found Liza a small pinto horse named Patches, and she galloped gleefully down the road to the gate and back again, her boundary for the time being.

CHAPTER
· 17 ·

It was a busy summer. There was so much to be done just to make things comfortable and attractive to live in. For one thing, the huge oaks that arched over the road dragged on the tops of delivery trucks and were now reaching for our station wagon. So Brooks and I formed a task force with long-handled clippers and hedge shears and began the job of trimming them from the stable down to the gate, preserving, of course, an artistic irregularity all the way.

It was on that day that I learned one of the wonders of pregnancy. As I reached for a high limb I stood still in amazement. A tiny flutter of butterfly wings inside me proclaimed that I was feeling life for the first time. It was a thrill not to be duplicated until I began to feel the usual hefty kicks and uncomfortable elbows in odd places, but this was a feeling impossible to share. I tried to tell Brooks about it as I waited for a repetition, and he insisted that I stop clipping, although I was so elated I wanted to continue in case it would activate the little flutter again.

When I had found I was pregnant, my doctor had typed my blood and had called me in to say, "Now this is not necessarily serious, as they are finding more ways to circumvent it every day, but I thought you should know you are Rh negative." He went on to calm my fears, but Brooks and I were a little sobered by the thought. Dr. Auerbach had also said Brooks should have his blood typed as well, so he had given some for testing. When I went in the next day for a lung X ray, Brooks went with me, and our doctor called down and said, "It's hard to believe, as the percentages are so far against it, but Brooks is Rh negative too!"

"Is that good?" I asked.

"Haven't you ever heard that two negatives make a positive?" He laughed.

So we went home with lighter hearts.

Since I'd discovered my pregnancy early in the second year of "Miss Brooks," I decided not to disclose it to my cast and crew right away, hard as it was to keep such a happy secret.

Then we did a show in which we were a hillbilly band, and I was Daisy Mae in a white blouse and tight black satin skirt. That was the night I knew I had to tell everyone concerned, as I struggled to conceal a shiny round protuberance with a tambourine held in front of me.

After the show, Brooks and I broke the news, and I was delighted with everyone's warm reaction. I still had almost four months to wait, two of those in front of the camera, and it took some maneuvering to conceal my burgeoning figure. Clothes were ordered in larger sizes, and story lines were invented to provide a cover. Miss Brooks studied art and a smock was very helpful, and in each show Miss Brooks stood behind a larger piece of furniture. I think we all heaved sighs of relief as hiatus time arrived.

Our family retreated to the farm and I could relax. I discovered that nature had taken care of all the fears I had harbored about childbirth, and the ones people had foisted on me about "having a child at your age." I felt a sense of well-being and a surety that everything would be all right.

The big day came in September. I arrived at the hospital at 8 P.M. and was sent to be "prepped," always an embarrassing moment. The nurse turned out to be an ardent "Miss Brooks" fan and told me how much her family loved the show. She quieted down as the "prepping" attendant arrived with her pan, shaving cream, and razor. The preppy worked efficiently and swiftly in complete silence. Finished, she was walking away when the nurse made a fatal mistake.

"Isn't it lovely to have Our Miss Brooks with us?" she asked.

The eyes of the stolid little woman flew open, and the utensils in the basin rattled like castanets. "OUR MISS BROOKS!" she gasped. "Oh, could I please have your autograph?" As I signed it I could only think, Thank God she wasn't in the middle of the prep! And that wasn't the end. Later, as Brooks sat with me in the pre-labor room, little gremlins in green uniforms with caps and masks appeared with the same requests . . . I couldn't believe it. Here I was, in the most "expectant" moment of my life, with pains making me jump at regular intervals, and I was signing my name.

Brooks was sent home to get some sleep, with the promise that he'd be called when I went into "real" labor. What did they call this?!

Douglas Brooks West, nine pounds and six ounces, was born around 6 A.M. Meanwhile, Brooks had arrived in a state of anxiety and sat alone in the father's waiting room for over an hour. Finally, an attendant arrived to pick up the fathers' discarded gowns. Looking at the lonely survivor, he said, "Congratulations!"

Brooks leaped to his feet. "Is it born?"

"The doctor will tell you," was the reply.

"Is my wife all right?"

"The doctor will tell you." The attendant smiled.

"Is it a boy or a girl?"

"The doctor—"

"I know!" said Brooks. "He'll tell me." And he sat dejectedly for another half hour before he was told. Finally, in a hallway, the family came together while we had the pleasure of counting the baby's fingers and toes.

The days in the hospital, with visits from my new son, from my cast and some of my crew, with flowers arriving constantly, and with Brooks sneaking down the hall, to take a forbidden picture of Doug in the nursery, were exciting and fulfilling. Even Papa Freund, our outsized German cameraman (whose theory about children was, "Dey should be sent avay to school at five, und not come home until tventy-one—vell-trained und mit pyootiful manners") surprised me with a visit and stated that Doug was too "pyootiful" to be a brand-new baby, that I looked twenty years younger, and he'd like to photograph me right then. My cup ran over.

I got a welcome laugh when Reggie, our little prop man, who'd been puzzled by my constant yearning for pickles and watermelon (out of season yet), brought me a tiny wicker wash basket, beruffled and holding a watermelon with a baby's face drawn on it.

When Doug and I came home, there were letters cut from newspapers and tacked to the canopy of our big pine bed, saying, WELCOME HOME, MOM AND DOUG! The three siblings, who had not been allowed to visit at the hospital, were ecstatic about meeting their new brother.

When Doug was three months old, we spent his first Christmas at Westhaven. A month later we decided that the farm was where we wanted to live. Eventually we sold the house in town and cast our lot with the country folk. The girls started school in Thousand Oaks. It was nine miles away, but the school bus stopped at our gate. There Brooks built a little red structure with white trim and a bench inside and called it Westhaven Waiting Room. The rainy weather had begun.

Before we moved to the farm for good, there was a dreadful period when I ran the gamut of "Hollywood nurses." Rosalind Russell had warned me about a group of them who constantly orbited from one movie star's home to another, and the gossip sessions they held in the Beverly Hills Park each day.

What horrified me most was when she told me of a friend's experience. The woman had found that the nurse she trusted was giving her baby a slight dose of gas from the oven whenever she wanted to get away early to meet her boyfriend!

I was determined to find one whom I could trust as implicitly as I had Nanny, and that my kids would love as much as they did me.

I found Helen Swenson, who came to an interview with Mrs. West, not knowing we were a "show biz" family. When she saw the two baby boys who were to be her charges, and found that we were soon to live out on a farm, she happily accepted the job.

The new baby in the home had one strange effect on Liza. The nurse who followed Nanny (until she wound up spending the night in her car in a ditch, and thereby revealed her serious drinking problem) once told us that Liza was asking to be taken to veterans' cemeteries, where she seemed to think her "real" father could be found. We interpreted this as the same sibling jealousy that started her clobbering Connie.

On an inspiration one day, I asked Liza to walk up to the windmill with me. On the way I said suddenly, "Liza, who do you love the most, me or Daddy?"

Shocked, Liza stood still. "I love you both, Mommy," she cried.

"I know, darling." I smiled. "But you must love one of us a little bit more. It's all right. I won't be mad if it's Daddy. Anyway, it's our secret."

By now Liza was almost in tears, saying, "No! I love you both the same!"

After a few more protests I said, "I believe you, Liza. But why is it so hard for *you* to believe that you have your place in our hearts, and no one can take that away from you; but Connie has her place, too, and you can't take that from her; and Duncan has his, and Douglas has his, and we love all of you the same!"

That seemed to satisfy her.

We met neighbors: the Duntleys, with three girls around Liza's and Connie's ages—also the three peacocks who visited; and, up above, the Talleys, with five children of assorted ages. Next to us in the opposite direction was Alan Ladd's ranch. Alan and his wife Sue were there on weekends, and for longer stretches between his pictures.

As we got to know them, I began to realize what a complex Alan had about his height. He was extremely handsome and very sweet, but visiting there was a little like playing musical chairs. Since Brooks is six feet two and I am five feet eight and a half, Alan, five feet six, never approached the car when we arrived, but stood above at the door to the house. When we walked up, he quickly offered us chairs, and from then on, if we rose, he sat, and vice versa. After we knew him better, there was a moment when he broke my heart a little. He actually stood next to Brooks one day and, looking up at him, said wistfully, "I could use you in my pictures, Brooks, but why did you have to be so tall?"

On weekends he would drink to let down, and then he would mount a huge stallion he owned to show his mastery of it. I heard his foreman, Tex, mutter, in obvious concern, "It'll get him some-day." It didn't, but I really think Alan's overwhelming concern with his height made him, with everything he had to be happy about, an unhappy man.

It also made him a reckless one. I remember one day when he drove up to our house, wanting Brooks to drive his new Cadillac (he'd wrecked the other one, hitting the telephone pole on the curve above our guest house). Since Brooks was in town, Alan insisted that I drive it. When we reached a long straight stretch, he claimed I wasn't testing its power and clamped his foot on mine. The car leaped forward like a racehorse at the finish. I was sure it would be my finish too! Fortunately, Alan looked at my stricken face and removed his foot.

Alan raised chickens and sold their eggs to his studio and Chasen's Restaurant. He loved his ranch and seemed happiest there. Tex, his foreman, was very helpful to us in getting used to the vagaries of ranch life.

·   ·   ·

Six weeks after Doug arrived, I went back to work on "Miss Brooks." Now that we were living at Westhaven, it settled into an easy routine. People in the hectic world of television today refuse to believe that we made "Miss Brooks" in two and a half days.

I drove to the studio on Friday morning and we read the script and blocked it for the cameramen. Then I had most of Friday afternoon and all of Saturday and Sunday at the farm, watching Duncan take his first steps. On Monday morning, Brooks drove me to the studio, and I learned most of the script during the forty-mile drive. We rehearsed from 10 A.M. to 5 P.M., when we gave a dress rehearsal for the secretaries and others on the lot. I arrived at noon Tuesday, having had my hair done earlier. We rehearsed for the cameramen and lighting technicians until five-thirty, making any necessary cuts or changes, then had dinner in back of the set, showered, made up, and dressed.

Meanwhile, our audience arrived at seven and occupied the wooden bleachers that faced the set. When our announcer had completed his warm-up, consisting of a few jokes and the introductions of the actors, we began to film with three cameras moving in and out to catch the action.

We were usually finished by nine or nine-thirty. We worked as most of us had in the theater, knew our lines (cue cards were unheard of) and enjoyed our work. This schedule also gave me Wednesday and Thursday at the farm with my family.

Our animal population there was growing rapidly. Bill McCann, our real estate man and friend, had asked us to board his horse, Lady. Brooks rode her, and we had bought a nice mare for me named Dolly, who was already with foal. I didn't get too many rides in before she was too wide to straddle comfortably.

Alan's foreman Tex, accustomed to delivering colts, had instructed us to call him any time of the day or night when Dolly showed signs of labor. That happened when our man Buck was away, and Brooks and I returned home from a movie in Thousand Oaks at eleven-thirty one night. Deciding to check on Dolly on our way to the house, we found her streaming milk from every teat. I rushed to the phone and called Tex, who had obviously been sound asleep. He said he'd be there as soon as possible. In the meantime Brooks, who had read a book on the delivery of large farm animals, was prepared with a big jar of Vaseline. As I tried to guess what it was for, Dolly was falling heavily on the straw-covered dirt floor of the stall and then struggling to her feet again. I tried to offer her encouragement, having so recently been in her condition, but she would fall again with a terrible thud. She got up once more, and suddenly the colt's head appeared. It was very long, with a white blaze down the nose, and covered with a caul, or membrane, through which we could see the closed eyes with their long eyelashes. I thought it must be dead. A moment later a front leg fell out. Dolly went down again, and this time I felt certain the baby would be injured, but no, once more Dolly got to her feet. Now Brooks realized that the other foreleg was retracted and not coming through.

I watched my husband, sleeve rolled up, smear his hand and forearm with Vaseline and then gently insert his hand into the birth canal and carefully bring the leg forward and out. Still the colt gave no signs of life. Then one back leg was dangling beside the others, and only then did we see the eyes fly open, the head toss from side to side, and the legs begin to kick. Almost immediately the fourth leg followed and, as Dolly fell again, her new baby was lying beside her.

It was one of the most exciting moments either of us had ever known. I had only seen a few births, of kittens and puppies, but Brooks had never witnessed a birth of any kind.

Tex arrived in time to watch the colt struggle to its legs and Brooks rolling down his sleeves with the air of a captain who has safely brought his ship through a typhoon.

"Well, I'll be doggoned, that's some job for a city fella," he grinned. "Guess I shouldn't have taken so long to tie my shoe-laces."

He examined Dolly and the colt and pronounced them fine. "Guess I'll get on back to bed, nothin' to do here."

We thanked him anyway, then went up to get Liza to see our first colt. We hadn't wanted her to be traumatized by watching the birth, but seeing our "special delivery" was a must. We named the colt Prince.

Shortly after that, we acquired three heifers: two golden Herefords named Marilyn Monroe and Jane Russell, and one half-Angus, half-Hereford, black with a lovely white blaze down her face and unbelievable black eyelashes—Liz Taylor, of course. We named them because of their lush beauty, but were embarrassed when several movie gossip columns picked it up. Then I happened to sit next to Jane Russell at a party one night, so I decided I'd better explain that we meant it to be complimentary, in case she'd read it. She laughed and I felt better.

We were still pretty new to the wilds when, after bidding some guests good night after midnight, Brooks and I were sitting up in bed reading when we heard a low growl that made my hackles rise. Brooks put down his book.

"What the hell was *that?*" he asked.

"Well," I said, "that's the most menacing growl I've heard outside of a circus ring, and I think we'd better call Jungle-Land in Thousand Oaks and see if they're missing a tiger!"

Just then a louder *grrrr* rumbled right next to our window. Brooks dialed Jungle-Land while I tried to peek outside. Only utter blackness. Jungle-Land reported nothing missing, and on inquiring where we lived, said, "Oh, in that case it's probably a mountain lion," and hung up.

It took us a while to get to sleep, but we found later that there were indeed mountain lions or pumas in the hills behind us.

The only thing that really terrified us, though, was the night we sat bolt upright out of a sound sleep at a bloodcurdling shriek. We rushed out in our pajamas, sure that our babies below were being massacred. All was dark and quiet in the main house. Then we heard it again, a sound to chill the blood, but from the hilltop across the way. Even in the bright moonlight nothing stirred.

The next afternoon we had our answer, when, not fifty feet from us, a magnificent bobcat came out of the bushes and strode boldly across the tennis court, his white-tufted ears, short tail, and white furry face proclaiming his species. Our nurse Helen was warned to keep the babies away from that area and the girls were told to play elsewhere, but we never saw him again.

CHAPTER
· 18 ·

We had taken an apartment in town when I first started filming "Miss Brooks," thinking I'd spend the nights there before and after shooting, but it only lasted a few months when we discovered we'd much rather be home to see the kids off to school.

On this evening, though, our anniversary, we were at the apartment with Helen and the kids when the doorbell rang. I had one baby in each arm as I went to answer. There stood a little brown burro with white-ringed eyes and mouth who resembled Al Jolson in blackface makeup. She had a huge red bow on her neck that said her name was Molly Bee and she was our anniversary present from our friend and my manager Glenn Rose. There was a man with a truck and trailer to drive her to the farm. After the show, we started through the canyons, following Molly Bee in the trailer in case of a problem. It was dark, and all we could see were her Jolson eyes and mouth. On some of the curves she'd slip down out of sight, but she always fought her way up again. When we got to the farm, I rushed to welcome her and held out my hand. She promptly bit it to tell me what she thought of the trip!

Around that time we weathered our first disaster at the farm. It was on a Monday during rehearsal when we got a phone call from Helen. She reported a huge fire over the hill and that she could already see flames at the top of it behind the farm. Should she bring the children into town? she asked. "But immediately!" we answered.

Brooks, who had driven me in, leaped into the car and drove at high speed toward the farm, passing the family on their way in.

When he reached our gate and drove toward the house, he could hardly see it for smoke. He found the firemen, their backs to our kitchen wall, turning their hoses on flames in many directions. Brooks then turned his mind to what might possibly be saved. It all seemed pretty futile, but he drove the car up to the guest house and began throwing clothes and books into the back of it. A slightly hysterical neighbor, wanting to help, grabbed my elderly mink coat and threw it on top of the pile. When she rushed back, Brooks, thinking he might offer the weary firemen a drink, handed her a couple of bottles of bourbon, which she promptly tossed on top of everything, breaking them both!

Back at my rehearsal, through calls to the caretaker, I was getting messages such as, "Mr. West says he thinks the house is gone" and then, "The last time we saw Mr. West . . ." I was frantic and felt more helpless than I ever had. I knew Helen was in town with my children, but did I still have a husband and did we still have a house?

Hours later I got the news from a grimy, tired Brooks. "Honey, the firemen, God bless them, saved the houses, but the fire came to the edges of the tennis court and went beyond it along the hillside, where it burned our wooden water tank to the ground. We still have the cement tank, though. The bridge was cracked when the fire truck drove over it. But, thank God, no one was hurt, and the animals are all okay." We were a grateful group that night. I did the show the next night, but the fire was still raging, so we didn't return to the farm until Wednesday afternoon. As we drove through the valley, we saw Old Boney burning in a straight line down the whole mountain. Every now and then there would be a burst of flames as a pack rat's nest high in a tree caught fire. It was terrifying to see flames and smoke in such quantity.

As we drove into our property and neared the house, I could see the hills behind, now a mass of gray ashes, with only a few black stumps and grotesque limbs reaching for the sky. I wept. I couldn't see how our beautiful hills could ever look the same again. Brooks put his arms around me and said, "Darling, it will all grow back so fast, you'll see."

He was right. A few months later, green shrubbery was creeping over the ugliness, and though the black sticks still poked up through the green, we managed to knock most of them down and gradually were able to forget the horror. There was still so much to be enjoyed.

Molly Bee proved to be very loving as well as independent and funny. Occasionally she'd allow me on her back, holding Duncan or Douglas, but when she'd decide the load was too heavy she'd run us off the road and dump us on the bank. Her favorite game, though, was in the pasture, where she spent most of her time with

Lady, the large, dignified mare. While Lady was munching on hay, Molly Bee would sneak up behind her and nip her on the buttocks. Then, as an indignant Lady would turn in pursuit, she would race down the pasture, hee-hawing with glee. Lady could never seem to catch her, so the game was repeated until Molly had had her fun. Then the two companions would munch peacefully together.

When Doug was two years old, we took him to Austin to a reunion of Brooks's large family. With my family gone, I had been thrilled to find that Brooks not only had an older brother and a younger brother, but an older and younger sister and extended family of in-laws and nieces and nephews. Brooks's mother, in her seventies then, had already been to visit us on the farm.

It was a wonderful reunion, but I had begun to realize a couple of things about my husband. Brooks's family tree, with ancestors tracing back to before the Revolutionary War and many more to the Civil War, southern branch, of course, had a direct line of Southern Baptist ministers, and his whole family was a deeply religious one. That is, except for Brooks, who had, early on, rejected organized religion, more from the bigotry he had seen in the small town of his early youth than in his close family.

The other thing I noticed was the casual Texas drinking that went on during the several days' celebration, and how Brooks responded to his family's admiration and deep affection for him by increasing his own drinking.

Having inherited my mother's tendency to worry, I began to nag a little about "moderation," and when we returned home, Brooks, in an effort to please me, seemed only to join me in my single drink before dinner.

What I didn't know was that his drinking had gone underground and that, between the dozens of activities he took on himself as our lives grew more complicated with more building and putting in a pool, he had begun to take a nip of vodka on frequent visits to the kitchen. Brooks was such a vigorous and vital man, who sprang out of bed early each morning to tackle chores with joy. I never knew him to have a headache and certainly not a hangover.

It was only when our four kids were getting to ages more difficult to deal with and I began to realize my inadequacy in handling four such individual characters that I could see, when we sat down to dinner each night, that my pleasant husband seemed to develop a personality that I didn't recognize—a tendency to play devil's advocate with the children and question their ideas and interests. I attempted to smooth things over, without much success. When, in the hope of getting good advice from a close friend, I mentioned my problem, she said, "That's typical behavior for an alcoholic."

I was almost too stunned to speak. "You mean you think that Brooks is an alcoholic?" I stammered.

"Oh, I thought you knew," she said with concern.

I thought back over the anger he had been expressing for the last year or so, which had been so unlike him. I'd attributed this to his disappointment with his career at the moment.

As I worried and continued to nag, Brooks insisted he didn't have a problem, so I cut out the nagging, as the kids knew only that Mom was becoming a bore. Until Brooks drove me into town one day, and suddenly I heard him say under his breath, "Help me!" I knew then that he *was* aware of his problem. From then on I tried to initiate action by suggesting that he go to some Alcoholics Anonymous meetings. The stigma of the disease was intimidating to both of us then, but I only knew that I wanted him well. I finally convinced him to go to a newly opened facility not too far from us for a ten-day stay.

For two people who were as private as we were, it was agony to walk into that unfamiliar place, make all the arrangements with strange faces, say our good-byes in his large lonely room, and then face our first voluntary separation.

Three hours later I answered the phone. Brooks's aggrieved voice demanded: "Do you know that you've left me in a nut-house?"

He told me that, just before dinner, as he was sitting on his bed feeling very alone, his door opened suddenly and a tiny white-haired woman entered. With a bright smile and nod, she crossed the room. Throwing open his window, she caroled, "Wasn't it a beautiful day?" Then, as swiftly as she had entered, she exited, climbing through the window!

Inquiring, Brooks had discovered that the psychiatric ward was next to the alcoholic ward and the doors between them were open all day. But Brooks went through the detox program and the lectures and we thought our problems were over.

That summer we met a charming neighbor at the end of the valley. Eleanor French was the widow of a Major French who, at one time, had owned most of the valley. She was a lady whose love for dogs, indeed for all animals, outdid even Doris Day's. She

found homes for most of the strays in the valley, but was unable
to find a home for eight of the most peculiar animals I'd ever seen.
They all appeared to have shared a common dachshund mother,
but several had curly hair. The thing that made me laugh out loud
when I saw them was that nature seemed to have omitted something in their structure. They all had enormous heads, ears, and
paws, and huge fluffy tails, but the legs were almost nonexistent
and the bodies negligible, so that when they streamed out of her
station wagon, you saw eight heads followed by plumy tails, running about on twenty-four fat feet. They had to be seen to be
believed.

Mrs. French had another loving peculiarity, as we discovered
when we went to buy a rooster from her. She led us to a coop
containing five very depressed hens and thirteen roosters. She
explained that she couldn't bear to kill them. We relieved her, and
the hens, of two roosters, which were all we could handle. I don't
think it ever occurred to her that in kindness there could be a bit
of cruelty as well.

We also looked at her flock of sheep, as we were thinking of
buying a few to keep down the grass on our hillsides. I had never
known that sheep actually had long tails. Mrs. French's did. Another
case of misguided kindness, as I realized when we had our own
flock. Long tails carry filth and pick up ticks and are uncomfortable
for the animals, but the remedy itself brings a week or so of intense
discomfort. A metal stretcher opens a heavy rubber band and slips it
over the sheep's tail, releasing it to clamp about two inches from the
base of the tail. The poor little lamb doesn't know what struck him
and is miserable for a day or two until, with the blood supply
completely shut off, the tail begins to deteriorate and finally falls off.
Then the lamb begins to frolic again, and if you've never seen a
lamb frolic you've missed an enchanting sight! They leap high into
the air a few times, butt each other like small boys in a fight, run
races down the pasture, and finally regroup near their mothers, to
start leaping and repeating the whole process.

We started with a flock of four and a ram, black-faced Hamp-
shires, who soon began to reproduce. One day we watched the
arrival of twins. Then a phenomenon fairly common among sheep
took place. The mother nudged one lamb to its feet, happily
cleaned and nuzzled it, and trotted off, her pride and joy following
in her wake. The other lamb lay where it had dropped, and we
could do nothing to inveigle the mother back to finish her duties.

I looked at the poor little thing lying in the hot sun and I couldn't stand it. I picked it up in a couple of towels and carried it to our enclosed porch to dry it off. Then I got one of Doug's bottles, cut a larger hole in the nipple, and filled it with warm milk. Little Orphan Annie, as she became known, was showing signs of life and eagerly finished the bottle. Then we got to the difficult part. When we tried to return her to her mother, there was no way. Not only would Mom have none of her, Annie would have none of Mom.

What I didn't know was that, being the first to breathe on her, I had now become her mother. I hid behind trees after putting her near the ewe. She bleated pitifully and then quickly located me. Strangely, although she bleated an answer each time she heard her lamb, the mother repelled any attempt to put Annie with her twin by butting her away. Annie, acknowledging only me as her rightful parent, trotted right back to mother Eve!

Finally I gave up and took her back to the house for another bottle. Since she needed feeding often, we made her a bed in a large cardboard carton filled with towels and straw, cut a window in it by my side of the bed, and I fed her several times during the night and took her outside on the lawn at 5 A.M. to housebreak her. Finally she slept through the night and during the day played happily near the children down at the lower house, following me whenever she could.

It was Brooks who gave the ultimatum. "Either she goes or I do," he said. So I took her to the barn one day and waited, hidden behind the hayloft, for the flock to return from grazing. I hoped that in the dark they would accept her as one of them and perhaps her mother would finally have a shred of decency and acknowledge Annie's birthright. No such luck! Instead, in the dark, push became shove and angry exclamations rent the air. Above them rose the pitiful bleats from Annie, calling to her adoptive mother, so I leaped into the melee to rescue her. She didn't return to the bedroom, but slept in her carton outside. Eventually she did go out to pasture with the others but, a loner to the end, she always came back to the gate to call me.

We had several more sets of twins, but by now we were smarter. With the next reject, Buck and Brooks wrestled the ewe to the ground and turned her on her back. Then, as the men held her legs, I was elected to milk her! The idea was to get the milk flowing and the lamb nursing, then to smear its back with the mother's milk so she'd recognize it as hers. Milking is not an easy process, even

with a subject right-side-up, and sitting on the stomach of a struggling ewe and trying to get a grip on her slippery faucets was more
work than fun. Especially with my two "helpers" guffawing as the
Lady of the Manor gave herself an occasional squirt in the eye. But
at least we spared ourselves another pitiful Orphan Annie.

Later, when the boys were old enough for school and lambs were
being weaned, one of their jobs was to feed them a supplementary
bottle on the way to and from school. It was funny during weaning
to see lambs, almost as large as their mothers, kneel by them to
suckle and then bump the mother into the air with their foreheads
in an effort to bring more milk down. Of course Mom didn't stand
this for long, and would shake them off and go trotting down the
pasture in search of grass. Gradually the lambs learned to appreci-
ate the green stuff too.

One elderly ewe called Grandma Gabor (we also had Zsa Zsa,
Eva, Magda, and Mama G) performed the miracle of triple birth
and then proceeded to care for all three herself.

We finally had the good sense to get rid of the ram when the
flock reached twenty-seven. Particularly after he'd butted poor
little Dunc in the seat of his pants one day and sent him flying.

When shearing time came, a couple of men arrived to do the
work, and in no time skinny little sheep were running around
bewailing their lost modesty, and an enormous pile of wool was
lying on a tarp. This was bundled into sacks and sent to someplace
in Salt Lake City. A few months later, before Christmas, we received in return some beautiful, heavy white blankets striped in red
and green. Each of the kids was given one, along with our nurse
Helen and a few treasured friends. It was great fun.

At the top of the big pasture we'd found some pig pens, and
Helen conceived a plan for the boys to invest their allowances in
a couple of pigs for profit. So Chlora and Phyl arrived half-grown,
no longer sweet little piglets. Since they grew enormously in a
short time, and since carting slops and pig feed to two unapprecia-
tive swine was not a popular sport with the boys, there were no
tears when Chlora and Phyl vanished and were replaced by new
bankbooks.

Building was going on constantly at Westhaven. Brooks created
two more stalls out of part of the hay barn, and painted the whole
structure red with white trim. He cut wooden outlines of a cow and
sheep, painted them black and white, and hung them on chains

over the doors. On the sides of the barn he painted large Pennsylvania Dutch hex signs.

We hired a contractor who cut through a wall in a small den where Duncan slept, added a hallway and bath, then, a few steps down, built a large new bedroom for the boys and Helen. We also extended the kitchen and, much later, redid the guest house, turning its sitting room into a farmhouse kitchen with its own fireplace, and enclosing the outdoor fireplace to become a living room with a bay window, and adding a powder room. And Eve could decorate again.

The boys, from the time they walked, had projects under Helen's supervision. Back in the draw where the well was housed under a purely decorative windmill, they built a tiny lean-to workshop. It was amazing to watch two small boys, two and half and four, casually clamp a board in a vise and saw it in two, then nail the pieces together as they constructed a birdhouse. They made at least six of these, painted them green with white trim, added "West" under the doorway and nailed them up in our trees.

Their apprenticeship over, they proceeded, with help from George the gardener, to lay a rock-and-cement foundation for a two-room playhouse made from a piano crate. They cut out windows and made bunk beds. Then Helen bribed the carpenter who was working on the main house, by cooking him a special dinner, to crown it with a beautiful shingle roof and a chimney.

Helen's grand coup was to get a bargain rate on a huge waterwheel made by a local craftsman, which the boys attached to the side of the playhouse. A hose placed at the back supplied water, which turned the wheel and spilled into a cement channel, courtesy of George, down to a small pond where a tiny gnome sat fishing. The project kept growing, with a picnic table and chairs under an umbrella beside the waterwheel. Then later, another larger piano crate made another room a few steps up, to house the boys' electric train set.

The next thing they tackled was at the top of the pasture. On a hillside above the pigpens they built a two-story tree house in a huge oak tree and made a crow's nest from a tin washtub nailed to the trunk high above. Farther up on the hill sat a tall narrow crate from which they fashioned a jail with one barred window, a bench inside, and a door that clanged shut and fastened with a metal hasp and padlock. After I spent twenty minutes in it one day before the jailer would release me, I decided that crime didn't pay and refused to enter it again. Next to the jail they placed a tombstone, for their own macabre reasons, with the epitaph, "Here lies a bad guy." Protruding from the foot of the grave was a pair of George's discarded shoes.

The projects were endless. A hole in the arroyo bank was deepened and a sign went up: WEST BROS. GOLD MINE. An unused water trough sprouted sails and took them to new adventures. The pigpen, after Chlor and Phyl, became a fort from which to shoot Apaches.

First they paddled in a big portable pool, then swam by invitation in the neighbors' pools. Later we built our own.

I remember when Helen, who was quite plump, decided that for safety's sake she had to accompany her boys into the neighbor's large pool. She bought a bathing suit, and one evening she sat the boys in front of the TV and went to her room to try it on secretly. It was stuck somewhere between her thighs and considerable buttocks when, to her horror, she heard the door open behind her and three-year old Doug's gleeful laughter as he said, "Gee, Helen, you sure look funny trying to get your big butt into that teeny little bathing suit!" Thereafter Helen was careful to lock the door.

CHAPTER
· 19 ·

Warner Bros. decided to make a movie of *Our Miss Brooks,* and Al Lewis and I were co-producers. We used the original cast and added a millionaire with a yacht, played by Don Porter, who hired Miss Brooks to tutor his "rich brat son," whom she tamed completely, of course. Unfortunately, the movie was released after the studio had done one about Liberace to cash in on his popular TV show. That one turned out to be a disaster and Warner Bros. promptly tossed us right after him, giving us no publicity or support of any kind. But during the shooting of the picture the PR man brought several little 4-H Club girls to have their picture taken with me. One adorable little girl had her "project" with her, a small white goat with curved horns. To make conversation, I asked her what she was going to do with "Billy" when he grew up. To my horror her lips began to tremble, and she answered, "I'm going to have to put him away."

I looked at the beautiful little goat and back at her brimming eyes, and that was it. "You call my farm when you have to get rid of Billy and I'll take him for you." The child cheered up as I gave her my number and they left.

Fade out. Fade in six months later. I got a phone call and a sad little voice reminded me about Billy, then said, "He's got to go." So Brooks and I got in the truck and drove out into the San Fernando Valley. The little girl met us in front of the house and led us around to the back where, in a cage, were two enormous white goats. By the beard and the large curling horns I identified Billy. Ye gods! Then I made the fatal mistake of asking, "What's going to happen to the other one?"

I realized what I'd done when the lips started to quiver again and she said, "He has to be put away."

Brooks and I drove the truck home with two monsters peering

113

over the panel. We loosed them in the part of the pasture where we fed the sheep and gave them some oats and they found the water. For two months we counted ourselves lucky to have fallen heir to Billy and his brother. They were insatiable devourers of weeds, unwanted sumac, and poison oak. They even climbed on high boulders to munch on lower limbs and new growth on the oak trees. Our pastures and the hills surrounding began to look positively parklike.

Then one day I discovered Billy's drawback. With his gorgeous horns, he was butting our pregnant ewes! His motive was hard to discern, but he had to be discouraged. Since the vet arrived that day to operate on a new lamb, born with one more sexual organ than he absolutely needed, I asked Dr. Borden if he could remove Billy's horns without pain to the goat. He said yes, and he'd remove them right after he finished with the lamb.

I went back to the house, where I was busy for an hour or so. As I approached the barnyard again, I was horrified to hear deep guttural groans that sounded like a man in agony. Rounding the corner at a fast trot, I beheld poor Billy on the ground, legs tied, and Dr. Borden with a saw buried in Billy's forehead, which was wet with flowing blood.

I screamed, "Stop! You're killing him!" Dr. Borden stood up, leaving the saw embedded in Billy's head. Patiently he explained that it was necessary to get to the root of the problem or the horns grew back. I protested that Billy needed some painkiller. The doctor sighed and said that he'd already been given all he should have, and he went back to his work. I left.

But for two weeks, every time I passed the barn, there was Billy with no horns, but blackened dried blood surrounding his eyes, out of which he stared at me reproachfully.

One of the scariest nights we spent at the farm began with a phone call from our neighbor on the hill above. He said that his housekeeper, returning from the late movie in Thousand Oaks, had seen a man, stark naked, leap from the road down into Westhaven. He suggested that we call Camarillo State Mental Hospital, eight miles away, and see if they were missing anyone.

To put it mildly, we were a bit "shook," but Brooks dialed the number and they admitted that "someone had left."

We dressed, woke Liza and put on her robe but told her nothing.

Brooks secretly strapped on his Smith and Wesson .38 and escorted us to the lower house, where everyone else was fast asleep.

Three white-coated, very polite gentlemen drove in, sans guns, sans flashlights, even. They said that "Harry" had somehow escaped the padded cell where he'd been incarcerated in his birthday suit to prevent his injuring himself. Brooks and I looked at each other aghast.

They then invited Brooks to accompany them on the hunt, suggesting that I stay put and lock all the doors. You bet! Brooks supplied them with a few extra flashlights and carried his own pistol. They parked their car, "locked," near the top of the hill where their escapee had disappeared, and all four went crashing into the underbrush.

"Hey, Harry" they called, "you better come out and get some clothes on. You'll get all scratched up."

"There's poison oak in there, Harry!"

"C'mon, Harry, you know we'll find you anyway, and you'll save us a lot of time."

After an hour or so of friendly persuasion, they threw in a few threats.

"This guy's got a gun, Harry, and he's getting mad."

"Ya better watch out, Harry, he's a crack shot!"

Meanwhile, back at the ranch, a very tense Mrs. West was jumping at every sound. Up in the hills the flashlights of the searching party had roused a bunch of coyotes, who were howling their resentment. I was getting worried about my husband, when suddenly what sounded like a large body landed on the roof above me and I heard soft footsteps.

I swallowed my Adam's apple but stayed put. It wasn't Harry, but I didn't know that then. We later figured out that our friend the mountain lion had been driven down by the flashlights.

At around 2 A.M. they returned my husband to me, but they hadn't found Harry and back they went to the hospital. However, they had asked the sheriff and his deputy to look in on us every half hour or so, which they conscientiously did, waving their flashlights everywhere and ruining any sleep that night.

They found Harry the next afternoon miles away, wearing jeans he'd stolen from the clothesline of the neighbor on the hill.

Only a week later, the kids playing outside in the dusk came running up the path to say, "Momma, momma, those men with the white coats are here again!" This was too much! As they greeted me I cried, "No, not again!"

"No, not really." They smiled. "Harry was a little dangerous, but these . . ."

"You mean there's more than one!" I bellowed.

They nodded. "Three."

They went on to explain that most of the escapees were harmless fellows who just got homesick, or wanted a drink, or found a gate unlocked. We finally got used to it, and when we'd see one walking along the road in the valley, we'd just call the hospital and say, "Anybody missing?"

On Connie's eighth birthday we presented her with a sturdy little quarter horse named Chico, and his care and training became her main occupation and delight. She even trained him to jump, and Brooks and I were surprised one day to receive an invitation to a girl's school that had recently opened in the valley, where our daughter had been invited to appear in their horse show.

Puzzled, since Connie had told us nothing about this, we sat on a hillside with other parents and watched the girls jump their mounts. As the last of the girls finished, we saw her dismount near a tree where Connie was standing with Chico. She slipped out of her jacket and handed it to Connie, along with her riding helmet. The colonel who was conducting the meet said, "Ladies and gentlemen, we've invited a neighbor's little girl, who has been riding with us daily to jump her horse, Chico." There was a polite patter of applause as Connie entered the ring. He continued, "I want to ask you to watch the expression on Chico's face, particularly on the final jump, when he's absolutely determined to risk his all for his little mistress."

It was true. Chico took each jump dutifully, but his intent was clearly visible as he approached the last and highest bar and, with a tremendous effort, cleared it by inches. The audience laughed and applauded vigorously. They awarded Connie third prize, which was very decent of them, although privately we thought she deserved first.

By now Liza had given up horses for boys, so Connie became our equestrienne and later went on to ride, by invitation, with the West Valley Hunt Club, which came from Los Angeles to ride in the mountains behind us.

Pat Boone, who'd been given a Tennessee walker while doing *April Love*, had asked us if we'd keep Stepin' (his name) for him, and attempted to interest his girls in riding him, but it was a long trip to Hidden Valley and none of them was really interested.

Since Connie was working on Stepin's gaits, Pat decided to give him to her. We offered to buy him, but Pat refused. He said, though, that Mrs. Boone loved a small painting Brooks had done, and so a first-time-ever trade of a horse for a painting was concluded.

When Connie was seventeen and in her rebellious stage, I had the only moment when I regretted her horsemanship. After an argument with her dad one night and while her unsuspecting parents were watching TV, she slipped out of her bedroom window. When I came for her, hoping to heal the breach, I found her missing, leaving a curt note: "I have gone."

Before I got hysterical I decided to check her closet and found only her hacking jacket and boots missing, so I knew she was on Stepin'. We drove around the valley until midnight when, really alarmed, we called the police. They couldn't locate her either. Finally I insisted that we give it one more try. As we reached the bridge, Connie rode toward us, with a triumphant gleam in her eyes. She later admitted she had sat on the horse on a side road and watched the police search for her. That time I really had the urge to spank her, but since it was the only real scare she'd given us in seventeen years, I felt we owed her one.

My memories of Liza mostly concern clothes. On Christmas or birthdays I usually bought her outfits that I considered stunning. She thanked me graciously and they were retired to her closet. Occasionally, she even burst into tears on receiving them. I was vaguely affronted, considering myself somewhat of an authority on fashion and not at all "square." But I finally discovered that she lacked the confidence to try new things. Eventually, on a day when she'd complained of having nothing to wear, I'd casually suggest that she put on the dress she'd gotten for Christmas (this being the following June!). She would then leave reluctantly for school. On her return, all smiles, she'd say, "The girls really loved my dress, Mother," and it became part of her wardrobe.

On the day she was sixteen, she was to go on her first formal date. That afternoon our storage room behind the kitchen caught fire, and the firemen's hose spread havoc and lots of mud behind the house. Into this walked Liza in a long white organdy gown and matching faille slippers with her first high heels.

The young volunteer firemen were really impressed. We only

hoped we could remove the mud splashes in time for her date. Vanity! Thy name is sweet sixteen.

Our help at the farm had now stabilized. We had a new caretaker, Earl, who adored the kids and all animals. A young Mexican couple, Angel and Josefina, had come to us married only five days. She spoke no English but in a few months was far more fluent than he.

Our Danish gardener, George, had finally moved out from town and established himself in Thousand Oaks, building stone fountains and pools. He still worked for us a couple of days a week, but with our new couple he was really a luxury, and since he was working steadily on his own, we gave him notice and explained why. He accepted it genially, but the next day we found him collapsed against a wall he was finishing. We took him to the hospital and he seemed to be okay. But three days later his doctor came to see us. He told us that George had inoperable cancer and reported that George had no relatives to notify and had said that we were the people closest to him. The doctor hadn't told him of the seriousness of his condition. He said George would probably be able to work quite vigorously for six months or so before the end, and he might as well be free of worry.

Brooks and I found it difficult to believe that our dear old George, who had so patiently and lovingly taught our boys to do stonework and allowed them to "help" him with everything, was not going to be with us for long. We decided that we should have him near so we could keep an eye on him.

We explained to George that we now wanted to develop the rocky hill behind the tennis court into an oriental garden. There was a natural run-off from the hill above, and George had always wanted to build a waterfall up there, so we had a good excuse to bring him back. George was delighted and built us paths and rock walls and a waterfall from which a cement channel with several pools led down to a fish pond. He also helped a carpenter build an oriental teahouse and a soji gate. He lived well over a year longer.

We never knew if he suspected our ruse, but once we heard him mutter, "Well, I think I'll go out and work on my memorial now." And our little oriental garden was always known as George's Memorial.

26. From sergeant to commander in chief! That's quite a promotion!!

27. Director Irving Rapper watches as the star of *Bedtime for Bonzo* and I rehearse for *Voice of the Turtle*.

28 & 29. This is about as glamorous as I get.

30. Joan Crawford's best friend again in *Goodbye My Fancy*.

31. I'm thinking of something clever to say, while Frank Lovejoy tells Joan off in *Goodbye My Fancy*.

32. This was taken shortly after Brooks and I were married.

33. Sending Liza and Connie off to a friend's birthday party.

34. I was pregnant and was telling the girls we were expecting a new addition to the family—Connie hoped it would be a goat.

35. Fulfillment.

36. The scarecrow was for the birds, but Brooks made it and I loved it.

37. As you can see, I went from summer stock to livestock with equal abandon.

38. Eve's little lamb was not as white as snow, but Orphan Annie slept by my bed every night.

39. Connie is in a jam again, but Brooks finds it more amusing than I do.

40. Brooks grew a mustache for *Anatomy of a Murder*, and I recorded it for posterity. I think he looks like Clark Gable—don't you?

41. A happy family portrait at Westhaven.

43. At least Brooks and I
have fun building blocks.

42. Momma gets a rose from Douglas.

44. The boys put their mother in the slammer.

45. This picture of Doug and Duncan always reminds me of
Tom Sawyer and Huckleberry Finn.

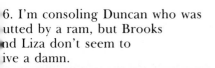

6. I'm consoling Duncan who was
utted by a ram, but Brooks
nd Liza don't seem to
ive a damn.

47. Come on! Molly Bee!

48. From left to right, Brooks, Liza, Doug, Duncan, Connie, Patches, Mollie Bee, and me.

49. I ride off into the sunset. The tale end of the story.

· · ·

In 1958 the "travel itch" demanded another scratch. This time the ship we took was the *Independence* of the United States Line.

Bette Davis was a fellow passenger. I had never worked with Bette and knew her only well enough to say "Good morning" under the hair dryers in Warner Bros. makeup department.

I was surprised when Bette told me she'd never been to Europe before. She said, "I was sent to London by the studio twice to do pictures, but then flown home immediately to start new ones. "When I had the time," she said, "I didn't have the money to travel, and when I finally made enough money, I never could take the time."

Bette was on her way to Madrid to film *John Paul Jones,* in which she would play the Queen of Spain; but this time she hoped to see some of the country when she finished. We were no blasé travelers. We entered the hat contest wearing creations by her sister and my husband, and each of us won a prize. We went down to the economy class, where students and sensible people who save their money travel. We sang for them, which took a lot of nerve, since neither of us was noted for her singing voice. It was made more difficult by the fact that Bette is around five feet two and I am five feet eight, so we couldn't hear each other well enough to stay in the same key, but our audience loved us anyway.

Brooks and I were met in Algeciras by Connie and Mike Raffetto, who'd been living in Rapallo, Italy, for over a year. They had driven all that distance to meet us and travel with us to Madrid. Bette was delighted, as she'd done a picture with Mike, and liked him very much, so she invited all of us to have dinner with her when we reached Madrid. We picked up a green Hillman station wagon that we'd ordered delivered in Gibraltar, and followed their Mercedes, spending the next two nights in Córdoba, birthplace of the Magnificent Manolete, bullfighter extraordinary. When we arrived in Madrid I was persuaded to attend a bullfight, my first and my last.

We had dinner that night with Bette in her suite at the Hilton and the next day visited her on the set of the Palacio Real, and watched her regally enacting the Queen of Spain.

Unfortunately, a family emergency called Connie and Mike away and cut short our trip together. We continued, as we had reservations in

Zaragoza, Barcelona, Montserrat in Spain,
Carcassonne, Avignon, and Cannes (in France again),
Portofino, Italy, and *bella Roma* (same),
Siena, Florence, Salzburg, and Vienna,
Munich, Heidelberg, and quaint Bavarian towns
like Rothenburg and Dinkelsbühl.
Then boating down the Rhine to
Cologne, on to Brussels for the Fair.
Paris, for a last good-bye.
The *Queen Elizabeth,* BACK HOME!

CHAPTER
·20·

In our fourth year, "Miss Brooks" had a new executive producer. As in all such cases, new producers think they have to make drastic changes. The fact that we were down a few points in the ratings was the excuse to get rid of all our beloved characters except for Gale Gordon and me. They moved us to Hollywood, put me in charge of a school for younger children, added a physical education teacher played by Gene Barry who was to become my new romance. I was furious but had no recourse. I made a bet that I would have Crenna, Rockwell, Jane Morgan, and the rest back within three months, and that's what happened. However, by then the boat had sailed and we were dropped at the end of the season.

The following year "Miss Brooks" was put in syndication. That's when people began seeing it every day while they ate their breakfast, and I still hear from a lot of those people to this day. Just a year or so ago I got a call from a woman saying that the people in her office had a betting pool, and the one who came up with the name of the cat in "Miss Brooks" was going to win quite a bit of money. I thought back all those years to that marmalade striped cat and up from the depths it came: Minerva. She must have won the pool!

I remember once telling an actor friend that my only real ambition was to find a play whose name would become synonymous with mine, as Judy Holliday's was with *Born Yesterday*.

He replied that if that happened, perhaps only a few hundred thousand people would see it in New York and, if I was lucky enough to make the movie, not too many more than that would see it in movie theaters. Then he said, "Don't you realize how many millions have seen you as Miss Brooks and, as long as there are reruns, will go on getting joy from them?

I had no idea of the impact that "Our Miss Brooks" had already made on my life and the lives of others, but I remembered being

121

in the audience at the Theater Guild one night and, while Brooks chatted with a friend from the University of Texas, I noticed a very attractive young man staring at me. Caught in the act, he crossed over to me and apologized. He said, "It took a lot of nerve for me to speak to you, but I just had to, Miss Arden. You see, as a young boy I was seriously ill, as a matter of fact, my parents were warned that I was not expected to recover. I was crazy about 'Miss Brooks,' and literally lived from one day to the next to see your show." I looked in amazement at this bronzed young man, and could only say, "You certainly look very healthy now!"

He smiled. "I've just taken my bar exams, and hope to be a good lawyer; but I just had to tell you how much 'Miss Brooks' has meant in my life." I thanked him and rejoined Brooks to report the conversation.

Two weeks later Ann Amster and I were Christmas shopping in Beverly Hills when a young woman stopped me and repeated the exact story, of extreme illness as a child, crediting "Miss Brooks" with her recovery! Ann and I looked at each other in disbelief at the coincidence, but I couldn't dispute my own theory of the need for laughter in everyone's life. It was strange to think of something you regarded as just another job, although one performed with love and satisfaction, having such a positive effect on people's lives.

When "Miss Brooks" finished after eight years, four on TV and five on radio, one of those years overlapping, CBS was readying another pilot for me. It was based on Emily Kimbrough's book about her lecture tours, called "It Gives Me Great Pleasure." CBS called it "The Eve Arden Show." They assigned a very good producer and director and excellent writers. The pilot sold immediately, to go on in the fall.

Then the network told me that I couldn't have the same producer, director, or writers since those people had done the pilot between their regular series.

I was very unhappy about this turn of events, but they assured me that they would put fifteen good writers on scripts. It was a case of too many cooks with conflicting ideas, which spoiled the broth, and a potentially good show went down the tube. Of course, in these days, the twenty-six segments we aired could be considered a success! All I had to show for that experience was a beautiful black-and-tan collie, which my director promised a Europe-bound friend I would be happy to adopt. His name was Bart and all of us adored him.

On one Christmas morning as we sat replete with breakfast, surrounded by the trappings and presents of the night before, Connie's little friend Gale arrived on horseback carrying a good-sized wooden box, which she said contained her Christmas present to Connie. She placed it on a large hassock in front of our fireplace and we saw that the box had a glass front. Connie peered inside and said, "What is it, Gale?"

"It's an iguana, a green one."

We all came closer and looked in silence at the creature, which was about ten inches long with tail, and was definitely green. There was a long pause as we considered the question of how to say thank you for something we wished were back in the jungle or desert or wherever it came from.

Gale, in an obvious attempt to make conversation and break the deadly hush, said, "They grow to be ten feet long!"

That garnered a little hysterical laughter, and Connie finally found the words to thank Gale, and the girls went out to saddle Chico and go for a ride.

Brooks and I were left alone to face the little green creature staring back at us. I said, "Well, when he gets to be ten feet long, we can tether him in the oriental garden and have our own dragon." We fell apart with laughter at the thought, and I went to see if I could catch him a fly. We named him Iggy (short for iguana, of course).

One day when I couldn't stand his lonesome look, I reached in and picked him up. He seemed grateful, but he felt so cold that I tucked him between my sweater and blouse to warm him. I really grew fond of Iggy and took to carrying him around now and then to give him a change of scenery.

I began to plead with Brooks to create something so Iggy would be able to run on the lawn for exercise, and Brooks came up with some fine wire mesh on a big wooden frame that we could set over him and allow him a good run. Our kindness was poor Iggy's undoing. As we sat on the porch one day, I became aware that Bart, our collie, had stepped on the frame, overturning it, and was busily pursuing our green friend through the grass. As I yelled at him to stop, he grasped poor Iggy by the neck and literally shook him to pieces. I think I was the only one who really missed Iggy, and with his departure went the dream of the ten-foot dragon in our oriental garden.

With the finish of "The Eve Arden Show," my contract with CBS had finished too. Since at that time no one realized what residuals from syndication could mean, I was delighted when my agent settled my rights in "Miss Brooks" for what seemed like an enormous amount. He then had them spread this over six years. This would cover the basic expenses of the farm and our help.

In our second year at Westhaven we had paid off the mortgage, and the owners had sent us the legal papers tied in a red ribbon. They had tucked in it a package of matches and that debt had gone up in flames. Now we felt free to accept some of the theater offers we were getting from around the country. These would allow us to play several weeks whenever and wherever we pleased, then we'd get back to the farm and the kids.

Sometimes during vacations they came with us, or stayed at the Amster farm, where we could see them on weekends. It also gave us the freedom to do an occasional picture or TV show in between.

So during the following years we played Kennebunkport, Ogunquit, and Skowhegan in Maine while the kids went to camp nearby.

In New Jersey, where John and Elaine Steinbeck had come to Princeton to see us before we were married, we went on to play the Paper Mill Playhouse and the Grist Mill. We added *Marriage-Go-Round* and *Beekman Place* and *Natural Ingredients* to our repertoire.

We did our own casting, sometimes in New York, where we'd see close to one hundred actors, and where we often found people we'd use again in other plays.

Through the years we played Saratoga, Syracuse, and Nyack in New York State.

In Massachusetts we played Marblehead and Beverly. We played Boston, where much earlier Brooks had tried an engagement ring on my finger under the table, while we lunched at the Copley-Plaza.

We worked during a storm in Somerset, in a reconverted movie house. Each time we stepped through a door off the set, we found ourselves outside in the rain. Prepositioned umbrellas kept part of the downpour off, but we reentered wet below the knees and with sloshy shoes.

In Dennis, on Cape Cod, I had first met Gertrude Lawrence,

when we followed her in one of our plays, and a couple of years later we'd again followed in her footsteps at the Falmouth Playhouse, owned by her husband, producer Richard Aldrich. There, in her cottage, which we occupied, I found the flowers she'd left me, with a sweet note of welcome.

In the cove below the cottage I waded out one morning. Several freezing yards later, I waded right back again, only to find that my diamond wedding ring had slipped off my cold, wet finger!

It seemed an impossibility that I'd ever find it, but I was going to give it a try. To make it more difficult, the wind came up and ruffled the water so that I couldn't even see the pebbles I stepped on.

I waded on, saying a fervent prayer. As I did, the wind ceased suddenly, the ripples cleared, and at my feet the diamond in my ring twinkled up at me, and I knew once again why I can't doubt a higher power.

On the summer we played *Here Today*, the English actress Viola Roache went with us. Vi had replaced Kathleen Nesbitt as Rex Harrison's mother in *My Fair Lady* in New York. When she came to California, we'd worked together in *Goodbye My Fancy*, with Joan Crawford, and Brooks and I knew she'd be perfect for the Boston matron in our show that summer. Vi, English elegance personified, had a slightly malicious sense of humor and kept us constantly amused, along with another cast member, Bert Thorn, a good comedian.

During this engagement we took side trips antiquing in the perfectly preserved Early American towns of Essex and Sturbridge.

At Sturbridge we had lunch in the beautiful tavern, and the routine was always the same whenever we stopped for lunch or dinner. Viola had with her the ancient Scotty she called Sally. Vi would say, "Eve, dear, would you sneak Sally into the dining room? You do it so much better than I do." And Eve, the patsy and dog lover, would hide Sally under our table. There she'd sleep peacefully except for an occasional snore.

On this day in old Sturbridge, we finished lunch in time to mount the buckboard waiting to return us to the area where all cars were parked. We were the only four aboard.

As the four horses stepped onto the great wooden bridge spanning a turbulent stream below, a cannon began firing a twenty-one-gun salute. We'd forgotton that it was the Fourth of July!

Four Clydesdales leaped into the air, crashing down in several directions. They seemed certain to plunge us onto the boulders in the wild waters beneath.

Brooks and I clutched each other and searched for words for a fitting good-bye, as Bert attempted to wedge himself under a seat.

In the midst of chaos I became aware of Viola's calm English voice saying, "It's all right, Sally darling. Don't be frightened, dearest. Mother will *not* let you be hurt!"

In spite of staring death in the eye, Brooks and I burst into laughter. Then the cannon shots ceased, the driver got the horses under control, and Viola patted Sally and said, "You see, my love, Mother can take care of her Sally." And the danger was over.

In Westport, Ruth Gordon and Garson Kanin came backstage, and Ruth told me how hard she'd tried to make *Here Today* a success years before. Then I thanked Ruth for the opportunity of doing her own play, *Over Twenty-One*, which had introduced me to my darling Brooks.

CHAPTER
· 21 ·

One day Glenn called me at the farm to say he'd just read a book in galleys that was due to be published soon, and he wanted to buy the rights for me. The thought of someone spending his hard-earned money for me threw me into panic. Glenn said that he would send the galleys out and I must read them immediately, as he was sure there would be offers made on this book as soon as it came out.

So I read *Auntie Mame* and saw its possibilities as a play, but then negative thinking set in. I thought that if the playwright was unable to translate it into a viable play and I didn't choose to do it, Glenn would lose all his money. I told him how I felt and he said I was wrong, that he still was going to make an offer. He got there the day after Freddie Brisson bought it for Roz Russell. The rest is history, except that when I was offered the West Coast production to play Los Angeles and San Francisco, I was not only delighted to play *Auntie Mame,* but anxious to do it for Glenn.

Auntie Mame was certainly one of the highlights of my professional life. Not only did I get the kind of notices an actress dreams of, but I had my choice of Rosalind's cast from New York, Brooks, who made a wonderful "Beau," and Morton de Costa to direct.

We opened in San Diego in a huge auditorium. The first dress rehearsal was frantic. I had to make the changes first without the seven wigs. We played only two weeks in San Diego, but the opening in Los Angeles was smooth as cream. Our eight-week engagement at the Biltmore Theater was so successful we could have played for months, but the theater had already booked shows behind us, which made them very unhappy.

In *Auntie Mame* the changes of scenes were so fast that I was usually being led through the dark by a dear old character actor named Frank, to leap off a moving set and run toward a tiny dressing room nearby. There my hairdresser and two wardrobe women waited, to strip me of my wig, jewels, furs and dress, and just as quickly get me into my next costume.

I remember a change I had to do onstage (curtain down, of course) as the set decoration was being similarly altered. In San Francisco, several of the stagehands were quite ancient. One night, one of these oldsters was carrying a portrait to be hung on the wall behind me; as he tottered toward me, the wardrobe woman suddenly stripped me almost nude. The tiny stagehand faltered as my bosom suddenly appeared level with his uncertain eyes—then he lurched in a seemingly safer direction. As the curtain went up, the memory of his bewildered face was still making me giggle.

As I often made my entrance down a high curving stairway onto the stage, I had to climb an equally high ladder backstage from which I stepped onto the hidden top of the stairway. Then stagehands would move the ladder away. I remember turning one night to ask a question, only to find my extended foot hanging in midair.

I also recall a night when I couldn't think of the name of the Connecticut town where my nephew's snooty fianceé lived. Since its name was in my first line as I made a speedy entrance down the stairs, I turned in panic to look down where the ladder was being moved away and the Connecticut group was waiting to make an entrance at the front door below. Only one face was looking up at me, Frank, my darling scenery guide.

"Quick, Frank," I hissed, "where do you live?"

Frank looked up at me innocently and replied,

"The King's Arms"—his hotel in Los Angeles. As I made my spectacular entrance down the stairs, I was laughing all the way. Fortunately, as usually happens, the name of that Connecticut town popped into my mind as I reached the final step.

In San Francisco we played the Geary, a great theater, but the dressing rooms were disgraceful, as they are in most theaters. I could not see spending eight weeks as the fabulous Mame in a dreary dressing room, so I promptly ordered it painted, papered, and decorated to suit the character.

When the excitement of opening was over, I began to notice the wistful looks on the faces of my cast when they poked their heads in to say hello while I was making up. They loved the gaiety and warmth of Auntie Mame's cubicle. I contacted Lou Lurie, the owner of the theater and a friend, and asked if something couldn't be done backstage in the way of painting. He said he'd think about it. So in the meantime, Brooks and I began a project of doing something to cheer up the dressing rooms, two each night.

We started with the character actress. We found a little Victorian lamp and mirror and, since she dressed alone, we got her a live orange canary called Mame.

One dressing room with three of the girls in it had the usual hanging naked light bulb in the middle of the room, unnecessary with the mirror lights. With some wide turquoise ribbon, stiff enough to swirl suspended around the light, we added some white feather doves. Turquoise pads from Woolworth's and a vase of flowers created quite an effect.

One boy who loved animals received a bowl of goldfish for company.

Our first efforts created a sensation, and every evening the cast could not wait to see whose room had been done. Two of the boys caught the fever and made a little museum of their room, to which we added tiny paintings and artifacts. A reporter got wind of the fun and we were all in a two-page newspaper spread.

Our "topper" was the juvenile's room. He'd been banished to a third floor "cell" because of his obstreperous German shepherd, which couldn't be left at his hotel. That one almost stymied us! Finally we found some placards for the walls that said things like: POVERTY IS NOTHING TO BE ASHAMED OF, BUT THIS IS RIDICULOUS. In the prop room we found a huge and hideous cushion with Chinese trim and gold tassels. We put this on the floor for the hound and, above it, going up the wall, we hung a white China cat looking back with terrified eyes. Two bowls for food and water sat by the cushion. But there still wasn't a note of beauty, and above hung that naked bulb. We had an inspiration. Below it we hung a metal collander, with the holes refracting the light, and filled it with fake ivy falling down over the sides. From its three curved feet we hung one can opener, one spoon, and one leather bone. Everyone climbed to the third floor to see that one.

About halfway through the run my voice began to give me trouble, so I spent most of the day quietly in bed. On a walk through Maiden Lane one afternoon, I saw in a pet-shop window a tall flight cage containing a number of tiny birds. It was so lovely that I promptly lost my head and bought one, tenanting it with my own selection of finches—seventeen of them—of different kinds and colors. I filled my day caring for them until it was theater time. I wisely sent Brooks out sightseeing to keep him from insanity, between a speechless wife and chirping birds.

On the final Saturday morning of our show, Brooks was out renting a large trailer. It would carry all our luggage, the Christmas gifts we'd shopped for there, and our aviary back to the farm. I was finishing my packing as the birds were happily bathing in several cereal dishes. The phone rang, and one more bizarre episode in our life began.

"I'm very sorry to disturb you, Mrs. West," the soft voice of the desk clerk said, "but there are two FBI men here who insist they must see you. I've checked their credentials, or I wouldn't have called you."

"Send them up," I said, wondering—what on earth!

In came two conservatively dressed young men with short hair-cuts, gray suits, and plain ties. They looked ever so slightly discon-certed at the sight of seventeen birds flapping in their dishes, then sat at my invitation as we studied each other for a minute. Then one of them reached in his inner pocket and produced a letter. He asked me if I recognized the name in its signature. It did seem vaguely familiar, but I said I couldn't recall it. He then handed me the four-page letter that said the writer was going to have to kill me and my husband because we had strange mental powers that we used to force people to drive their cars off the freeway, thus killing many of them.

As I read, I realized I had gotten the same kind of letter a month or so earlier and had discarded it as just another crank letter. What had amused me were the three people named as our accomplices: Bob Hope, Bing Crosby, and Audie Murphy!

The FBI man then told me that the letter had been sent to the Los Angeles Postmaster, thus making it a federal offense. They had traced it to a young man, probably a veteran of the Korean War, who had recently left to hitchhike his way to San Francisco, which made us his probable first target. They'd actually found someone who had picked him up and taken him as far as San Jose, where the driver's mother had offered him dinner and a couch on which to spend the night. In the morning he had left and was presumably on his way to us.

I couldn't believe what I was hearing, but there *was* that first letter.

Brooks arrived about then and was briefed. Then the FBI man said, "We can't offer you protection, but you can call the sheriff's office and arrange for them to put men in the theater, and we'll be there to see if we can spot him from the description."

Brooks and I agreed that the sheriff's man wouldn't be much help if a lone gunman suddenly took a potshot at us, but I said I was worried about our kids and asked if he could notify the sheriff in Thousand Oaks to watch out for them at the farm, since we were now late for the matinee. To our surprise, he said that had already been done, which gave me the chilling feeling that they were taking this very seriously indeed.

We left for the theater with their assurances that they'd be in the audience (to identify the bodies?). We were torn between laughing it off and feeling strangely creepy when we made an entrance. I told our cast that if they heard a shot, they'd better fall on the floor, and they'd find us waiting there.

The last night of a successful run is generally sort of sad. This certainly did add the spice of danger.

They finally found the young man a few nights later and sent him where he could get the care he needed. When we reached home after driving all night, there was a guard at the gates who had refused to let our caretaker in after his weekend off. Helen said the sheriff had been driving in all night long and she'd been told there was a bomb threat on the property.

CHAPTER
· 22 ·

When Otto Preminger was casting the picture *Anatomy of a Murder,* he asked me to play the part of Jimmy Stewart's secretary and offered Brooks the district attorney role. We were delighted to be able to do a picture together, especially one as exciting as this true story of a murder trial. The book had been at the top of the best-seller list for over a year, and it was to be filmed in Ishpeming, Michigan, in the inn where the murder had taken place, and the courthouse where the trial had been held.

We went to Chicago, where we boarded the train with Jimmy Stewart, Lee Remick (who had her baby and the nurse with her), Ben Gazzara, Arthur O'Connell, Murray Hamilton, and some other members of the cast.

Arriving in the middle of a snowstorm on the Upper Peninsula, we were met by a red-nosed, ear-muffed Otto and a battery of photographers.

They put all of us up in the only building of any size in the small town, a red brick inn which was very comfortable. That evening the cast met en masse in the dining room, except for George Scott, who wasn't due for a couple of weeks.

Brooks started work the first morning of shooting. Knowing that I would have many free hours during the eight-week schedule, I had come prepared with projects, sweaters to knit for the boys, books I had neglected to read, and something new to try, mosaics. I became intrigued with these and started a Modigliani-type portrait of Liza. When Brooks, with a 6 A.M. call, would go to sleep, I was wide awake and would crack the glass squares with a heavy steel cutter to fit my design, inadvertently spraying little shards of glass on the floor. Brooks, leaping out of bed at the sound of the alarm, would utter cries of pain and frustration as his feet landed on the slivers. Gradually I tempered my enthusiasm and he grew more cautious, and, at last, I started work on the film.

The picture went smoothly, with only occasional flashes of the well-publicized Preminger temper. All of us were delighted with the newest cast member, Joseph Welch, the witty and wonderful real-life judge, famous for his handling of the infamous Joseph McCarthy. He was playing "our" judge. His wife, an adorable lady, was acting as a juror. They were getting such a kick out of their "new" profession. One evening they surprised us by saying that they'd only been married a few years. They'd been friends for some time, a close foursome with their former mates. With the loss of his wife and her husband, they grew closer, and marriage was the natural result.

During the eight weeks, everyone had much time to spare between scenes, and since the huge courthouse wasn't the coziest place to lounge, we finally gravitated to an antechamber that had tufted leather chairs. There some of us knitted or made mosaics, Lee Remick did needlepoint, others sketched, read, or played Scrabble or gin. Jimmy Stewart, watching the group of busy bees, dubbed us Hobby Lobby.

At night after dinner we gathered in the inn and told stories and played games. One evening someone brought a large canvas, paints and brushes, and we began a collective painting, each one filling a small section in any way he was inspired to.

Occasionally, in an attempt at variety, we'd go to a small bar that had an Italian restaurant downstairs where Tony, the owner, prepared his own chicken diablo, and the next day the set was filled with whiffs of garlic.

There was a wonderful evening when they were shooting the roadhouse scene, with Duke Ellington and his band filling all our requests between scenes.

The night before we left, we partied at Tony's, where we all signed our names in red paint on the white walls and Brooks painted a copy of the "Dead Man" logo on one, all to the owner's delight.

I remember we had a discussion with Otto about children. His opinion was that actors and other creative people should never have them, and he was dismayed to find that we had four. When we heard some months later that Otto's wife had presented him with twins, we were very amused. Sometime after that we ran into Otto to find him transformed into the total doting father, of course!

We had arrived in mid-March in a snowstorm and left in mid-

May in a flurry of snowflakes, with the feeling that we'd been part of a memorable picture. Indeed, I think it's fair to say it did turn out to be a "classic."

In 1962, Glenn came to me with an offer for me to headline at the Sahara Hotel in Las Vegas. When I finished laughing he mentioned the sum they'd offered, and I sobered considerably.

I said, "But, Glenn, what on earth would I do?"

He said, "You've done several revues on Broadway, and I know you've done some impressions. We'll put together some good people and build an act. You'll be great!"

That's Glenn's method, to challenge me, then encourage me.

So, with Glenn producing, and gifted Jerry Fielding to do the music, Sid Miller to write material that excited me and Earl Barton to choreograph, I found myself on the stage of the Sahara that summer with four very talented boys.

All I remember about opening night were Carol Channing's two enormous eyes staring at me from where she rested her chin on the edge of the stage, next to her front-row table.

When the first show was over, I fell on my face on the dressing-room couch and went sound asleep. In a week I'd adjusted so well that I was trying to see other shows before my second one.

I remember Shirley MacLaine coming backstage to say that they'd been trying to persuade her to play Las Vegas, and she thought she'd better come up and see what I did.

She said, "I thought if *you* could do it, I could."

I laughed and said she was right, and she certainly could! And she certainly did. These reviews will give you an idea of my act.

I never would have thought such a grueling act could be fun, but it really was.

A highly competitive phase of the entertainment world was invaded with markedly successful results by Eve Arden last night as she made her debut in a night club.

The comedienne . . . scored an overwhelming triumph, one which easily could open an entirely new career for her. The question on many lips prior to the performance was, "What can she do in a night club?" The answer was not long in coming and it is that she can do just about everything. She sings, she dances, she reminisces about her long career, but she scores her biggest hit with a series of hilarious impressions. . . . It's top quality entertainment as she lampoons such likely targets as Bette

Davis, Loretta Young, Zsa Zsa Gabor, Melina Mercouri, and, best of all, Jackie Kennedy and Marlene Dietrich.

—Los Angeles Herald-Examiner

* * *

Eve Arden is as star bright in person as in motion pictures and as TV's "Our Miss Brooks." Chic, blond, and exquisitely wardrobed, she wins the audience immediately with her clever, special material song number, "Everybody," then sails into a witty monologue, full of the acid wit for which she is famed, for applause and howls.

—Fabulous Las Vegas

* * *

It is doubtful that the student body at the mythical Madison High School ever saw the side of "Our Miss Brooks" that is on display at the Sahara, but boy! What they missed! Eve Arden delivers the sharp, biting Sid Miller material in a glossy polished way that seemed natural and was warmly greeted by first-nighters. Of the nine outstanding impressions, the most outstanding are Dietrich, Jackie, Zsa Zsa, Loretta Young and Melina Mercouri.

—Hollywood Reporter

* * *

Eve Arden enlisted the aid of some of the sharpest pros in the biz to whip up this act for her. . . . Gone is the film character imbued with sophisticated boredom; gone, too, is the man-chasing "Miss Brooks" of TV. From the beginning of the turn, Miss Arden says she's going to play Eve Arden, and in so doing she unveils many hidden talents . . . a disarming personal charm and drive.

—Daily Variety

* * *

PART THREE

CHAPTER
· 23 ·

I had done the Vegas act for the challenge and the money, but with no thought of becoming a night club performer. Although I enjoyed performing, the daytime life—sleeping late (since the two shows were pretty exhausting) and not able to go anywhere without walking through miles of blackjack and crap tables, keno games, and dozens of one-armed bandits—depressed me no end. But when the boys in my act said, "You're not going to just quit, are you, when you got such good notices and you've invested all that money in it? We'd like to go on with it, too." Then I began to feel guilty because I hadn't realized that they also had a stake in it. So I said, "Let's see what offers we get."

The first came from Australia, for twelve weeks. It would mean leaving Brooks and the kids for three or more months. I would have to fly, which I wasn't happy about then, and I would really be in a new business, hiring a conductor and having to pay social security for the four boys. So, feeling like a coward, I decided not to mention that offer to them.

The second one came from the Waldorf Astoria in New York. This intrigued me, so we went east to investigate the Grand Ballroom, where Sheila and Gordon MacRae were appearing.

Sheila did impressions, and had to go to a dressing room to change for each of them while Gordon sang a song or two.

In Vegas I had been on stage, could slip behind the wing curtain, where my dresser stripped me of my wig, my jewelry, and whatever I used over my basic dress. I put on my new wig, slipped into different shoes and jewelry, and reentered. I knew there was no way I could do eleven changes in fourteen minutes in the Grand Ballroom, the logistics were just too difficult. So I relinquished that idea.

Then I had an offer to appear on the "Jack Paar Show" doing

139

my impressionist number. Since it seemed foolhardy to feed into the maw of television the best piece of material in my act, I said no again.

At last my business manager threw me a lifeline. "You've been wanting to take the kids to Europe and stay for a year, and now you have the money—why not go?" I seized on this idea for several reasons. Brooks and I were beginning to think that our children had been living in a comfortable cocoon too long, dependent on a nurse and housekeeper a lot of the time. We wanted to get away from familiar surroundings and help, and to live as a family sharing new adventures together.

Furthermore, Liza, in junior college in Santa Barbara, was seeing her friends fall victim to marriage one by one, and was casting eyes in every direction for "Mr. Right" herself. Connie, a few years younger, was so shy that a year of traveling in other countries and meeting different kinds of people could only be helpful. The boys at seven and eight were as absorbent as sponges.

The decision made, we took Connie to Santa Barbara for a dinner with Liza and broke the news. To our relief, both girls were ecstatic. Then the boys were told. There was great excitement. Maps were studied, the travel agent visited, and we made reservations on a ship of the United States Line, *The Constitution.*

Brooks and I enrolled in Berlitz and struggled with Italian. One glorious day we descended en masse on the passport office, applied for the children's passports, and renewed ours. One by one we filed into a nearby photographer's and had pictures taken. Then, as we watched our children solemnly take the oath that used to be required of all U.S. citizens going abroad, we began to believe in the reality of our dream.

By mid-January, resistance had set in. Departure was becoming a disturbing reality. Home with a capital *H* and romance with a capital *R* were not to be relinquished lightly. Pets were more cherished than ever. There were numerous rebellions and demands to be left behind with family friends. Brooks and I took on haggard looks and worried in the middle of the night.

Finally the day dawned. It dawned with so much left to be done that leaving seemed improbable. There was a constant frantic do-si-do of six of us rushing in and out, and up to the guest house and down again. Liza was all packed, she assured me smugly. All packed, except for two heavy coats, a sweater, a raincoat, and at least a dozen books.

A trip to Connie's room revealed utter chaos. Her large suitcase was bulging clothes and refused to be zippered. Alongside, five pairs of shoes she'd neglected to pack (outside of boots and sneakers, they represented all the shoes she had and couldn't be left). Schoolbooks were piled drunkenly next to a dotted swiss bag full of gargantuan curlers.

Helen had the boys well organized, but ruefully revealed that another suitcase would be necessary for coat linings, boots, and long underwear. Brooks, his things meticulously packed, took over this desperate situation, and I rushed to complete my own packing.

The time came to part with our pets. Chessie, our well-loved cat, and my tiny finches were taken to be cared for by the Dominican Fathers of a nearby novitiate. The girls returned from this mission with tear-filled eyes, and I was glad Helen had kept the boys busy. But I was beginning to wonder how well she would hold up at the moment of departure. I was feeling great pangs myself as I looked around our warm and memory-filled little house. Our Mexican couple, who had come to us after their marriage five years before, and whose baby girl, Chayo, had been born two years later, were close to breaking down. I dreaded the moment when "Helen's boys" and mine would fully realize we were leaving.

By now the skies were dripping in anticipation. Brooks was struggling baggage into the station wagon and the luggage compartment of our other car. Finally, all assembled with coats and hand luggage, we began saying good-bye. Josefina and Angel were crying, while Chayo whimpered an *obbligato*. An agitated Helen was trying to convince a frantic Douglas to get in the car with a sobbing Connie. Liza, weeping softly, climbed into the station wagon with a sniffling Duncan, and Brooks took off down the road to the gate and disappeared.

I put the car in gear and released the brake, but it was not to be that easy. Douglas, almost hysterical now, was wailing, "I don't want to leave hoooome, I'm homesick!" Then, as I started the car, he screamed, "Helen!" and, opening the door, tried to jump out. I grabbed him, closed and locked the door and, not daring to wait, put my foot on the gas and pulled away from the sad little group in the rain. Behind me, Doug's howls rose to a crescendo: "I love my home. I'm homesick. You're taking me from my home!" Connie's sobs intensified.

Their mother was suddenly heartsick, accusing herself of disrupting her children's lives to fulfill her own fanciful dream, and feeling along with them the anguish of leaving familiar and loved places and people.

Not until we picked up our business manager Bernie and reached the railroad station did Doug's wails cease from sheer weariness, and he was yawning apathetically.

The girls had perked up at the sight of the train, and Duncan, ever ready for adventure, was in fine fettle by now.

Brooks and I clasped hands and smiled encouragingly at each other. But only the sight of Bernie's face watching the huge amount of luggage being piled into our two drawing rooms broke the dismal mood, and we rocked with wild laughter. Then the *Superchief* pulled away from his grimaces, and we sat staring tiredly at each other.

To my surprise, Doug fell asleep as soon as he got in bed, worn out from his emotions. The others were beginning to look forward to what lay ahead. The next two nights were difficult ones. Doug, fine during the day, cried heartbrokenly for home and Helen at bedtime, and blamed me for the separation. Brooks gave me the bolstering I badly needed, and assured me that all would be well.

Chicago was a flying visit to the Pump Room for lunch and then back on the train overnight to New York. As we walked through Grand Central the next morning, Brooks grinned as Doug slipped his hand in mine and asked, "Mom, will we get to see the boat tomorrow?" The breach was healed.

The days in New York flew by with visits to the Amsters and other friends and a few nights at the theater. Then one morning, in three cabs, we arrived at Pier 84 and boarded *The Constitution*.

There is no mode of travel in which the "Bon Voyage" is as exciting as sailing aboard an ocean liner. The cabin was full of the happy chatter of friends. Flowers and champagne and gay cards were everywhere. Then the "all ashore," and we were hanging over the rail trying to snap pictures of our friends on the dock below, and tossing serpentine and confetti. The boat whistle blew its last shuddering blast. Waving toward the receding faces on shore, we felt a lonely little pang as Manhattan faded from view.

We went below to unpack and get ready for lunch. In the state-room Brooks and I shared with Doug and Duncan, we found a belatedly delivered "Bon Voyage" gift, and one I enjoyed for the entire sailing. It was an enormous yellow balloon that floated on the ceiling, trailing long silver and gold ribbons, down the length of which were tacked gauzy flowers of pink, blue, and yellow. It was outrageously extravagant and the kind of beautiful nonsense that gives the spirit a lift every time you look at it. As I turned out my light each night, the sight of it gently swaying there sent me to sleep in happy anticipation of opening my eyes to its morning greeting.

The ship, as far as the children were concerned, more than lived up to expectations. This was Disneyland on water. For the boys there was exploration: the play area, the pool, the many decks, and the movie theater. With their sisters they were invited to visit the kitchens, and all of us were taken on a tour of the bridge.

The girls investigated the beauty salons and the shops, which were full of bathing suits, hats, bags, scarves, sweaters, slippers, books, souvenirs, and postcards. They also prospected for possible dance partners.

At night there were parties, movies, the Captain's Gala, the Western Dance, and the Mad Hatter's Ball, in which the three West "girls" each copped a prize, thanks to our talented designer Brooks: for the most original, the funniest, and the most beautiful hat.

The dining room, however, was our downfall. The selection was so tremendous and varied that we didn't have to worry about our two finicky eaters, but the other two had to be watched carefully. As for me, for once I got my fill of caviar—and what caviar! At lunch and again at dinner, Fred our friendly waiter put before me a huge mound of the heavenly stuff, and I ate it happily if guiltily.

All of us were suspended in a dreamworld of comfort and fun, with no screaming headlines or blaring radios to shock us into reality. Life stretched ahead like the Yellow Brick Road to Oz, and we had the eager anticipation of Dorothy. Oh, there were minor rumbles and a few outbreaks of hostility between the boys and the girls, or the two boys, or the two girls, or one boy and girl against the other pair. But that was to be expected, and soon it was time for lunch or a movie or a costume party and all was forgotten in the preparations.

We celebrated Liza's eighteenth birthday, with Fred and Mario (the maître d') and the waiters singing as they presented a becandled cake. Liza had whispered to me earlier that she would really feel eighteen if Dad ordered her a special drink when he ordered ours. I said I thought that would be okay, and what was the special drink she wanted? She said, "A mint julep." I gulped a bit, but quietly passed on the information.

When Brooks ordered three drinks, Connie's eyes popped, along with the boys', in surprise. Liza was blasé, but she looked strangely disappointed. She toyed with her glass often, but ineffectually. Finally she whispered, "Mom, I thought you always had a mint julep in a tiny glass with ice and straws, and that it was green."

A light dawned! "No, darling, that's a crème de menthe." Brooks's eyes met mine with a secret smile; our girl was eighteen. On the last night aboard we stayed up late and I was hard put to ward off would-be buyers of "just a Coca-Cola for the boys" as people swarmed around our fellas, who were looking solemn and captivating in their new black suits.

Connie, who only six months before had sworn allegiance to horses and expressed complete disdain for boys, had been the surprise of the trip. Mr. Gorie, the nice purser who emceed the entertainment each evening, had asked her on the first night out to draw a number from the usual hat. When he saw how she blushed in embarrassment, he announced loudly, "Oh, that's *my* girl," and for the rest of the trip had worked to overcome her shyness. Evidently he'd succeeded only too well, for during the last dance that night we heard calls of "C'mon, Connie," from various people. Suddenly the floor cleared and there was our Connie, long blond hair swinging to the floor and back, dancing the "Fever" as we'd never seen it danced before.

We had enjoyed the halcyon days on the ship, unaware of how abruptly our idyll was to end. Our first sight of Naples was prophetic. Brooks had set our brand-new never-tested alarm clock the night before, and at 6 A.M. our nervous systems were shattered by a banshee scream of unbearable intensity. The man in my life bounded from his berth like Nijinsky suddenly bee-stung, and cracked his head on the upper. He groped frantically for the alarm button. I groaned and tried in vain to recapture my interrupted dream, but at Brooks's exclamation of "Hey, there's Naples," two small pajamaed figures made it to the porthole before I did, and four heads jockeyed for a first sight of *bella Italia.*

Though this low-lying strip of land covered with nondescript buildings wasn't our idea of the legendary Bay of Naples, it was a dramatic sight, due to a brilliant shaft of sunlight striking it through lowering clouds. That was the last bit of sunshine we saw for days.

Landing was the usual tedious combination of red tape, passports, landing cards, and much waiting. But in a short time we found ourselves ensconced in two dreary, if expensive, hotel rooms, overwhelmed by luggage and depressed by the weather, which was steadily growing worse. We mourned our beautiful ship.

Reaction set in with a bang. We were very far from home, surrounded by the strangeness of foreign tongues and different customs. Brooks and I could have dealt with our own feelings, but to see our young feeling so lost was hard to combat.

We washed up listlessly and trailed into the hotel dining room. It was bristling with waiters, but there were few diners, and we sat staring at menus for which six weeks at Berlitz had left us unprepared.

Thoroughly spoiled by ten days of unlimited selection and completely readable menus, we stared uncomprehendingly at such things as *tagliatelle romana, pètto di pollo alla Napoli,* and *cannelloni Sicilia.* With a battalion of waiters breathing down our necks, we hastily settled for spaghetti in some form or other. We were to learn to adore cannelloni and to accept spaghetti as a daily necessity, but this pasta was cold, and it certainly left us that way.

Back to the room we trooped and tried to encourage everyone to unpack or write letters. But this was our first taste of togetherness in dismal circumstances and we reacted accordingly. A quarrel broke out between the boys. The girls, annoyed, spoke sharply to them and then got into an argument of their own. My patience was wearing dangerously thin.

Suddenly, Doug wailed, "I'm homesick. I want to go home." My irritation turned to sympathy for all of them. Doug had put the basic problem into words.

We tried to cheer them with predictions of a change in the weather (not likely!) and the happy thought of picking up our new Volkswagen bus in the morning.

The phone rang. It was Ciro from our local travel agency offering to show us Naples. We were galvanized into action. Clothes were changed, hairdos fussed with, coats buttoned, and we piled into Ciro's small car and were off through the rain-drenched city. Our first sight of Naples did little to cheer us. It was our children's first taste of really brutal poverty, and even Brooks and I had seen nothing before to equal this. In the narrow, dirty streets, all doors seemed open to the rain and cold, probably because crowded living in the small rooms became unbearably claustrophobic. What lay beyond the doors was a far cry from any "home" we'd ever seen. Our children sat stunned and quiet at this revelation of what life was like for a great many people of the world.

Soon, though, the car was climbing the hills of Naples and the character of the scenery changed for the better. Nice residential sections and small shopping areas came into view. We all tried to guess the meanings of signs on the shops. "*Drogheria,* that must be a drugstore."

"*No, signorina*"—from Ciro—"that is what you call a grocery store. The *farmacista* is the druggist."

"*Pasticceria,* oh, that's easy, a pastry shop, but what is a *macelleria?*"

"Oh, I can see it's a meat market."

The meat market startled us at first, as we were used to meat in glass counters behind glass doors. Here you usually entered through a "door" of long, colored strips of plastic, somewhat like an oriental bead curtain. Inside, the meat lay on open counters or hung against the wall. But the walls and counters were of marble and, in most places, spotlessly clean. Each evening the meat was put away, and the empty shop hosed clean, walls and all.

As we drove, Ciro told us about his five children (a blow to the girls) and entertained Duncan and Douglas with stories of his war experiences, during which he'd found himself drafted into the Italian navy one day, spending six days going in the direction of action against the Americans, and two days later, after the fall of Mussolini, heading back to Naples to fight the Germans!

We reached our destination, a museum high above Naples in an old palazzo. Ciro had recommended it, sure that the boys would enjoy its hundreds of models of ships that had fought sea battles in the bay. There were huge galleys, one all gold and red, owned by the King of Naples, conjuring up the hundreds of galley slaves, backs bent over the oars. The girls were entranced by paintings and memorabilia of Lord Nelson and Lady Hamilton, and of Napoleon and Josephine. There was a tiny chapel where a whisper in one corner could be heard distinctly in the one diagonally opposite.

By now the complete lack of heating in the drafty corridors and rooms, which seemed to be solid marble throughout, was taking its toll on the older generation. Brooks and I were congealing with cold, along with the red-nosed, purple-fingered museum guard, and we were happy to rejoin the patient Ciro in his car.

The way back was sparked by the astonishing sight of a Neapolitan hearse, rococo white and gold, with glass sides revealing a bronze coffin heaped with flowers. It was drawn by two black horses tossing white-plumed heads. A most impressive VIP exit!

Back at the hotel, warmth, lights, and hot baths transformed us into agreeable human beings again. While I attempted to make a hotel a home with pictures, books, and scarves over unattractive lamp shades, Brooks called the Neapolitan garage to check on the arrival of our ordered Volkswagen bus from Stuttgart.

There is no agony like conducting a business conversation over the phone in a foreign language, particularly when the local dialect cancels out any resemblance to the vocabulary you've learned so far. Brooks did manage to gather that our bus was not there as promised—but perhaps *domani. Domani,* however, brought only another *"non c'è"* and *"forse domani."*

"Perhaps tomorrow" was frustrating us in our desire to reach Rome. The next day Ciro was waiting to drive us to Pompeii, so we started off with a promise from him to phone the garage later and straighten out our difficulties.

We'd prepared our young with various books and stories on Italy before leaving home, and the results were happily evident in Pompeii. It was easy for them to picture the chariots that had worn the ruts in the huge cobblestones of the roads and marketplaces. The past seemed to come alive as we wandered through the Forum and the Temple of Apollo, and the great public baths with their hot, tepid, and cold rooms. The pools evoked the young athletes and the Amphitheater recalled the fearless gladiators.

The hundreds of objects in the adjoining museum won their rapt attention as they looked at pins and needles, dental equipment, and beauty aids, so modern in concept. The dog, trapped in his death agony and reproduced from a mold formed around his body by cooling ashes, got clucks of sympathy. The beautiful colors in the frescoes, some as fresh as when they were painted, were admired. Now we knew the exact color of Pompeiian red.

When Ciro called the garage later that day, we found to our amazement that our bus had been delivered by train two days before. What the garage man neglected to tell us was that Brooks needed to bring his passport in order to get it through customs by the next morning.

So Brooks and Ciro, an irritated twosome, went off to deliver the passport and a few irate words, while I made arrangements by phone for my Foster Parent child, little Maria, who lived in Naples, to have lunch with us the next day.

The following morning there was another bilingual discussion with the garage man, from which Brooks managed to deduce that the bus's status was still *"non c'è"* and that, when it did arrive, it would need to be put into condition, and therefore would not be ready once more until *"domani."*

At this point Brooks, who had been alternately boiling and simmering, finally erupted. English or no English, there evolved an understanding that the bus was to be ready by six o'clock that evening.

At noon we met Maria, with the charming lady representative of Foster Parents, along with Maria's mother and fifteen-year-old cousin, Mima. Maria, now ten, had been my foster child since my French boy Daniel had reached his eighteenth birthday. I'd become so involved with Daniel and his whole family that when I was assigned Maria, I decided to remain more impersonal, and took, along with her, a young Vietnamese girl and a small Chinese boy in Hong Kong. I knew they all benefited through the plan in clothing, bedding, food and schooling, and from time to time I sent them packages, but I'd always felt a sneaking guilt that I couldn't find the time for more of myself than a none-too-frequent letter. Now, sitting beside Maria and watching her radiant face as she looked at "her family," I was glad that I was her Foster Mother, no matter how unsatisfactory.

My children were sobered when they realized, as we ordered lunch, that Maria and her sad-faced cousin could eat only simple pasta and a few greens because their stomachs couldn't accept the richer foods that formed most of our daily diet.

We learned an expressive Neapolitan gesture from Maria when I asked her if she liked chicken. She jerked her chin sharply into the air twice. I took this to mean "yes" and started to order it, but the woman from Foster Parents said with a smile that this meant "absolutely not." It was a wonderful gesture of disdain that the kids soon adopted for their own.

Our lunch over, Maria kissed us all good-bye, and we watched a little sadly as she, her mother, and Mima disappeared into the misty rain of Naples. I tried not to think of the sort of place they were probably going back to. The hotel room we'd been complaining about suddenly looked very wonderful to all of us.

We spent the afternoon repacking so that we'd have time to go with the men to collect, at long last, our bus. We drove some distance through a storm that was rapidly getting out of hand. Trooping en masse through a courtyard, we entered the garage and, behold, there was our gleaming gray-and-white microbus. It took over an hour, and a burst of temper from Brooks, before, at last, gas tank full, we were on our way.

CHAPTER
· 24 ·

In the morning we caused a slight sensation loading all our luggage on the bus. Even we couldn't believe how much we'd brought, but, we told ourselves defensively, it was for a whole year!

Ciro came to see us off, bringing the boys a wooden Pinocchio, and we waved a teary *arrivederci* to our new Italian friend.

The trip north on the autostrada was easy and the countryside beautiful though bleak, in mid-February. The mountains were topped with snow, and Duncan and Douglas were diverted by the sight of Monte Cassino, the monastery as pristine as if it had never known the touch of war.

As we neared Rome, excitement grew. "Look, Connie, that big dome over there must be Saint Peter's, isn't it, Dad?" "I've never seen so many people on bicycles!" "We'll take you to lunch at the Casa Valadier someday. You'll see all Rome spread before you and it will help you to orient yourselves."

We drove into the Piazza di Spagna. "Those are the famous Spanish Steps. We used to sit there and read our mail from you. This spring you'll see the steps banked with blooming azaleas at Easter. Our hotel, the Grand Hotel de la Ville, is right above here, on the Via Sistina. We'd better get there and get settled before dinner."

We were always a little embarrassed and felt like "those crazy Americans" when we pulled up before a hotel and unloaded four children and all that baggage. But the embarrassment was soon dissipated by the warmth with which the Italians enveloped our children. Doormen, elevator operators, maids, and waiters, they all adore children. "*Èccola! Una bella famiglia!*" "*Questi bambini sono molto delizioso.*"

Even young salesgirls in the shops would pinch the boys' cheeks with "*cherubini.*" The "pinchees" would stand rigid with humiliation. I would smile and, seeing signs of anger appear, would hastily shepherd the boys out of earshot.

"Why do they do that, Mom? Do they have to act so silly?" But eventually they learned to relax and, if not enjoy, at least accept it.

Again we were in two hotel rooms, large enough until all the luggage was deposited therein, which promptly cut down our living space by a third.

The first few days we were so happy just to be in Rome that nothing bothered us. After continental breakfast we'd set out for Saint Peter's or the Coliseum or the Forum. Brooks and I were delighted with the kids' response to everything they saw. They really "dug" the whole idea. Several hours in a row of the Vatican Museum didn't faze them. The Egyptian Room in particular was a whole new kind of adventure. Duncan, of course, questioned us constantly about who, what, where, and when, and I realized we were going to have to do a certain amount of homework.

We were amazed when, after coming out of the Senate Building in the Forum and reminding Duncan that that was where Caesar was assassinated, he was furious that he hadn't been shown the exact spot and went back in to confer with the guard on the complete details. Later, he asked me to get him a book on Caesar's legions.

We were even encouraged at the interest the girls were showing. At an age when one's social life supersedes all else, they'd had none of that since we left the ship. But Connie had always been talented in art, and Liza found a new interest in sculpture and asked for reading matter on Bernini.

Our cultural lives were progressing famously, but family life was running into a snag. The hotel rooms were closing in on us. We had never lived in such close proximity before, and our dispositions were undergoing a severe test.

It was simpler to have the continental breakfast together in one room before the arduous chore of finding clean shirts, underwear, and socks for the boys and locating that just-right dress or blouse and skirt for the girls. Since the closets were minute, clothes surrounded us, hanging everywhere.

Brooks and I, creatures of habit, deprived of our morning papers, would try in vain to restrain our annoyance as the boys teased each other and wrestled suddenly into breakfast, laid out on trays on the bed.

Lack of privacy and sleep was demanding its toll, along with minor vexations, such as the sliding bathroom door, which daily trapped me inside, my lack of mechanical skills being notorious in the family. I must admit I laughed after one of these struggles when I heard Duncan call, "Dad, I suggest you come to the rescue of a damsel in distress."

The lack of sleep, however, was our basic problem. Our rooms were directly above the Via Sistina, which we discovered was a sort of testing area used by sports-car owners. At any time after 10 P.M. they would pass the Trinità del Monte at the head of the Spanish Steps, rev up their motors, and then *Vrooooom*—they would practically lift our beds from the floor as they passed under our windows. This was an all-night diversion, and the bags under our eyes began to rival the ones heaped on our floors.

Our original idea had been to take an inexpensive apartment from which to sortie to Greece or Austria or Switzerland. Now, however, we were finding the apartments far from inexpensive or even attractive.

One day we rushed with the agent to see *un bello appartamento* before anyone else could snap it up. It was still February and cold, but the chill was nothing to that which struck us to the marrow as we entered the available "mausoleum." It was marble-floored throughout, with no sign of a rug. The living room looked like a good place to hold the reading of a will, if the deceased had only three relatives, that is. The urn with the ashes of the departed was already on a marble pedestal. The hall would have made an ideal skating rink. As we skidded uncertainly toward the bedrooms, my teeth became castanets. I looked at Brooks, whose face was congealed in despair. There were rooms and more rooms, upstairs and down, and we went through every freezing one.

We escaped thankfully and made for the nearest espresso bar to thaw out, a very discouraged pair.

That night, even dinner at George's, our favorite little restaurant behind the Excelsior, couldn't raise our spirits. The young, taking their cue from us, were edgy too. As we walked toward our hotel along the Via Veneto and down to the Via Sistina, my redhead, resenting a comment from one of his sisters, took a swing at her. His complaints of persecution were many and loud. A tall man wearing a chesterfield coat and a derby, obviously English, stopped and smiled at Duncan. Then, transferring his smile to me, he said, "You seem to be having a little trouble, Miss Arden."

Always confounded by my professional self being recognized in the midst of private difficulties, and not sure if this was someone I'd met and should recognize, I replied politely that Duncan was a bit "pent up" from hotel life and that we hoped soon to find a place to "release" him.

The charming gentleman then said, "Have you tried the Principessa yet? She's very good at finding the right place."

Having recently seen the film *The Roman Spring of Mrs. Stone*, which dealt with a *principessa* who arranged assignations between American widows and handsome Italian *giovani*, I was slightly taken aback. He quickly went on to say that this Principessa, although a real one, was also an agent of real estate and knew all the good houses in Rome, and that he'd be glad to leave her number at our hotel. Then he bowed ever so elegantly and moved off into the night.

I reported this incident to Brooks and we chuckled over the idea of a *principessa* finding us a house. But the next morning there was a message in the box with the number of the Principessa Soldatenkov!

As the sports-car races had been particularly bad the night before, I was desperate enough to call her immediately. The ring was answered by a hacking cough that lasted a minute or two, then a deep voice said, with weary disdain, "Heylo."

I introduced myself, explained our problem, and said we'd decided to find a house outside of Rome, since we seemed to operate better in the country. She inquired, without much interest, what we had in mind to pay for rent. I mentioned the fairly modest sum that was our starting price. There was a deathly hush at the other end of the line, and I thought I'd lost her for good. Finally a stricken voice said, "Oh my dear, nothing like that in Rome. Florence, perhaps, but Rome, nevah!"

I allowed as how we might raise the ante a little, but she left me with scant hope.

I'd received a letter from a "friend of a friend" welcoming us to Rome and asking us to call her. She was the wife of a screenwriter and invited us to visit their villa on the Appia Antica, and "could we come to lunch?"

We were delighted to have a day off from dreary apartments and anxious to see the outskirts of Rome where we too might find a house. After a delicious luncheon that introduced us to spaghetti carbonara, our hostess suggested two towns in the Alban Hills,

Frascati and Grotto Ferrata, where we might find a small villa, so we decided to drive up and see them after lunch.

Driving through vineyards, orchards, and odd little villages, we arrived at Frascati and were charmed by its quaintness and the lovely view toward Rome, but it was siesta time. So we planned to return during the week.

One of the few drawbacks of living in Rome is the siesta. To Americans, most of whom conduct business from nine to five daily, the Italian habit of closing shop from noon to four, for lunch and siesta, is hard to accept. Weeks later, we would drive into Rome with film to be processed, or groceries we needed from the *super-mercato* (newly opened in Rome), or wanting to pick up mail, only to wait, fuming and frustrated, until languid workers strolled back from siesta and leisurely prepared to open doors.

On our return from Frascati I found a message from the Principessa. When I called she told me she thought she had a wonderful villa for us, although it would not be available for two weeks— would we be interested in seeing it? Would we ever!

Things were looking more hopeful, but we decided to move out of the hotel in the meantime, so we could get some sleep. I had been reading the ads for *pensiones* for several days, and had been intrigued by one that sounded too good to be true. "Children welcome. Garden with restaurant attached, can even do your own barbecueing." Now I asked Brooks if he'd look at it while I stayed with the boys and the girls went for the mail. If he liked it, we would all go later.

After an hour he returned elated. "Honey, I think you'd love it. It seems to me to be just right for us."

So we hopped into our bus and headed for the Parioli, a section much favored by Americans. It's very easy to get lost in Rome, so we twisted and turned as Brooks tried to remember the way, and I endeavored to make sense from the map. Eventually we turned the right corner and there it was, the Villa Eva.

In a courtyard off the tree-shaded street, steps led up to the front door of what had once been a large family villa. On one side, doors opened on a patio, and beyond that was a raised dining terrace, covered with gay canvas awnings.

Mine Host came smilingly toward us. A genial Polish gentleman, Mr. Landesburgh, with a twinkle in his eye, led us to the top floor and opened a door on the right. We followed him down the hall-way, off which opened four bedrooms and three baths. The bedrooms were curtained in different patterns of cotton, with headboards and beds covered in the same fabrics. Each room had its own bath, with tiled walls in a cheerful, if rather startling, pink. The whole effect was so inviting and spacious that I turned and asked, "How soon can we move in?"

Mr. Landesburgh smiled and said, "Today, if you like."

I looked at Brooks, who nodded and said, "We'll be back in an hour," and we were.

Mr. Landesburgh strolled to meet us as our bus drove up in front. "I'm glad to see you travel light," he said solemnly. "So many Americans carry too much luggage."

I did a double take at our suitcase-laden vehicle, and then I saw the eye with the twinkle.

After a delicious dinner, we sat in the dining room and chatted with our amusing host, as we seethed with contentment. Our boys were up in their room unpacking their toys and the girls in theirs writing postcards. I had made my nest with the usual pictures and books, et cetera, and now, after a liqueur proffered by our host, we were ready to call it a long day.

Upstairs, I could barely stay awake to see that the boys were bathed and in bed with lights out. Liza and Connie were already sound asleep. Finally, in utter peace of mind, I was drifting off when I heard the patter of little feet, the door opened, and in the darkness came a small voice.

"I just have to sleep with you, Mommie. It's too lonesome in there." I got out and led Douglas back to bed, speaking soothingly. There followed an hour of travel between beds, with assurances of our nearness and Duncan's proximity. Nothing did any good. Finally I tried God's ever-present nearness, a mite late, to be sure, with an exasperated answer from Douglas: "Well, *he* won't discuss my problem." Eventually, he slept.

I realized Douglas's confidence needed a little bolstering, so the following day, when Duncan was out with Liza, I encouraged Douglas to take a walk alone around the block. Then I watched from an upstairs window as he left the courtyard and disappeared from view. As I stood there, wondering how large a block it was, he came tearing back in and hid just inside the villa gate. A moment later two people passed by. He ventured out again, and this time was gone so long that I returned to the window to look.

Suddenly Doug darted in the gate and looked frantically for shelter, then hid behind a bush by the wall. I stood watching, puzzled. Then a large black dog walked purposefully into the courtyard and began a search. I felt helpless up there on the fourth floor, but as the dog got nearer to him, I called reassuringly, "He wants to make friends, Doug."

At the sound of my voice, the dog looked up, wagging his tail. Doug, encouraged, emerged and patted the dog's head. "I found him down the block," he said, with only a tiny quaver. "At first we were kind of scared of each other, but now he's my friend." And he was right. The dog came daily to play with Doug, and was dubbed Fiocchi, after the cornflakes that were Doug's favorite breakfast dish.

CHAPTER
· 25 ·

The morning we were to look at the Principessa's prospective villa, we went almost reluctantly. We were comfortable and happy in our little *pensione*. But as we followed the man sent to lead us to the Marchese di Spinola, the villa's owner, our spirits began to rise as we drove into the countryside. Even though the vineyards and trees were still leafless, the moist earth was sprouting green with a promise of spring. We swung farther into open farmland and then turned sharply up a hill between rows of alternating pine and plane trees.

In front of us, the tree-lined road swooped down and then up again to a Roman red villa with dark-green shutters. We drove through its tile-roofed gate into a graveled area where a youngish man waved and came forward to greet us. We were staring, entranced, at the garden that surrounded the house. It was at least two hundred feet deep and planted with many varieties of trees and shrubs. Enclosing it was a high wire fence covered with climbing roses just begining to bud. Beyond the garden, on all sides the ground dipped away into meadows and then rolled up to the horizon. The Marchese owned 158 acres of this, and the only other buildings to be seen were those of his adjoining farm, and a few other farmhouses on the skyline.

I was so spellbound, I could hardly answer the Marchese's nervous greeting. He was nervous because he felt his English was inadequate for all he wanted to explain to us.

The house, he said, had never been rented before. It was only three years old, and he'd built it to get his wife and children out of Rome in the terrible heat of July and August. Therefore he could only rent it through June. Also, he apologized, it had been painted inside at the end of the previous summer, then the house had been closed through the unusually cold winter, and the paint was peeling off in places, but he would redo it before we moved in.

157

As we walked through the attractive house, I couldn't have cared less about the peeling paint. It was love at first sight. In the foyer was a Ping-Pong table. The living room was very large, but the furniture formed "chintzy" groups around the fireplace and at the far end. In the dining room he opened a sideboard to a lovely array of green-and-white China, and a drawer full of silver. The kitchen was a shock. It was split into three small rooms, with none of the conveniences of our American counterpart. But the thought of cooking our own meals erased this tiny drawback from our minds.

Upstairs there were five bedrooms and three baths, and the master bedroom had a balcony from which we could see miles in every direction. It was glorious! It was magnificent! It was ridiculous for us even to think of renting this dreamworld, and we were determined to have it!

For a cold moment we thought of the sum he'd mentioned. But after all, that was in lire and those figures always sound fantastic. We'd figured it out, hadn't we, and it wasn't too bad, was it? No, we hadn't, and it was, but that came later.

There was still the crowning glory to see, the pool. Out we went across a back garden to some stone steps that led down to a terrace, and there it lay, a sixty-five-foot pool, and at one end a half-moon pool for the children. My children were trying to contain themselves as ordered, but little yips of excitement were coming from the boys, and whispers from Liza and Connie.

"Oh, Mom, Dad, can't we live here? We won't ask for anything else, and we'll help to take care of it!" Little did they know!

We thanked the Marchese and told him we'd phone him that evening.

As we drove back on the Appia Antica, we discussed the pros and cons. Maybe it would be better to settle down and really get to know Rome until June, and travel later. We could study Italian, get brown and healthy by the pool, play Ping-Pong, and have games and conversations instead of television. At this, Dad looked happy. We built our castles higher and higher, then, with a bucket of cold water, they collapsed. We had figured out all those thousands of lire, and it was far more than first estimated.

I was unhappy as I dialed the Marchese's number. He listened as I explained that we'd added wrong and, as much as we loved his beautiful place, we couldn't afford it. He said he was very sorry, as he'd liked our family so much. I said I was more than sorry. Then, as an afterthought, I said of course we wouldn't really mind living with peeling paint, so that would save him some money, and (hopefully) that maybe if we came up a little, he would be able to come down a little. He said rather stiffly that he never discussed business, his lawyers took care of that, and maybe they'd discuss it with me.

I was pretty embarrassed and felt that I lacked any talent at bargaining, and we politely "good-byed." Well, I thought, that's that.

At this time our friend and former guide Iole Paglia came back from skiing at Cortina d'Ampezzo and had dinner with us at Villa Eva. That same evening, an American family with six children, all under ten years of age, moved into the *pensione.* Ted Mearns was a young lawyer from the University of Virginia who had been on a Fulbright Scholarship in Sicily for the past year. His wife Pat, a pretty, delicate blonde, handled six small children with nerveless efficiency. They too had a Volkswagen bus, in red and white, and it became our family joke to yell "There's the Mearns" at the sight of a red-and-white Volkswagen. Usually we were right.

The Mearns children spoke fluent Italian and this began to pique ours. A few times I took the boys to a nearby park to kick a ball around, as all little Italian boys do in imitation of their soccer-playing fathers and older brothers. I loved to watch the small *italiani,* with their olive eyes, pushing, scrambling, and yelling in mellifluous Italian.

One day a tall, quiet little boy of about ten stood watching my boys fly a toy plane. He was as handsome and aristocratic as a small prince, and he smiled shyly back at me. When the boys' plane landed high in a tree, he eagerly went to the rescue, and ingeniously managed to recover it. He spoke no English, but with my halting Italian I learned that his name was Paolo.

The boys were thrilled with their first Italian *amico,* and encouraged Paolo in a game; but they were constantly frustrated and came running to ask, "Mom, how do you say, 'Run after me and tag me'?" "Mom, how do I ask Paul if he wants an *arranciata* (orange drink)?" "Mom, can I ask Paul to the villa, and how do I say it?" This was the first time I felt the tug of my fish on the language hook.

Two days after we'd seen the Marchese's villa and had begun to resign ourselves to losing it, we came home from a day of trotting our four and four small Mearnses through Hadrian's Villa and the Borghese Garden's zoo. Exhausted, I fell on the bed and then jumped as the phone rang in my ear. It was the Principessa calling to tell us that the Marchese had reduced the rent for us, and if we would meet her at the Villa with the Marchese's lawyers, we could make arrangements for taking over. Happy surprise!

Then began the lengthy and complicated process of concluding an Italian lease. First, at the Villa, we listened to rippling conversation in Italian between the Marchese's sister-in-law, a doe-eyed brunette, his lawyer, and the Principessa. The Principessa was quite a character. A large gray-blond woman of Russian, German, and English descent, she was dynamic. She spoke Italian fluently and English forcefully. She was there to protect our interests, she said, and as we went through the house deciding what would and would not stay, she would halt proceedings now and then to deliver a two-minute harangue in Italian. Only when the lawyer and the sister-in-law nodded agreement would we continue inspection. I felt amply protected, but on the other hand, the Principessa's boon companion was making me very nervous. This was Basil, an outsized basset hound with a tendency to lift his leg in greeting to any other leg, such as a chair or table. The Principessa was completely oblivious to this little facet of his personality.

The tour concluded, we were told that the next step was to meet the Marchese in his office that evening and go over the lease, which by then would be typed in final shape. That evening we guided the bus through the ancient, narrow streets near the Pantheon. In the dusk the many cat tenants of the Pantheon were out being social and disdaining tidbits from human admirers.

We entered the courtyard of an old palazzo and walked up its stairs to the office. There were wonderful old paintings hanging on every wall, landscapes and portraits; it was like being in a small museum. The Marchese greeted us, and we sat at a long table to conduct our business.

I'm not one of those Americans who come to Europe to complain that everything isn't "just like home." I cherish the differences in countries and peoples. This to me is the salt and spice of life. But I reserve the right to small idiosyncrasies of my own, and one is about foreign lighting.

The Italians practically always seem to light with ten-watt bulbs. I like lots of soft warm light, and have paid a fortune to Mr. Mazda and General Electric to prove it. The Marchese's great drawing room of an office was lit by a few sconces that held those dear, weak

THREE PHASES OF EVE   · 161

little bulbs. Straining our eyes, we went over the lease from five-thirty dusk to seven-thirty dark.

Roman business never seems to be a matter of urgency. To two Americans, brooding over the possibility that their four children, left alone together for hours, would probably murder each other, it was torment. Finally we finished the corrections in the lease and prepared to sign it, pay our rent, and leave.

To our surprise, the Marchese refused the money. No, he said happily. The lease must be retyped and checked and in two days we would meet at the villa, sign the lease, get the keys, and then we could pay the money.

We forced our way into the rush-hour traffic. As most shops in Rome close at seven, traffic from then to eight-thirty is not to be imagined. Tiny cars dart like ants in every direction, and just as frantically dodging between them are hundreds of people heading for buses or nearby apartments. If you have not attained the perfect combination of bluff, steel nerves, and James Bond daring, just stay home or call a cabbie who has. Brooks was a great Roman driver, and we arrived to find our children intact.

The following Wednesday we moved, a little sad at leaving the Villa Eva. Mr. Landesburgh, his wife, and Pietro, our lovable waiter, gathered to see us off. Even the huge black cat we'd named George and had been plotting to kidnap, rubbed against our legs in farewell. Douglas wailed, "I don't want to leave the Villa Eva" as we pulled away. But Duncan, the practical one, said gleefully, "I just can't wait to get into that pool!"

There was still a complete inventory to be done, so the Principessa was there to meet us. The kids were consigned to the garden until we'd finished. The Marchese's man was representing him, and also there were the Principessa's assistants, an elegant young couple who turned out to be, of all things, a *conte* and *contessa*. This was the final fillip, minor royalty counting your spoons!

I followed, fascinated, as they efficiently listed *"ventiquattro forchetti, ventiquattro coltelli, trentadue cucchiaini."* Then, in the bedroom, *"diciòtto attaccapanni* (hangers, to you), *trentuno lenzuoli* (sheets)." There were a great many little cries of *"qui"* and *"la"* as they located various items. Basil, the Principessa's boon companion, was still giving his blessing to the furniture, and I gently called the Principessa's attention to this breach of etiquette. She drove him from the house with loud cries of "Basil, how could you! You *know* you shouldn't wee-wee in the house. Out, out, you naughty boy!" Five minutes later he was back, having saved himself for the indoor work he obviously preferred.

As the afternoon wore on, dark clouds gathered and the shadows deepened in the rooms. I switched on the lights. Sure enough, those tiny ten-watters. I made a mental note to replace all bulbs.

The children came in shivering and asked if they could make tea and move their clothes into their rooms. The inventory was finished by now and we had poured a drink for the group. They were toasting our occupancy when the lights went out. If there is anything that inclines me toward panic, it's being without electricity.

As no one present seemed to have any idea of what to do, I began to be apprehensive. But I should have known that my ever-reliable mate would deal with the situation. On our tour of the kitchen, he'd noticed a light bulb dangling from a wire, which had flickered madly when touched. He suspected a blown fuse from this source, and in a short time the lights were restored.

The aristocracy departed, and the bourgeoisie prepared to cook their dinner. It was cold in the kitchen, so we lit the gas oven and left it open. Then Liza took a pan to the sink for water. She turned the faucet and got nothing. I literally howled for Brooks. He was upstairs, and had discovered there was no water there either.

"No wonder it's cold. The furnace has gone off because there's no water in the steam-heat radiator." This was disaster indeed.

"Where is the number to call for Mauro, the Marchese's man up at the farm?" I located it.

"You'd better call him, honey," he said. "You seem to understand Italian over the phone better than I do." I managed to get the number and ask for Mauro, but explaining our problem strained my vocabulary. However, I dredged up a few words that left him in no doubt.

"*Aiuto, soccorso,*" two pleas for help. "*Non acqua, non caldo.*"

Mauro answered, "*Subito.*" In two minutes his little car buzzed up the road. There followed a great display of pantomime on both sides, and we were initiated into the mysteries of the water tanks. Huge, round metal ones in the attic, they were heard but never seen. They were filled by flipping an electric switch. Where was the switch? Out the back door, across the garden, around the pool, and in the toolhouse. There it was, in plain sight on the wall. This was a twice-daily operation from then on. Usually, we discovered we were out of water just as one of us had worked the toothpaste into a good lather or when I had a nice batch of laundry ready to rinse and the faucet gave an asthmatic cough.

The refill procedure was simple and required only a short time. Once you'd made your way through rain or wind to the switch, you flipped it and went back to the house to wait. Then, when a noise like Niagara overflowing came to ear, you yelled "Duncan" or "Douglas" or just "Turn off the water!"

As Brooks said with American practicality, "For twenty-five bucks they could put in an automatic switch, but they say, of course, what the hell, what are servants for?"

I felt, though, it lent a certain charm to living, and I even enjoyed the chore when there was no storm. For now, as though the weather had been waiting for us to settle in, it turned nasty. The winter before had broken records, and this one wasn't going to give up without a try. The morning would dawn, sunny and tempting us to consider the pool. Half an hour later, the skies would be gray and trees were whipping in the winds. Shutters, twenty-odd pairs of them, would start to rattle, and lightning would flash.

Our first days there were filled with indoor work, so we didn't particularly mind *"il tèmpo."* We were enjoying doing our own cooking. Brooks is a great chef, and Liza's talent was beginning to bloom. I stand a weak third in this triumvirate, being more of a "special dish" type. I'm a great dishwasher, however, and yield to none in my methodical approach to this art.

But the reaction from the long trip, sleepless nights in the hotel, and the strain of moving, carrying, and cleaning was beginning to tell. Brooks, for one, came down with a cold that developed into a terrible coughing fit one night, and we got no sleep. The next night I insisted that he take two of the smaller variety of sleeping pills our doctor had prescribed for emergencies. I took one myself, which, as I wasn't used to them, was enough to knock me out. I slept a deep, dreamless, bottom-of-the-sea sleep, through which I fought my way to the surface to find Brooks gasping for air in his sleep. I tried to rouse him and he sat up, groggy and in pain. It seemed to be bronchitis. I quickly woke Liza and explained the situation, and the two of us went down to the kitchen. We put water on to boil for a croup kettle. Liza, calm and helpful, tended to this while I went to the phone.

It was four in the morning, an awful time to call anyone, but

Brooks was more ill than I'd ever seen him, and it had to be done. Fortunately I had the number of a doctor, given me by a friend who'd recently been in Rome. I got what sounded like a busy signal. I remembered hearing that by dialing 110 you could get an operator who would break in on any number, if necessary. I got a male operator who spoke no English, but who made me understand, by patiently repeating the number and then correcting it, that I had the wrong one. I checked it and dialed more carefully, and this time I got an eldery Roman. *"Il dottore non c'è, è fuori di Roma."* Thanks to Berlitz, I understood that the doctor was out of Rome.

I ran upstairs with a bucket of boiling water, threw some Vicks in, arranged Brooks so he was breathing the steam with a towel over his head, and ran downstairs again. Hospital! I found the number of the Ospedale del Salvatore Mundi. The man who answered spoke English and gave me the phone number of a Dr. Nick. In heavily accented English, Dr. Nick told me that I must bring Brooks to the hospital as soon as possible. It was now 5 A.M. on a Sunday morning. Brooks's coughing had eased, and he seemed so tired that I allowed him to sleep for as long as he could. Then the coughing recommenced, and we all dressed hurriedly and got into the bus. One of the wildest hours of the entire trip followed, as the patient, surrounded by his worried family, drove himself to the hospital. Except that we couldn't find the hospital! Cleverly hidden in the wooded hills, it takes an experienced native to locate it. Maddeningly we circled and swooped, but no hospital.

As we drew up at a stop signal, I said to Brooks, "The only thing to do is to get someone to lead us there. I'm going to ask this young man on the motorcycle." I did, and the young man beamed happily and said, *"Ospedale, sì, sì"*. With a sweep of his hand and a rev of his motor, he urged us to follow. "You see," I said to Brooks triumphantly, "ask and ye shall receive."

Over hill and dale we swept in pursuit. It seemed a great distance from where we'd been looking. Then at last, our young man waved toward an imposing hospital gate, smiled, gestured good luck, and was gone.

We drove in, parked, and entered the main building. Brooks, in misery, looked relieved. Two Italian sisters walked toward us. I asked for Dr. Nick and drew a great blank. Black eyes questioned, foreheads furrowed, and no one spoke a word of English. We were in the wrong hospital! As arms began to wave directions, we beat a hasty retreat. We'd been through that bit.

This time Brooks solved the problem. "We'll go back to the Vatican and hire a taxi to lead us to it." And we did. The empty taxi went up a little alley behind St. Peter's, a turn to the left, a zig and a zag, and we were there.

I never thought I'd see the day when I'd be glad to leave my husband in a hospital, but that was the day. Brooks was almost at the end of his rope. To see him settled in a clean, soft bed in a cheerful room, with doctors and nurses making him comfortable, to know that his breathing would be eased and every care taken was almost too much for me to bear with equanimity. I kissed him and promised him we'd be back tomorrow. As the children said good-bye, I stumbled into the hall to weep a little and get it over with before they joined me. The times Brooks and I had been apart since we had been married could have been counted on one hand: when I was having Doug in the hospital, and once or twice more. From an independent career-type woman, I had turned into a large ivy plant, I thought miserably, alone in bed, trying to read myself to sleep.

Then came the gala celebration of Dad's return four days later. We'd picked some pretty leaves and early-blooming flowers for the table, and dinner was planned. Everything was beautiful but the weather. On the way home in the bus we sang and laughed. Dad was home again!

He admired the table and the polished floors, then the two of us sat in front of the fireplace and sipped champagne while the girls served dinner. Suddenly a bolt of lightning flashed. All the lights went out as thunder crashed. There was a great scramble for candles. We were well prepared this time, and lit quite a few. Rain began to pelt and wind blew.

Liza said suddenly, "Oh heck! I left all the windows in the guest room open to air it." Liza and I rushed upstairs and ran into the guest room, which faced the storm. Rain was pouring in and we couldn't close the sticking window, so Liza tried to push the inner shutters closed. As I came forward to help her, they blew open with a clatter and a veritable wall of water drenched us both. We gasped, then struggled them shut and locked them. Dripping, we walked back across the room and the door blew shut in our faces. I grabbed the door knob, which came off in my hand.

We were soaking wet, in the dark, and locked in, and Brooks on the outside couldn't open the door. It was too much for us and Liza and I shouted with laughter. With the boys holding candles to see by, Brooks finally got the door open and we went down to dinner, still hot, thanks to the gas stove. Dinner by candlelight was a merry one, in spite of banging shutters. As we carried dishes out, on came the lights.

All was right with our world again—Dad home and well, lights and warmth, and a good dinner in our stomachs.

I decided to spring my discovery. I sneaked out while everyone was talking and went down the cellar stairs, snapping on lights as I went. I opened the door on the other side of the furnace, snapped on more lights, then came upstairs and announced, "Ladies and gentlemen, if you'll follow me, please, I think I have a little surprise for you."

Mystified, they trooped after me. I flung open the furnace-room door. "Will you step into my cantina?"

The preceding day I had found, beyond the furnace, a perfect little barroom with murals on the wall, a stag's head hanging over the little bar with its four stools, and a couple of tables with chairs. The kids squealed in excitement. Another door, when opened, led us up some steps to the corner of the house nearest the pool. What a spot for a party! My surprise was a wow! Brooks agreed it was a memorable homecoming.

The next morning was clear and sunny. As we sat at breakfast in one third of the kitchen, we heard a sound at the back door. Not ten minutes before, someone had mentioned missing George from the Villa Eva. We opened the back door and there, on cue, was a shiny black cat.

"George!" we shouted, but Duncan, psychic for once, said "Georgia," and he was right. She seemed a gift from heaven, and we accepted her in the spirit in which she was sent.

In the mail one day I received two scripts from my agent in New York. I settled down to read one. It was better than a lot I'd read, but not really tempting. It was night before I had time to look at the other. I sat in bed reading it as Brooks slept.

I wanted to cry, and I did sniffle, waking Brooks, who asked what was wrong. I said I'd waited years for a part like this, and it seemed unfair to find it now.

Brooks said, "Well, honey, if you want to do it enough, we'll go back."

"And give up our year in Europe? Never! Maybe we'll do it in summer stock." I sighed. And we did play Neil Simon's *Barefoot in the Park* in Atlanta two years later.

As the days grew more beautiful, the garden stirred under its winter wrap and began to leaf out and even bloom here and there. One day I found a magnificent shrub of bridal wreath shooting great sprays of white blossoms in every direction. The plowed fields of the farm, which had been sherry brown, were rich with green, and signs of spring were everywhere. Connie Raffetto wrote from home requesting a run-down on our average day in Rome. Here is my reply:

Dear Connie:

Outside of a few social nights during our first weeks here, we've been an early-to-bed and the same to-rise group. As you know, we're living in the villa about thirty kilometers out of Rome, which is negligible to us, living twice that far from Los Angeles at home. As far as our kids are concerned, we don't seem to have raised one city dweller. So here we sit in the middle of the Marchese's 150 acres and, for the moment, it's all ours!

As for our day, Brooks wakes on the button of seven-thirty, and with him that's it, he's up. I'm a little slower type, which gives him ten minutes for a shower and shave, and he goes downstairs to put coffee on. Then I get up and open the shutters in our bedroom. I remember our first sight of Italy ten years ago. When we descended from the Alps into Turin on a hot summer's day, I thought the city had been stricken by a plague! All the windows were boarded up with large, ugly wooden shutters. This was to keep out the heat during siesta. Our Villa has a more attractive version of these in green, with a small decorative cut-out.

I throw the shutters open and stand there in admiring awe as I do a few deep-breathing exercises. The villa is surrounded by lawn, and a wide strip of garden planted with dozens of varieties of trees and shrubs. An enclosing fence is thick with climbing roses beginning to bud and promising to overwhelm us with their beauty.

The villa sits on a softly rounded hill from which the earth sweeps down in all directions, and then up to the horizon, where only a few farmhouses can be seen.

Over the hilltop to my right comes a rush of woolly sheep. Tiny lambs, still newly white, trot at their mothers' sides. The shepherd descends the slope, crook in hand, giving eerie whistled commands to five huge white dogs as they drive the sheep toward our fence. I cringe slightly. A few days before, I'd come out to call the boys to lunch. They were in a swing by the gate which opens on the fields. I stood in the warm sun watching the boys and had that strange familiar feeling of being watched myself. My eyes went to the gate and there, leaning on it and staring intently, was what the girls have come to call "Mom's sheepherder."

For a long moment I tried to outstare him, then gave up. *"Buon giorno,"* I said. The effect was electric. The round face cracked smilingly in half, arms waved, and the shapeless object that was his hat came off as he responded, *"Buon giorno, signora."* I was encouraged. I tried again.

"Oggi è una bella giornata, non è vero?" I'd overdone it. The return flood of Italian swamped me. With a surrendering wave of the hand, I went indoors, forgetting to call the boys to lunch. I "took five," then came out again. There was my shepherd, still in his leaning trance, still staring. I bellowed "lunch" at the boys and retreated, disconcerted.

Since then my shepherd has become a fixture. When I guiltily sneak branches of magnolia from the gardener's precious trees, my eye is caught by a figure at the gate, staring at me. When I hang the boys' jeans and some of my unmentionables on the clothesline, there is the silent one, staring. Even as I move from table to mantel in the living room I can see him through the long glass doors, at his post peering in. I don't cherish any notion that my person is irresistible to him, although I did give up wearing shorts for a few days. He is nerve-wracking only in his complete concentration. It made me jittery until I figured the cause of it. Logical reasoning gave me the answer. I merely put myself in his place and thought of watching a batch of sheep, which, though they vary personally from year to year, certainly do not vary in appearance or habits, grazing inch by inch across the same hills for three hundred and sixty-two days a year (that's allowing a day off each for Natale, Pasqua, and the shepherd's saint's day) without letup. No wonder he was compelled to stare at any manifestation of human life, be it hanging out laundry or emptying garbage—particularly when performed by a tall blond *donna* in pants.

Accepting this fact, I'm able to bear the stare with equanimity and an airy wave of greeting as I carry on with my day.

After enjoying the view from our balcony, I go to brush my teeth and then dress, which I do in the bathroom to the strains of our transistor radio.

I am captivated by Italian radio, which has a laissez-faire all its own. The morning broadcast generally begins with a lark calling to its mate, followed by several moments of silence while, I imagine, sleepy announcers are finishing their morning espresso, yawning, or gathering up odds and ends of paper with news items on them.

At first I would strike the transistor a blow or two or turn the dial because I just couldn't believe my ears. As a performer who did "Our Miss Brooks" on radio for years, I can still remember the panic in the control room if an actor happened to swallow the wrong way and, strangling, left a second or two of dead air. I must say I admire the Italian attitude: *"N'importa!"*

At breakfast we sit down to the only American meal of the day —cereal, toast, and instant coffee. Liza and Connie are only allowed espresso at siesta.

Then Liza, Duncan, and I, the fat-control group, set out on a brisk walk down the tree-lined road and up the other side to Mauro's farm to see the horses. We race and play tag, and sometimes pick the red poppies and lupines in the meadow. Lately a session of yoga exercises has followed the walk, and although it's filled with moans and complaints that "Duncan is just faking, he doesn't really touch his toes," or "Liza, you're not doing the cobra right," we still feel that any yoga is better than no yoga.

On Fridays around eleven, I hear the furious putter of a motor scooter, then a *beep-beep* at the back door, and I know that my *pescatore* has arrived. He catches his own fish in the morning and he brings them gleaming and bug-eyed for our inspection. *"Ombrine?"* he questions. *"Molto fresche,"* he assures me. Loath to send him away empty-handed, I purchase *quattro ombrine,* which he neatly scales and cleans before our fascinated eyes. *"Grazie, signora."* And away he putts on his Lambretta, the tassels on his knit cap flying and the aroma of brine lingering behind him.

Brooks returns with Luisa, our jewel of a *donna,* who prepares us cannelloni for lunch. She's a divine cook, having once been a chefess in a first-class *ristorante di Roma.* Then, with a heavy, damp cloth wrapped around each foot, she skates from one room of dull tiles to another, leaving in her wake a high-gleaming polish.

An astonishing racket outside announces that the Marchese's trio of gardeners is arriving by Vespa and Fiat. They deploy and snip, mow and prune, and sprinkle until our garden is shaved, trimmed, and manicured. Then they are off in a splutter of exhaust, to return *dopodomani.*

After lunch we are ready for Piera and the Italian lessons. She comes three times a week in her little white Fiat and teaches the girls first, then the boys, while Connie rides the lovely gray horse which belongs to Julia, the Marchese's daughter. Connie, who misses Chico, was thrilled when the Marchese asked her please to ride the horses whenever she likes.

Piera has a cup of Liza's espresso and drives off in a rattle of gravel; then there's a rush for coats and sweaters and it's aboard the VW and into Rome.

The siesta is almost over and the American Express will be opening, and that means *mail!* The most important factor in a traveler's morale is hearing from close friends at home. Mail-less days cast a pall over our spirits. Jackpot days, however, are exciting. "We got two from Connie and Mike and one from the Amsters." "A letter from Helen for the boys." "Who's the blue one for?" Liza wins the sweepstakes. Five letters! Yes, jackpots are the best.

Then we drive past the Spanish Steps, banked with azaleas for their Easter dress, a sight of incandescent beauty when they burst into red and pink blooms. Then we go to the *supermercato.* When we have time it's more fun to troop from the *macelleria* for baby lamb and beef (a different store for chicken and pork), *frutteria,* then the *alimentari* for pasta and groceries, the *latteria* for dairy products, the *pasticceria* for *dolci* and the *tabaccheria* for cigarettes and matches and, of all things, salt. But in a hurry it's the *supermercato* for almost everything.

Then down the Via Veneto to gape at the sitters at sidewalk cafés, who are gaping at the passersby. We stop at the *giornalaio* for the *Rome Daily American,* the *Paris Tribune,* and *Il Messaggero,* to increase our *vocabolario italiano.*

Occasionally we stay in for dinner at one of our favorite restaurants, George's, Tre Scalini, Taverna Flavia, or Angelina e Tor Margana.

But our villa has undeniable pull, so we scramble into the bus and once more we are knee-deep in Fiats as we fight Roman traffic. We drive through the Borghese Gardens, with a short stop at the *galoppatoio* for Connie to watch a horse taken over the jumps.

From the edge of the gardens we see all of Rome lying at our feet, tawny-brown and rose. Down we go through the Piazza Venezia, its empty balcony recalling the upraised fist and jut-ting jaw of Mussolini, now long gone. Past the huge white monument commemorating the unification of church and state, which the Italians have dubbed The Wedding Cake and up the Fori Imperiali to the Arch of Constantine. A comment comes from Connie in the back seat. "You know, when I thought about coming to Rome, I felt it was like a dream. And now we drive along here and Duncan says nonchalantly, 'Well, there's the Coliseum.' " We laugh and roll on through the Porto San Sebastiano, out the Appia Antica, past the catacombs, and veer off into the countryside. The last rays of sunlight touch the yellow or white farmhouses and the pink or red villas that crown the hills and terraced slopes.

On the car radio we hear a song we all know, so we are singing lustily as we drive up our tree-lined lane. Off in the distant Alban Hills the lights of Frascati twinkle like a Fourth of July sparkler.

Inside, our cat Georgia mews her welcome and Brooks lights a fire in the fireplace. Connie puts "Happy Time" on the record player, while Liza curls up with her diary. The boys start a Ping-Pong game and I settle down to finish my postcards home.

A couple of hours later, tomorrow's project—a trip to the Villa d'Este or the Baths of Diocletian planned; someone yawns and says, 'I think I will go up, I'm sleepy.' The boys run up wrangling, happily or unhappily, as the case may be. The girls follow with more dignity. Brooks and I rise in silent agreement and go about our final task, closing up our twenty-six pairs of wooden shutters for the night.

Well, you asked about "my day."

Love,
Eve

CHAPTER
·26·

Easter was approaching and tourists were arriving in a swarm like locusts. Brooks, coming in with the mail one day, slammed it on the table and said, "Let's go out of town somewhere for Easter. Rome is getting impossible to move around in. It took me a solid half hour from the Piazza Venezia to the Piazza di Spagna, and on Easter we won't get within miles of St. Peter's. Why don't we go to some small village and stay for a few days?"

We all agreed that would be fun, so out came the maps and we considered. Greece? Too far. Portofino? No, we'd save that until Barbara came (our friend Barbara Morrell would arrive in a couple of weeks for a visit). Positano? Yes, that was it, definitely. Our friends John and Elaine Steinbeck, if I may drop a Nobel name, had urged us to see Positano, as we'd insisted that they see Portofino. John had been named honorary mayor of Positano and we remembered that they'd recommended the Sireneuse Hotel.

Brooks picked up the phone, no procastinator he! He got the long-distance operator okay.

"*Positano numero uno,*" he said distinctly. He thought the girl rejected the number, then he heard distant sounds.

"They're getting it," he said, with the smugness of one able to obtain a number in a foreign tongue. Suddenly there was a rattle of Italian in the receiver, and Brooks looked stricken. "*Numero uno?*" he said hopefully.

There was a negative reaction in Italian. They didn't seem to be digging him. Brooks's ire was rising. "*È molto simplicato!*" he said. (He proceeded on the theory that if you use an English word with an Italian ending, eight times out of ten you'll get lucky.) Then, louder and clearer, "*Numero uno Positano.*"

The operator now had a helper, but *she* didn't speak English either. They were trying to explain something between giggles. If they were amused, Liza and I were convulsed. We were getting the picture along with the sound, and Brooks's expressions and gestures were far better Italian than his words. *"Positano numero uno, Positano"* he bellowed. Liza and I wept with laughter. Finally, as we were joined by cackles of merriment from the instrument, he roared into the phone: *"O, molto comico, non è vero?"* And, as they agreed, he laughed too and, giving up, hung up.

An hour or so later the phone rang and I happened to answer it. I was able to gather that the circuits were now free, and they had *numero uno Positano* on the line! Brooks was vindicated!

I talked to a Mr. Cinque, who spoke English of a sort, and was charming. He was, he said, devastated not to be able to accommodate us at Easter, as the Sireneuse was full to overflowing. He was even trying to find accommodation for some of the owners' friends in private houses.

I leaped at this. *"È possibile trovare una casa privata per la nostra famiglia di sei persone?"*

He thought that might be arranged, and on our arrival he would direct us to what he was sure would be pleasant lodgings.

The autostrada that had brought us to Rome was now in the throes of spring. The hills were lush with green. Many of the farmhouses that had looked so bleak were now sporting new coats of pink or yellow paint. Wild fruit trees spread a seafoam of blossoms across the landscape, and newly born lambs were frisking in the sunshine. I was with my family on the way to another new adventure. Happiness spread through me like some sort of delightful disease as I ran my blessings gratefully through my mind.

We stopped short of Naples and had a picnic on the shoulder of the autostrada. On we went past Naples, past Sorrento, looking as old and tired as the song, on to the high winding curves of the Amalfi drive.

After a few hours, the map and the time said we must be getting close to our destination. We swung around a curve and the town of Positano unfolded beneath us, its houses spilling down to the sea, looking like boxes of honeycomb perched on narrow terraces. With misty fog blowing over its mountaintops, it had an eerie quality that chilled and even frightened me a little. We wound down a torturous roadway into a rabbit warren of shops that comprised the town's *centro.* Then up another winding street to the Sireneuse.

We located Mr. Cinque, a chubby and amiable man, who had rooms for us at the Hotel Margherita, several layers above. The

Margherita also was crowded, so we were established in three double rooms in the annex on the hill behind. Our rooms were connected by a large terrace where we gathered a few minutes later for a look at Positano.

First impressions are often revised, but usually something of the original one remains. In this case it was a sense of living in the distant past, which we never quite shook off. The windows and archways of the houses, which were stacked like boxes in layers, looked devoid of human life. But my imagination peopled them with the Positanese of the tenth century or so, looking out to sea for the galleys that came occasionally, bearing silks and spices and other wonders from far-off places. I fancied I saw them beginning their long trek down to the beaches to barter and buy, then re-climbing the steep hills, arms filled with treasures.

It was too late in the afternoon and too foggy to attempt the three hundred and eighty-five steps to the beach, so we spent the time unpacking and getting ready for dinner.

After a delicious dinner, replete with food and growing sleepy, we crossed the road and ascended two more flights to our nest. The annex was a new acquisition, and the heating apparatus had not yet been installed. The cold of a dozen hard winters seemed to have settled in its plaster walls and tile floors and, in spite of eventual sunshine, it remained frigid for our entire stay. The only remedy at bedtime was to lie submerged in a piping-hot tub until fully thawed, then swiftly leap into the icy air, dry with an icy towel, get into icy pajamas, and dash for the icy sheets, where, after lying in a cocoon of coats-heaped-over-blankets, suddenly the ague abated, and you felt you had never been quite so warm before.

In the morning the overcast and fog peeled off into strips of sunshine, and when we went down for breakfast it was warm enough to eat on the terrace beyond the dining room. Potted geraniums, shrubs, and vines made it an attractive setting for our toast and coffee as we watched the sun glinting on the clusters of tile roofs below, and the blue-green sea beneath them, and planned our day at the beach.

Later, in bathing suits under terry robes, we descended the three hundred and eighty-five steps to the beach, passing shops and outdoor cafés on the way. The beach was a deep half-moon of sand, lapped by blue water and flooded with sunshine by now. We spent the whole day there, with time out for lunch in one of the cafés and the purchase of sun hats for all of us in the attractive shops. As the kids splashed in the sparkling waters, Brooks and I engaged in conversation with an Englishwoman who had lived in Positano for several years. Her husband, a painter, was presently in London at an exhibit of his paintings. I took pictures of Italian *bambini,* sand-digging nearby, and Brooks got snapshots of the beach and the surrounding hills, which later became two paintings of Positano. Then the sun went behind the mountain, dropping the temperature with a thud, and we started the long climb back to our hotel.

The next morning was Easter, so at midnight we awakened to the singing of a group of devout Positanese on their way up the mountain. They were carrying a cross to be erected at the top; and again, around 5 A.M., we heard them returning, voices still raised in song. It was an exciting and awesome sound at that hour of the morning.

The junior Wests were delighted by our idea of attending a Catholic mass, a new experience for them, so we descended a few hundred steps to the church with the green tile dome.

The interior was a surprise. Except for the elaborate altar it might have been an early New England church, almost chaste in its simplicity of line and pure white paint. Rough-hewn chairs replaced pews. But over the altar hung a glittering Byzantine madonna in gold mosaic, and below her, strips of brilliant red cloth alternated with enormous brass candlesticks, candles alight, and large bouquets of red and white flowers.

The sturdy, snow-thatched little priest was pure typecasting from an Italian movie, and I was frustrated at understanding only a word now and then, for he seemed to be delivering a strong sermon to his flock, who listened intently. As far as I could grasp, it didn't seem to have much to do with Easter or a mass, and I wondered, from the occasional word I caught, whether it concerned the coming elections.

Since the day after Pasqua is a big picnicking day for the Italians and everyone is on the road driving somewhere, we decided to spend the day at the beach.

There we found our English friend, Phyllis, waiting to invite us for a boat ride to Praiano, up the coast, and to lunch at Luigi's, a much-publicized restaurant since Mrs. Kennedy's visit there. The boat ride with Vincenzo, a burnt-leather character who doubled in brass as a fisherman and excursion boatman, was exciting. We took a side trip into a newly discovered grotto, which, Vincenzo loyally declared, was more beautiful than the famed Blue Grotto of Capri. Unfortunately, he said, the opening was a bit large, and let in too much light for the best effect. My tendency toward claustrophobia gave me a nasty moment as we slipped through the opening, which wasn't a *bit* too large as far as I was concerned. But the cave itself was amazing, a high-domed roof lined in the most unbelievable colors of blue and orchid. We attempted flash pictures that turned out the nicest shade of black you ever saw; but the memory of those fantastic colors still remains with us.

Luigi's was a thatch-covered open-air restaurant at the base of a rocky cliff and packed with vacationers. We had a long, cold wait as the wind came up, and we were grateful for extra T-shirts and beach towels. But the spaghetti and white wine and crisp, divine, whatever-it-was fish revived us and we laughed off the rigors of the return trip. The boys each got a turn at the tiller and Vincenzo praised them highly for their skill, as their chest measurements perceptively increased. The next morning the VW circled the hills as we took a last look, remembering Positano at night with tiny lights flickering behind the arched windows, and I thought of the weird feeling I'd had of living in the distant past.

We turned eagerly toward Rome again, and as we drove up to the villa, Georgia came to greet us with her kittens, Giampiero and his gardeners were snipping and clipping, and from the back door wafted the tantalizing smell of Luisa's cannelloni. Life was back to normal.

The next morning at the villa I got into jeans and prepared to take advantage of one of the newest joys it was offering. Almost overnight the fence enclosing the garden with its hundreds of feet of climbing roses had burst into bloom. In twenty-foot lengths there were red roses, then white ones, and pink, yellow, scarlet, and orange. I began to suffer from a sort of rose madness. I couldn't stop picking them. Where I picked one, there immediately appeared two even more beautiful. My fingers were etched with scratches and studded with thorns and I couldn't kick the habit. I picked armfuls after breakfast and more after lunch. I sent them into town to the Marchese and his wife. I gave dozens to Luisa, to the fisherman, and the laundress who did our *lenzuoli* (sheets). I took them to our friends in Rome, and put vases full in all our rooms and still didn't make a dent in a fenceful. But I never enjoyed an affliction as much as "rose fever."

With the weather at its best now and the kids kept busy with the pool, exploring the farm, Italian lessons, Ping-Pong games, and letters home, I decided to try my hand at sculpting. Through a little Frenchwoman we'd met, I set up an appointment with a sculptor named Cino (Cheeno), and Liza drove me far across Rome to his studio.

Cino told me that sculpture couldn't be taught, since it was an experience of the individual artist, but he'd be happy to show me the process. I told him I'd like to try doing a head and, as Liza watched with interest, he showed me how to make an armature. We took a central upright, nailed it to a base of wood, and secured it with crosspieces. We wrapped the column with woolen cloth and began to lay against it thick ropes of clay until it was the size I wanted, then I began to form a head.

Liza and Cino tried a little Italian conversation while I worked happily away. In my need for a guide for proportion, I glanced at Liza for a model. It was surprising how fast it took shape. I enjoyed feeling the dimensions rounding out under my hands. I was having a ball!

Cino turned to look, and said, "Oh, I see you've worked in clay before." What a compliment!

I laughed and said I'd once made an ashtray, but that it had been terrible. Cino kept insisting that I was an artist, not a pupil. Naturally, I floated home on a pink cloud, envisioning my first commission for a large bust of Albert Schweitzer.

Brooks's elation matched my own, as it always had. He even suggested, since I was so impatient for the next lesson, that I get some clay to work with in the villa meanwhile. It became a family project. Douglas did a small bust of George Washington and Duncan made soldiers. Brooks decided to concentrate on bone structure. To that end he produced an old man, bony and bald, with sunken eyes and a toothless mouth. It was so good that we could hardly bear to look at the poor fellow. I attempted a head of young Alexander the Great. Months later, when it became time to leave the villa, Brooks and I debated the disposal of our homemade art. At one point we thought of sneaking into the Borghese Gardens, where there are many pedestals with busts of prominent Romans, and placing my warrior and his old man on a couple of vacant ones, just to see how long it would take for them to be discovered and removed.

But when the day finally arrived, I carried Alexander to the ash heap. Giampiero, weeding the fragolini, was horrified that I would destroy a "work of art," and asked to keep it. I told him it would dry out and crumble, but he pleaded. Flattered, I gave it to him. Brooks had already taken his old man outside the back gate, where there was a compost pit. By now the old man was a hideous sight. Brooks had molded him on a piece of broom handle without any padding, so as he dried, the head slipped to the bottom, leaving the top of the handle protruding from the skull. With his occasionally ghoulish sense of humor, Brooks carved the wood into a wicked-looking knife handle. When he was buried in a mounded grave with the head partially exposed, he was a sight to give our unwary sheepherder quite a jolt. But my two days a week working in Cino's studio gave me tremendous satisfaction as I watched my head progress.

Our guide friend, Iole, called one day and said she had *biglietti* for the Wednesday audience at St. Peter's, and we were anxious to go. The personality of Pope John XXIII had won us all. There had been rumors that he had been extremely ill, and we hoped to see him recovered and well. Also, I had purchased some rosaries for our Mexican couple and some Catholic friends and I knew it would mean much to them if I had them blessed by Pope John.

On our first visit to Rome, when Pius XII was pope, and he had entered the church in his sedan chair borne aloft by the Swiss Guard, I remember how startled I was to hear a large group of orphan boys burst into what sounded like a school cheer: "*Il papa, yay! Il papa, yay!*" The pope, however, accepted it with a smile and a wave of the hand.

While waiting for the pope's arrival, I had been watching a plump little mother superior kneeling with a group of nuns. She was obviously very moved at the thought of seeing the pope. Most of the time her head was bowed in prayer, but occasionally she looked up with eager eyes. As they carried the pope closer, I turned to see how she was bearing up at the critical moment, and there she was, worshipful eyes filled with tears, with her forefinger buried to the knuckle, picking her nose! Complete Italian unselfconsciousness.

When we reached St. Peter's, Pope John was already seated on the throne of the Bernini Altar. In his white robe and cap he looked very pale, but his voice sounded strong as he spoke in Italian and French, and then his blessing was translated into English. It was

Pope John's last public audience, as we learned to our sorrow when his death came only a week later.

We took his loss very personally, as did everyone in Rome, so we were cheered when our friend Barbara Morrell came from Santa Barbara to spend a couple of weeks with us. Barbara was a particularly beloved companion of all of us. She had a great sense of fun, and was interested in all the things we were, from art and architecture to languages and people. The day she was due, the girls and I cleaned and polished frantically, and then we filled bowls and vases with all the different-colored roses from the garden. *"Molto bello"* was the consensus as we drove away to pick up Barbara at the airport. Her plane was delayed, and twelve hours after we started out to meet her, Barbara fell into bed surrounded by the scent of dozens of roses, and slept blissfully. I don't think we stopped talking for three days after that, but since she'd never been to Rome, we gave her the complete tour as we talked.

After dinner at our favorite George's or Angelino e Tor Margana, we went down the hidden little alleyways and stood in front of the lighted Fontana di Trevi as Barbara threw her coins into the fountain, guaranteeing her a return to Rome. We took her out of town to Hadrian's Villa, then to the Villa d'Este, where the German High Command stayed during their occupation of Rome. Its thousand fountains, which had been wrecked by bombing, had gradually been restored, and now eight hundred of them were splashing and tinkling and waterfalling all through the terraced gardens. Barbara was enchanted.

She went with me to Cino's one day to see my sculpture. She said she liked everything about it except the eyes, since the blind eyes of most classical statues had always disturbed her. Then she and Brooks went on to shop, while I pondered my great work of art.

Being more daring in clay than I was in paint, I decided I'd experiment. I had just gouged out both eyeballs when Cino entered the room. At the sight of the mutilation, he let out an anguished roar, like a wounded lion, and smiting his head in a distinctly Italian gesture, he left, slamming the door behind him. This broke me up completely, as I laughingly tried to repair the damage. He hardly spoke to me as I left, but he regained his equilibrium by my next visit, and I restored the eyes to his satisfaction.

We had dinner that night at a restaurant new to us, called Gigi Fazzo. It was an open, very well-lighted sort of place, and seated in the middle of the room, we were a conspicuous group of seven. In the middle of our salad course, Duncan clanged his fork down and announced loudly, "There's an ant in my salad!"

Aware of a plethora of eyes fastened on us, I cautioned him softly. "Duncan, I'm sure they don't have ants in this restaurant. That's a piece of pepper."

Duncan's reply was sorrowful and loud. "Pepper with legs?"

That night we went to the sound-and-light show at the Forum. It's a wonderful re-creation of the history of the place, with a narration taped in Italian and English. (We recognized Orson Welles's voice in that section.) The lighting effects move from the Senate steps where Caesar speaks to the tomb where his body was cremated. The sound effects thrilled the boys as the thumping feet of Caesar's legions were heard, while the lights led them below the cobblestones where we sat, and muffled drums rolled in accompaniment.

The girls provided us with our divertissement for the evening. They had been flirting outrageously with a couple of Italian soldiers sitting nearby, and when we left to go to our car, the men followed. As Connie and Liza got in, they smiled alluringly, feeling oh so devilish, and waved. As we pulled into traffic, the soldiers leaped into their car close to ours and took off in pursuit. At first, we were amused, and the girls were delighted, but as they followed persistently through Rome, out the Porto San Sebastiano in the old wall encircling Rome, and as far as the catacombs, the girls looked uneasy. And when we turned into the Ardeatina section, a good fifteen miles out in the countryside, even Brooks was showing annoyance.

A couple of miles before the turnoff to the villa he suddenly said, "Hang on!" And when the curving road hid their car from view, he gunned our VW ahead and then swung down a lane to our left and switched off the engine. A long line of heavy trees embraced us, and we sat silently until the lights of our pursuers appeared, then zipped past us down the road for some distance. Meanwhile Brooks started the engine and, as our ruse was being discovered and they turned around, our lightless car went back to our turnoff and then to the lane that took us over the long dip and up to our back door. We listened a moment in the dark, then quietly trooped into the house. I don't know why it was so scary, but the girls were noticeably chastened at how their harmless encouragement had backfired, and they learned to treat the Italian libido with more respect. The kids went to bed and Barbara, Brooks, and I relaxed with a glass of wine and toasted his ingenuity.

Our next trip was to Portofino, which we were determined both Barbara and the kids must see. At noon we stopped in a lush green field for a picnic, then drove to Pisa, where the four junior members climbed to the top of that tilted wedding cake, while their nervous mother prayed it wouldn't choose that moment to tilt farther.

Late in the day, on a tortuous winding climb out of Spezia, we hit a snag. A serpentine of cars stood static ahead of us. Brooks, on a forage afoot, came back with the rumor that a truck full of lumber had spilled its contents at the top of the hill, and it would be hours before it could be cleared. There was absolutely no secondary road to Portofino, and at this rate we wouldn't reach there until nine or ten that night.

Apathy set in, and a few moans were heard, but not from my husband. "Let's go up and take a look," he said. With a grind of gears we set off. Nothing was coming down, so we easily bypassed the long line. We arrived at the top and, sure enough, it was a mess. Huge flat sheets of lumber spread across the road, but to Brook's keen eye there seemed a spot with room to pass, even with our monster. He approached tentatively, with a questioning gesture to the swarming constabulary. To our amazement, after an uncertain shrug, they waved us on! From the back seat, Dad got a big cheer for his initiative, and a hug of appreciation from me.

As we wound into our favorite spot on the Italian Riviera, we worried that the third visit might break the charm. We needn't have. The ride through Rapallo and Santa Margherita along the water, then into Portofino itself, was greeted with ecstatic cries, and as we turned into the grounds of the Hotel Splendido, Barbara and the girls made sweet music to our ears. "It's so beautiful!" "Look at those terraces with the gorgeous flowers." "What a lovely pink hotel." "What a wonderful place!"

Our rooms, beautifully decorated with antique furniture, opened on balconies overlooking the tiny cove of Portofino, containing large yachts from many other countries as well as Italy.

Before dinner we sat on the side terrace of the hotel nursing an icy martini or a 7-Up, and sighed with contentment as we watched the intense Mediterranean blue darken to indigo, and lights sparkle on in the harbor.

After a delicious dinner, we wandered out on a long side terrace where white roses wound up tree trunks. Beds of countless flowers bordered the flagstones, and their aroma hung heavy on the balmy night air. Around us and through the trees below, the blue-white light of fireflies winked on and off. In the distance toward Rapallo, the bell lights of the fishermen hung suspended above the black glass of the ocean. Everyone, even the boys, was so filled with wonder that Brooks and I expanded with the satisfaction of parents whose baby has been suitably admired.

After breakfast on our balcony, we gathered to drive down to the cove. Although there are new and very chic shops now hidden behind the old facades, Portofino is virtually untouched. The buildings that sweep to the left of the cobblestone piazza and along the water to the end of the cove are so narrow and so tightly pressed together that they almost look like a wall of soft buff, pink, and green stripes punctuated by shuttered windows drooling bedding and laundry. Above them are awninged roof gardens bright with geraniums. We lunched on the second floor of a glass-fronted restaurant called the Pitisforo, then went to find the boatman from our previous visit—and there he was, white-haired, sunbaked, and bowlegged. His nickname was Tempi Duri, meaning "stand against the storm." He was one of the few to brave the winter seas. He welcomed us joyously, and we made a date to go to San Frutuoso the next day.

At 10 A.M. we set off in his comfortably sized boat. There was a fresh breeze and enough sun to take pictures, and the trip took a pleasant half hour or so. As we rounded the edge of the deep cove of San Frutuoso, he stopped the engine, first for a look at the ancient stone monastery which, besides two restaurants and a few fishermen's houses, is all there is to San Frutuoso. It's a lovely sight, nestled at the base of the mountain, with its unusual bell tower and graceful arched windows spilling flowers. The second reason for the stop was to see the Christus of the Deep, a huge white statue of Christ lowered into the water by fishermen some years ago. We had a clear sight of him, lifting his arms wide in benediction, in the green sunlit depths.

We had a lunch of *fritto misto,* a mixture of small fried fish, and lasagna, as we watched small Italians splashing in the turquoise waters below. After lunch we went to see the pretty little chapel at the rear of the monastery, and the Tomb of the Dorias, a noble seafaring family. The tomb is striking, in striped black-and-white marble.

50. As usual, I'm getting nowhere with Mr. Boynton.

51. I was hoping the tambourine would disguise the fact I was pregnant.

52. Robert Rockwell
(Mr. Boynton)

53. Richard Crenna
(Walter Denton)

54. With Gloria McMillan (Harriet Conklin)

55. Gale Gordon (Mr. Conklin

56. "AUNTIE MAME" PULLS OUT ALL LAUGH STOPS
by Philip K. Scheuer

"Auntie Mame" is staged like a revue consisting entirely of blackouts—with the difference that it is telling a story. I was about to write "one story," since Mame Dennis is the central figure from start to finish; but that wouldn't quite describe all the things that happen to this astonishing woman, or all the things she happens to, in the course of one evening at the Biltmore Theater.

. . . Mame is a creature who is scatterbrained and shrewd, Mrs. Malaprop and mastermind, in one—and the epitome of the "intuitive" female.

. . . We can go on to promise you an increasingly happy evening in the theater and, in Miss Arden, a star who would seem to bear out every demand that either reader or playgoer could make on any actress.

—*Los Angeles Times*

EVE ARDEN MOST FANCY, LOVABLE HEROINE MET IN "AUNTIE MAME"
by Harrison Carroll

A glorious romp, a shot in the arm to a timorous, stuffy world, that's the best way to describe "Auntie Mame," the Jerome Lawrence–Robert E. Lee comedy which burst upon the Biltmore stage last night with Eve Arden scoring an explosive hit as the zaniest, most uninhibited and most lovable heroine you have met in many a year of theater-going.

. . . Source of much of the comedy and also of the play's underlying tenderness is the love between Mame and an orphan nephew who comes to live with her and who grows up in her Bohemian world.

Even the timidest of viewers will be fired by Mame's courage in the face of adversity, her contempt for prejudice and her exultant pronouncement:

"Life is a banquet and most of the so-and-sos in the world are starving to death!"

Morton Da Costa's direction keeps the comedy at break-neck speed.

Among the many other excellent performances are those of Brooks West, as the Southern oil millionaire, who marries Mame. . . .

Whatever you have to do to get tickets, don't miss "Auntie Mame."

—*Herald Examiner*

57. "MAME" BRILLIANT COMEDY
by Patterson Greene

That threatened demolition of the Biltmore Theater may be simplified by its tenure of "Auntie Mame," which began last night.

The walls and ceiling shook and rattled with the billows and bellows of laughter from an audience that filled even the last rows of the second balcony—which haven't been warm since "Oklahoma."

This is rowdy, preposterous fun.

Everyone who reads is familiar with the vertiginous lady of Beekman Place created by Patrick Dennis in the novel that bears her name. Jerome Lawrence and Robert E. Lee have carried her to the stage without withering or staling her infinite variety.

And in the person of Eve Arden she becomes so beautiful, so delirious, so breezy and so lovable that you go along joyfully with her balmy excursions that range from the erotic to the equestrian.

Many of Miss Arden's lines are like tinseled hand grenades, and she tosses them with split-second timing and unerring aim. Best of all, she never departs into caricature. Her Auntie Mame is warm, winning and true, and her swift excursions in and out of pathos and sentimentality are as delectable as her wit and ribaldry.

She is potently aided in the first half of the play by small Dennis Joel as the youthful Patrick Dennis. Thanks to his own talent plus the glittering direction of Morton Da Costa, he becomes one of the most creditable and least artificial youngsters to grace the theater in many a season.

"A live little boy around the house!" she exclaims when he at first arrives. The emphasis is, significantly, on the "little." Mame is no saint.

Her struggle is chiefly concerned with keeping him from becoming a stuffed shirt—first in his schooling and later through a marriage into a family of upstate snobs. But these are only high points; practically everything in our civilization is burlesqued within the "scope and ubiquity" the authors have allowed themselves. And while not all the blackouts are hilarious, the average is on the plus side.

The same may be said of Miss Arden's support—from whom, notably, I must certainly single out Dennis Joel, the boy . . . ; Benay Venuta as Vera Charles, her closest pal; Brooks West, as Beauregard Jackson Picker Burnside, the southern gentleman she takes as a legal husband.

—*The Examiner*

58. EVE ARDEN'S ACTING A-1
by Lowell E. Redelings

All the good words written and spoken about "Auntie Mame" are obviously true. A jam-packed house at the Biltmore Theater last night sat enthralled, when not doubled up with laughter, as this renowned Broadway comedy opened a sure-fire smash-hit engagement. The news about "Auntie Mame" is so good, it is difficult to know where to begin. Perhaps with Eve Arden. The popular star of TV's "Our Miss Brooks" took a lot of curtain calls last evening. She deserved them. She plays the title role with poise, dignity (when called for), comic capers, warmth, reserve and all-around polish; it is a commanding performance.

—*Citizen News*

"AUNTIE MAME" A SOLID HIT
by Dick Williams

The utterly mad saga of that irrepressible character "Auntie Mame" has at last reached us with the opening of the Lawrence and Lee comedy hit at the Biltmore with most of the original New York cast. The comedy based on the Patrick Dennis best-seller opened an eight-week run last night.

And that is the only terrible mistake. The entire engagement is already sold out and the show could have played here at least twice as long.

Eve Arden, in a spectacular array of clothes, is marvelous as Auntie Mame. It is a singular triumph for her and she has given it everything from her famous dry wit to some genuinely touching moments that show us that Mame also has a wistful side too. As her housekeeper sighs, "You're a lovable woman—odd but lovable."

The entire company was really "up" last night. The show clicked off fast with its intricate and elaborate changing of sets. There was an electricity in the theater which I have rarely sensed for any stage production here in L.A.

—*Los Angeles Mirror*

59. "AUNTIE MAME"
by Forest Duke

In fact, this is a triumphant return to the stage for Miss Arden, confined in recent years almost exclusively to the limiting dimensions of the 21-inch screen, and it appears likely that she'll set new box office records at the Biltmore in her eight-week run.

To say that the show, as a whole, has pace is as limp as saying that the intercontinental ballistic missile has speed, since director Morton Da Costa has not only fired and flogged it to a high key, but invested it with a wealth of detail and invention. There are two acts to the comedy by Jerome Lawrence and Robert E. Lee, from the book by Patrick Dennis. There is one intermission, or breathing spell.

Mame's widely quoted philosophy of life, which permeates the proceedings, is that "life is a banquet and most poor sons-of-bitches are starving to death." Not Mame. She is the hostess, the cateress and her own happiest guest. She is rich, she is broke. She takes under her wing anyone with less exuberance than she and this includes almost everyone. She raises an orphaned nephew to enjoy life as she sees it and the crisis of the play comes when the young man defects to believe himself in love with a really dreadful young woman. Lissome, but loathesome. Stuffed shirts only make Mame yawn, but when she discovers the nephew is landing himself in a nest of bigots, whose loftiest boast is that they live in a "restricted" community, Mame is off like a brace of Valkyries. They must be put in their place and her nephew must be saved. They are and he is.

As for Miss Arden's dynamic contribution, on physical demands alone it's enormous. She changes moods as swiftly and blithely as she does costumes and wigs (seven of the latter). She is bawdy, tender, brazen and romantic, and in all she is bewitching, funny and believable.

Benay Venuta, as her drink-soggy actress friend and confidante, is another click, belting out her lines with authority and underscoring them with subtle gesture. Young Dennis Joel gives an excellent performance; Brooks West balances neatly between humor and caricature as the improbable southerner, and others in the huge cast who contribute vividly are Ray Fulmer, Manning Ross, Florence MacMichael, Willard Waterman, Dorothy Blackburn, Elizabeth Talbot-Martin, Loren Tindall, David Lewis, Robert Allen and Spivy.

—Daily Variety

60. "AUNTIE MAME"
by Colin McKninlay

Patrick Dennis' Auntie Mame was one helluva gal and Jerry Lawrence and Robert E. Lee evolved one helluva show from Dennis' novel.

"Auntie Mame" is a tour de force piece, and even to contemplate a weak star in the central role is painful, since she's onstage throughout.

. . . it remains to report that Eve Arden was a hilarious tower of strength in the title role and the play, in blithe disregard of the textbook rules, pleases immensely and with justification. As noted above, it's one helluva show.

The theme is neatly summed up by a tart Irish nursemaid early in the elongated first act . . . says she to Auntie Mame, "Yer a lovin' woman, ma'am. Yer odd, but yer lovin'." Tale revolves about Auntie Mame's decidedly odd, but lovin' upbringin' of her nephew, from the day he's delivered to her in the midst of a pre–1929 Crash N.Y. salon party, liberally garnished by mixed nuts, to his rescue from the clutches of a daughter of hidebound, "restricted" suburbia. En route, Auntie Mame fends off stuffy trustees, unsuccessfully copes with commerce, wins the love of a scion of the Old South . . . , becomes a successful author (with the dubious aid of an attractive Irish poet), marries her nephew to a pretty interior decorator and is off and running in another cycle with her grand-nephew at the final curtain.

Miss Arden again demonstrates that in the fine art of the double-take and the long sidelong glance, she has few peers. Additionally, she brings to the part the important element of warmth, without which Auntie Mame becomes a freak.

—Hollywood Reporter

That night after dinner at our hotel, we sat outdoors in the café of the Nazionale Hotel in the cove, enjoying the soothing laps of water and the warmth of the lights gleaming in the shops and aboard the yachts, and regretted that we were leaving in the morning.

Once back in Rome, we had only a couple of days before leaving "our villa" for good. The day before we left, we were invited for cocktails with the Marchese and his family. Besides Julia, they had another daughter and two boys about the same age as ours. During our stay they had built another pool and guest house at the bottom of our road, where the Marchesa brought us drinks and hors d'oeuvres. We thanked both of them for the joy of living in their villa and they replied that they had loved our family and hoped to see us again.

A week or so before this, as we went through the inventory with the Marchese's representative, we had mentioned that we had kept all the broken glasses (our only real casualties), so we'd know exactly how many we'd accounted for. Then a few days later we phoned his office about a broken windowpane needing immediate replacement. The Marchese, having translated our earlier report as *vietro* (window-type glass) instead of *bicchieri* (drinking glasses), said to his man, "Good God, there can't be a windowpane left in the place!" He was relieved to learn the truth, and we parted on a laugh.

Dinner that night had an undercurrent of sadness. Leaving here was different from leaving Westhaven. Our return there was a certainty. This place had become a part of us, yet we had no guarantee of ever returning. Brooks and I tried to raise group spirits by touting the excitements of Florence, where we'd be spending the next night, but it was a droopy group that kissed us good night and climbed slowly up to bed. Connie, in particular, seemed apathetic. She'd had a fall that afternoon while defrosting the refrigerator. Chasing Douglas, who'd been teasing her, she'd slipped on the wet tile floor and fell hard. I asked her now if she felt okay, and she assured me she did. I should have been suspicious.

This was the girl who, when she was eight, was pitched from her horse onto a neighbor's fence. She'd remained for dinner with them and, returning home, kept insisting it must be her bedtime. Finally I realized she'd been holding her arm behind her back all evening, and I demanded to see it. Sure enough, it was swollen monstrously and, when X-rayed, proved to be broken clean through.

At this moment, however, I was too tired to be my usual nasty, suspicious self. In spite of my weariness, I lay awake that night as a montage of memories projected through my mind. The time I'd spent in this place had been among the most meaningful of my life.

The next morning came the moment of good-bye. Mauro, our ever-present help, was smiling warmly. Giampiero, our young gardener, was wielding his camera as we lined up by our bus. He'd found homes for Georgia and her kittens, Romulus and Remus.

The usual shot of waving a tearful farewell had an unexpected finish as Doug, carried away with emotion, wailed loudly, "I don't want to leave Rooooome! I'm Romesick!" Our efforts to cheer him carried us through the worst of our last drive down the road from the villa.

By the way, ten years later, when Sean Connery came out to the farm, he saw hanging on the wall Brooks's painting of the villa, and in a dramatic voice that reverted to his original Scotch he exclaimed, "Good Gawd! That's the villa we rrrented in Rrrome last year!"

In late afternoon we reached Florence and the renowned Ponte Vecchio. Doug and Dunc were spellbound by the story of how the retreating Germans, after blowing up every bridge across the Arno to delay the pursuing Allies, and crossing this ancient one, had blocked each end with rubble. The American forces first on the scene had cleared the way in a matter of moments, carrying on in hot pursuit of the surprised Germans.

We continued down the edge of the Arno River until, about twenty minutes out of town, we reached the Villa La Massa recommended to us by Fay and Mike Kanin. They had spent some time there working on the play *Rashomon* for Broadway. The villa had been an old ducal palace at the time of the Renaissance, and Fay said it was an experience we shouldn't miss. It sat in spacious gardens at the edge of the Arno, now a torrent from the early rains.

As we changed for dinner, a white-faced Connie came into our room. "Mom and Dad, I'm afraid I can't make it to dinner." She admitted that her fall had been bad, but she hadn't wanted to spoil our drive, which, of course, had made it worse. It was evident from the swelling of her leg that it was something pretty serious.

We put her to bed and finally located a doctor who said he'd be there early the next day. The next morning his verdict was that the knee joint was badly bruised and the ligaments of the leg were strained, and that she must have an X ray and a cast put on. He gave her something for her pain and then, in our bus, we followed the car of the nice little doctor. A more hair-raising ride outside of Rome I've never known. I was sure he'd once done a stint in ambulance driving, but we held on tightly to our patient, stretched out on the middle seat. Dr. Mori took Connie and me in the emergency entrance and left us in the hands of the intern in charge. He was an Italian version of Dr. Kildare, handsome and blue-eyed, with a sexy touch of Dr. Casey. My sufferer, expecting more of a Dr. Zorba type, lay blushing furiously as he thoroughly examined her leg. He was pretty sure there was no fracture, but he had to have an X ray and only then would put the leg in a cast. It was a stark-white Connie who finally had her cast on from thigh to ankle. Worst of all, she must be immobilized for two days, until it set properly; all that was left of our Florence stay. While she, poor darling, spent those days reading books on Florence, her luckier relatives toured the Uffizi Palace and the Pitti Palace, among the world's greatest treasure troves of painting and sculpture. We saw the loveliest church in Italy, to my mind, San Croce, containing the tombs of Michelangelo, Galileo, and other great Italians, the Medici Chapel containing Michelangelo sculptures of *Night and Day* and *Dusk and Dawn,* and his scupture of David at the Accademia. In between we visited Harry's Bar in Florence, which, with his one in Venice, has the best hamburgers outside of America.

By now we were looking forward to Venice and Gianni Giovanni. Gianni was our favorite gondolier, a friend from our first trip. We always gave Gianni's name to anyone going to Venice, thereby doing a favor to both. Once, out of the blue, he asked a passenger what part of America she came from. Gianni doesn't speak English but conversed with her in French. When the lady answered, "California," Gianni asked, "Do you by any chance know my friends the Brooks Wests?" Incredibly, she turned out to be a neighbor from Hidden Valley!

No sooner were we settled in our rooms than the concierge called and announced that "our gondolier" was in the lobby.

The West horde rushed down to see him. We had sent him a family picture at Christmas, so he recognized the kids and greeted them by name, which thrilled them. We arranged to meet him after dinner on the Piazza San Marco.

It was a moonless night as we stepped onto Gianni's gondola. The Grand Canal was rimmed with the large hotels, like the Royal Danieli, the Gritti Palace, the Bauer Grünwald, and the dozens of villas, all centuries old. They twinkled softly with lights, but hardly intimidated the velvet black of sky and water.

Far ahead, from a barge decorated with hundreds of lights, came the sounds of happy music. Gianni swept us toward this vision in the center of the canal. As we got closer, the mass of lights separated into fruits of glass—bunches of purple grapes with green leaves, peaches and apricots, all glowing with Italian gaiety. Beneath them sat a band of musicians, bundled in coats against the chill, playing accordions, violins, guitars, drums, and flutes. Dozens of gondola prows massed together around the barge. It was fascinating to see a gondolier who wanted to withdraw from the center of the group give an almost imperceptible signal to his cohorts and see them silently part to let him out, and then close ranks again.

Since there was a *serenata* that night, we left the barge to join it. A *serenata* is a parade of gondolas through some of the narrow side canals. The gondoliers sing as they maneuver their way, and the tenants of the buildings stand on their balconies and watch. In the black night, with only tiny gondola lights gleaming below, the people on the balconies above, in the spill of warm light from their open doors, join lustily in the singing. The whole scene is magic.

The next day was a special one for Connie, who finally had her cast removed in Venice. We said good night to Gianni the night before we left, as we needed to take a *motoscafo* in the morning to carry all our luggage. We looked at every gondola we passed, hoping to see our friend, but we reached the mainland with no luck. We packed our luggage in the VW and drove down the ramp in the garage. At the bottom a figure stood framed in the doorway, arm held high to wave us good-bye. Gianni, of course.

CHAPTER
· 27 ·

London has a pleasant pattern of houses enclosing a "square" with a lovely garden in the center to which each house has a key. Almost all of the houses are five-story: basement kitchen, ground-floor dining room, second-floor sitting room, bedrooms above, and, on top, servants' quarters. Most of the bathrooms are afterthoughts of a century or two later, and since there was no room left, they are built outside the house from the landings where the steps make a turn. The endless narrow stairways have banisters with polelike railings, and I could envision my two "athletes" whizzing down them five times a day. I figured the odds leaned toward losing at least one to a broken neck, so I looked for alternatives. In back of the houses on the squares are alleyways where two-story stables once held the carriages and horses. These have long since been converted into snug little houses and were now the most chic dwellings of all. Ours took five weeks to find, but it was worth it.

Behind Cadogan Square in Clabon Mews was a house owned by an American who worked at the embassy. It was presumably too small for us, having only a master bedroom, another small bedroom, and a tiny library or bar. Since Liza was going away to college in a month or so, I converted the library into a "one bed one cot," changed the bar into a closet, and it became Connie's bedroom with room for Liza on vacations. The small bedroom I outfitted with bunk beds, which the boys loved, and Brooks and I hogged the master suite. Luckily, there were two bathrooms. Downstairs were a cozy living room with fireplace and niche for dining, and a none-too-large kitchen. Off the tiny hall, a door led into a garage. The house was beautifully decorated, but a bit too elegant for our tastes. One day, when I asked the owner if he'd mind removing some of the expensive ormolu, since I didn't want a heart attack every time I heard objects crash, also one or two large oil paintings, as we wanted to hang the ones Brooks had done in Rome, he said, "Look, I have a ten-room flat in Mount Street, where I was persuaded to move to let you have this. It's almost empty, and anything you don't want here, I'll use. I'll go further. I can tell you have taste [nice of him], so if you find something you like to replace things, bring me the bills."

Naturally I had a ball buying antiques, white enamel and brass beds, recovering sofas in cheery green-and-white print with orange and yellow chrysanthemums. When we came in from "a foggy day in London Town," our spirits would rise considerably, then, with a "noice 'ot cuppa" (tea, that is) we'd sit by the fireplace and purr. When I'd finished, I'd made it ours, and we were "at home" in London. One day I received a call from Laurence Olivier's secretary. Would I, he asked, do Sir Laurence the honor of appearing on their *Night of 100 Stars*? It was *the* night each year when British actors appear for the benefit of their peers (like American actors support the Actors Fund). I said that I had no material with me, and I was sorry. He then asked if I'd mind just appearing for a bow, that Sir Laurence and Miss Elizabeth Taylor would be greeting the guests as they entered down the stairway. I agreed, but since "Our Miss Brooks" had never appeared in London, I was afraid no one would recognize me. But during the next weeks British cabbies reassured me as they mentioned various movies I'd done. So I turned up, nervous but comforted, at the Palladium. Brooks and I sat out front during the first half of the show and watched many British stars, who'd been in our favorite English pictures, perform.

On stage, Peter O'Toole, whose *Lawrence of Arabia* was one of the most recent, was doing a take-off from *West Side Story* as a "Dead End Kid" in the number "Oh, Officer Krupke." He suddenly let loose with *that* four-letter word and shocked me out of my senses. Lawrence of Arabia?

Later, backstage, he and Richard Burton smiled a greeting, and I remembered my first meeting with Mr. Burton at a dinner party in Hollywood. He was the newest heartthrob in town then. As I was about to sit down at my dinner place, my chair was slid deftly under me, and the memorable voice vibrated in my ear with something like "I've admired you for a very long time" and I was left, shaken, until I recovered enough to pick up my soup spoon and return a smile across the table. Recently, in Rome, we had just been through the seething caldron of "their romance," still in its paparazzi stages, so I was intrigued to see them here.

In the dressing room, Hayley Mills and her sister Juliet gave me a welcoming word or two. Constance Cummings, whom I admired, gave me a look that said, "Oh Gawd, another American who wants to work in London," so I forbore speaking to her. Brian Aherne, whom I'd known in Hollywood when he was married to Joan Fontaine, *I think,* took me in tow as my escort, and down the steps we went for the "royal greeting," Liz smiling graciously and Olivier shaking hands warmly. I was very touched by the response of the audience. Later, many of them told me I was a particular English favorite, as they had no one like me. Anyhow, it was wonderful to feel so welcome in London.

It was now time to find schools for all the kids. They'd had six months off, but what they had seen and experienced in that time was an education found only in travel.

The British have certain men who specialize in education counseling. They suggest schools that might be suitable for each child, and are paid a small fee. Near the center of the city of London, we found our man in a bombed building still half open to the sky. A rickety iron elevator, still working somehow, bore us aloft, and a moment after we located the office, a gentleman in a derby, chesterfield, and umbrella arrived to unlock it and invite us in. He asked each child's qualifications, and our specifications. Then he suggested the American College in Leysin, Switzerland, since Liza's grades weren't all that good (did he raise one eyebrow?), and Arts Educational Ltd. for Connie, who'd expressed her first interest in show business. It would give her half a day of academics and an afternoon of drama, singing, and ballet. For the boys he recommended Sussex House in Cadogan Square, a hop and a skip down the mews from our house.

Then came the fun of outfitting Connie and the boys. Connie's uniform was fairly nondescript, something like a gray flannel jumper and white blouse. The boys, however, were resplendent: peacock-blue jackets, gray short pants, blue caps, maroon tie, and maroon tops on their long gray socks. I loved seeing in London the lines of small boys and girls in different uniforms, shepherded from place to place by a teacher. The line was called a "crocodile."

Liza, meanwhile, was attending a modeling school. We thought it would give here more assurance on entering college. We were invited to "graduation" and were delighted at the poise with which she entered, twirled, and smiled.

Then came the day to put her on the *Golden Arrow,* the train that boards the Channel boats and goes to Paris, where she would catch her train to Leysin. We all stood smiling bravely at the first to leave the nest—except Doug, who cried, "I don't want Liza to leave!"

We were settling in nicely now, reading English papers, full of juicy divorce stories and what was known as "The Profumo Affair," about a respected statesman and a couple of English call girls, Christine Keeler and Mandy Rice-Davies. We followed the pregnancies of the Queen, the Duchess of Kent, and "Lady What's-is" to see who'd give birth first. We watched the BBC and ITV and saw a wild group of boys called the "Beatles." The shaggy hair of most of the English youths and their eccentric clothes were a step ahead of their counterparts in the USA. We picked up on English expressions: "a bit iffy," "not to worry, mum," "suuuper" (which I loved), "you-lot," "have a go," "I've been lumbered" (clobbered), and "a bit dodgy" (not on the up and up).

We were enjoying London theater, including Vanessa Redgrave in *The Seagull.* Vanessa was a client of my French hairdresser, Paul, and I was surprised to see how tall she was. Then one day I sat next to a pudgy young girl having her hair done, who was talking about making a movie, and I thought, Poor darling, who'd give her a part, so fat? Of course it was Vanessa's younger sister, Lynn, who made the wonderful *Georgy Girl,* and is a very successful actress now and extremely slim.

We saw Maggie Smith in *Mary Mary,* and Sir Michael Redgrave, and Sir Laurence Olivier in *Uncle Vanya* and *The Cherry Orchard.* We were invited to parties at the Savoy, where we met Sir Michael Redgrave and the adorable Margaret Rutherford. She lived at Brighton, and someone told us about her going out on the pier in her bathing suit at six every morning, where she'd pause for a moment on tiptoes and then, soaring into the air, dive in. I also was thrilled to meet Rebecca West. We "took to" each other, and she invited our family to visit her farm. It was a great temptation, but my boys hadn't settled down yet, and I regretfully declined. I think she was already Dame Rebecca West then.

A friend had asked a wonderful English couple to call us. Sadie and Harold Goldman not only called, but took us in hand. First, luncheon at the Caprice, the Sardi's of London, where we saw Laurence Harvey and blinked, as we'd seen him earlier in Rome, and in Venice. Actors were certainly getting around these days. Sheilah Graham dropped by and deftly dug from us any Hollywood gossip we knew (which was almost nil), and left us for greener pastures. We stared, impressed, when our host pointed out the empty seat occupied the day before by Princess Margaret.

Harold Goldman was an alderman in the city of London and could've been mayor but elected not to. It's an honorary office for one year, which leaves the mayor "out of pocket" by about a hundred thousand pounds at the end of the year's entertaining. We were invited to the Mansion House, where Harold and Sadie were receiving with the mayor and his wife at a formal banquet. The mayor wore around his neck a huge medallion of gold and diamonds that was so heavy I wondered how he held up his head. He saw my eyes pop, I guess, and sweetly explained that he never even touched it. It was placed around his neck by a flunky (my word) and later removed by the same man and locked in a vault —in case an out-of-pocket mayor might choose to take off to Tahiti, I suppose.

There was a funny moment during a traditional ceremony where everyone stands at the long rows of banquet tables below the dais where the mayor and speakers are sitting. Then huge gold goblets are passed around each table and sipped from. Each man takes a little cloth that hangs at the side of the goblet, carefully wipes where he's drunk, and passes it to the lady at his right, who curtsies as she accepts, and repeats the action. We were a little nervous about how seriously they take these rituals, and when Brooks was handed the goblet by the lady on his left, he threw in a curtsy for good measure. Our group had a low-key case of hysterics.

Being an adoptive mother, I was invited to (now Sir) Lew Grade's home, where Mrs. Grade presided over a group somewhat like Foster Parents. There I was presented to Princess Alice, who was the only living grandchild of Queen Victoria, and very warm and charming. We went to a charity ball at the Dorchester soon after, where we met her again.

Almost every weekend Harold and Sadie drove us out of town —to Henly on Thames, for lunch at Ye Olde Belle, built centuries earlier; to Windsor Castle, and to Eton and Cambridge. We went to Petticoat Lane, where the 'costers or pearlies (people with pearl buttons covering their costumes, the women wearing huge plumed hats) tend their barrows and sell everything you can dream of and more.

One evening we took the boys to the Mayfair Hotel for dinner (Con had a date). In their black mohair suits they looked especially handsome. We suddenly realized how our months in Europe had affected our "country boys" when Douglas, half hidden behind the enormous menu, started a dialogue with the waiter.

Douglas: "Is your vichyssoise good and cold?"

Waiter: "Oh yes, sir, nice and chilled."

Douglas: "I'll have it." A momentary perusal of the next course. "How do you do your chicken à la Sophia Loren?"

An interval while the waiter described the processes of chicken à la Sophia.

Douglas: "I see. No, I think I'll just have the blue trout, some asparagus hollandaise, and a small green salad. I'll order dessert later, thank you."

Ye gods, a gourmet! Brooks and I sat, stunned. Ray Milland, sitting at a nearby table, seemed to find it amusing. After all, he didn't have to pay for those newly acquired champagne tastes.

CHAPTER
·28·

Our immediate need was for a "daily" (prounounced "dyly"). The last in a long line of also-rans was Rosie, a tiny sparrow-like creature with a high pompadour of dry, over-bleached hair. This strawlike substance hung to her shoulders behind her ears. She had a calcimined face with painted-on, star-tled eyebrows and light eyes that blinked constantly. I was called "modom" so many times a day that I began to get a complex, and asked her to call me Mrs. West. Rosie gave it a try, but it never took. After chattering a blue streak all day, she prepared to leave each evening with a half-hour silent ritual that held me a captive audience. Behind the open door of a closet under the stair, she would change from her uniform to her dress. Then she would pull on high-heeled, red patent boots. A trench coat was bound tightly around her with its belt. In front of the mirror, she would begin the back combing of her pompadour, carefully smoothing over the top of the huge mound she'd created. There was a painfully delib-erate stretching of her scarf across it, and the final knot under the chin. After this followed an application of calcimine over the whole face, two high, narrow arches of eyebrow pencil, and a Cupid's bow of lipstick. Then, tote bag in hand and teetering on her high heels, she would bid me a squeaky "good day, modom" and dart off to some mysterious assignation.

Just before Christmas, she beat me to the punch by quitting before I could fire her, or, as she told me on the phone, "Me back's gone out on me, modom." When, however, I called her three days before Christmas to find out how she was doing, she had "gone off" for the holidays, leaving "modom" in a bad way for the festivities.

A quick call to the agency brought us Scottie, our savior and comfort and our love. A most remarkable button of a woman, Scotty called us "modom" and "the guv'nor" and spoiled the boys with taffy she sneaked in. She not only worked for us from eleven to five (and usually stayed until six because she hated to leave) but she got up at 5 A.M. to clean an office and then "did" for her own flat at night. She was "on the list" for a new flat, a process that took years, but the one she lived in was a walk-up on the fourth floor and, it's hard to believe, but to go to the bathroom she walked down the four floors, crossed the street, and climbed two floors in another building.

She'd never been anywhere in London, never had the time or the money, and when I found she'd never seen Harrod's, London's most spectacular department store, I said, "Then take off your apron and put on your hat." I took her through the Halls of Harrod's. First, one with trees and flowers and, that week, a water-fall. Then the Food Hall, filled with gourmet goodies and a deli and bakery; the Fish Hall, with an Alaskan Crab stretching its claws over a bed of shaved ice on a center glass case. All around us fish and crustaceans of every description. Scottie was overwhelmed. "Oh, modom, it's wonderful," she said in her brogue. "The most wonderful thing I've seen in all me life!" Then I took her up to the seventh floor to Harrod's Zoo. There were puppies and kittens galore and dozens of exotic animals, even snakes. A large macaw wandered free on the floor and took an occasional nip out of an ankle. One cage contained five puppies: two cairns on each side of a small white "Westie." While the cairns yipped ceaselessly for their dinner, she sat quietly and looked at us with round black eyes.

"Oh, modom," breathed Scottie, "isnt' she a wee smasher?"

I asked for her to be taken out of the cage, and she trotted to us wagging her tail.

Doug had been having a small attack of homesickness and I thought, maybe a dog! I mentioned it to Scottie and she asked, "Couldn't we get the guv'nor to see her?"

I took a reluctant Brooks back that afternoon, and he lost to those eyes. He stipulated only, "No sleeping in the bedrooms." We named her Chelsea for the area where we lived, but to Scottie she was always the "wee smasher."

When our three-month visa was almost up, we had to register as "aliens," very strange when we felt so at home. Doug was getting a bit of "alien" treatment, though, from some of the older boys at school. Also, while his marks were incredibly good, he was almost paranoid about tests, sure that he'd fail. Nothing helped, and one day he refused to go to school. There was a test in "Scripture," and I knew he knew the answers. I called the head "mahster" and explained. He talked to Doug. No results. So I dragged my unwilling captive down the mews and into school and left him petrified. When he came home he refused to discuss the results. I called later to check, and Mr. Roberts said patiently, "Mrs. West, Douglas was given thirty-four questions and answered thirty-four right," and he hung up with a slam.

Then one day he called to say, "Mrs. West, I'm afraid Duncan's in a spot of trouble."

"What's he done?"

"He got angry at being teased about his weight, and picked up a chair to hit his tormentor, but unfortunately hit the boy behind him and cut his eye."

"How bad is it?" I groaned.

"The boy's been sent to hospital and is being treated. We hope it hasn't affected the eye."

My heart sank, but the worst was yet to come. The headmaster hesitated and then plowed on, "Even more unfortunately, the boy is the son of the Dutch ambassador here, and it is of some concern to all of us."

Ye gods! I thought. An international incident! But he had more. "It was the boy's birthday today, and his party had to be canceled. I'm sending Duncan home now."

I stood in the mews waiting. When I saw the little figure appearing through the fog with slow footsteps, my heart cracked a little. "Hi, Dunc, I hear you had a little trouble?"

"Yes, Mom." His voice quavered a bit.

"Well, come on in and have a cup of tea and we'll talk about it." He'd never been able to stand any teasing, particularly about weight.

"And Peter was my friend, Mom. I didn't want to hurt *him*."

"Well, why don't you sit down and write a note to tell him so, and I'll run out and get him a birthday card and a present."

I had the address of the Baron and Baroness Vander-something, and we delivered the things to a servant, who said Peter seemed "quite all right except for the eye," and that the baron and his wife were at a dinner. Much relieved, we came home.

Later, I spoke to the baroness by phone. She was lovely, and said the doctor just wanted to watch Peter's eye for a while. We agreed she would send us the bills. A few days later she called and said, "I just couldn't *mail* you the bills, it seemed so cold. Could we meet?" So we invited them to tea.

When the bell rang I went to the door, smiling straight ahead. I saw only vest buttons that went up and up and then a neck, and a head with a pleasant face, and a voice said, "Mrs. West, I am the Baron Vander-something. May I present my wife." And the six-foot-seven baron stepped aside, revealing the six-foot-five baroness! They entered with Peter, a tall, handsome blond boy. There wasn't even a scar left over his eye; and only a small one on Duncan's conscience, which I nevertheless hoped would give him a twinge if he ever again raised his hand in anger.

We sat down to tea with the ambassador and his wife, and found them delightfully "jolly" and the international incident was over.

A week or two later in Sloane's Bookstore I ran into Tilli Losch, the dancer who was also Lady Carnarvon, widow of the Lord Carnarvon of King Tut fame. Tilli was delighted to see me, as we'd had great fun doing a picture together at Universal. She invited us to a cocktail party at her flat in Eaton Square, where we met a lady in a large flowered hat with lots of feathers on her. She was very "Auntie-Mamish" and fascinated me. We found out that she was the Guinness Stout and Ale heiress, and probably the richest woman in Britain. She called us the next day to invite us to her son's birthday party. They had a "small town house" that happened to be two large houses with walls knocked out to make them one. A band was blaring rock music, so Brooks and I gratefully accepted the invitation of Lady Guinness's husband, a judge, to come up to his study and inspect his collection of letters from people like Washington, Lincoln, Napoleon—I can't remember them all—but they were very impressive. He also had an indoor aviary containing the most beautiful birds: a red cardinal, a blue-bird, a yellow oriole, and others. I asked how he kept them so beautifully neat. The trick, he said, was to have only male birds, the most colorful. Then there was no one to "nest" and make a mess!

We were happy by now to have the Steinbecks, John and Elaine, come to town on their way to Moscow. I adored John Steinbeck, not only for his writing but for a story Brooks had told me about him. He'd met John through John's wife Elaine. She and Brooks had been classmates at the University of Texas and become great friends as members of the Curtain Club, together with Allen Ludden and Zachary Scott, Elaine's first husband.

When Brooks was having particular trouble reestablishing his career after the long interruption of the war, John and Elaine invited him to dinner one night.

After dinner, John said, "Brooks, I have noticed that when actors sign a contract, they always seem to be offered another job right away. So I have drawn up a contract between us that I want you to sign." So saying, John picked up a "contract" for Brooks's signature. Sure enough, within a week Brooks had a job! It was such a perceptive and kind thing to have done that Brooks loved him forever, and so did I. We gave them a party and invited only John's close friends, since he was an extremely shy man. Among them were Alexander Knox and his wife, and Joan Bennett and her friend John Emery, the actor. Joan seemed very nervous, and only later did we learn that John came directly from his doctor's, where he'd been told he would soon die of cancer. I also invited Tilli Losch, as we knew the Steinbecks would like her. It was great to talk "Amurrican" for a change!

One day I got a call from Harry Ackerman, my "Miss Brooks" producer from Los Angeles. He had an idea for a pilot to be made in London, about an American travel agent who comes to London with her teenage daughter to run an agency for an American tycoon. Brooks and I thought it had scope, with tours to the continent, et cetera. So I made it, and it turned out very well. My London producer was Walter Shenson, an American who'd lived in London for years. He'd made some successful British movies with Peter Sellers and Margaret Rutherford. I loved working with the English actors and the wonderful crews, although I was surprised when we took a break twice a day: for "elevenses" and at four o'clock for tea.

Only much later, when the pilot was "sold" to two sponsors—General Foods, my former one, and Kaiser Aluminum—did we find that neither network would allow us to do it abroad, having been burned before by several productions overseas, which cost them a fortune and then failed. They wanted me to come home and make it at the Beverly Hills Hotel and change all the English characters to Americans. I didn't think this would work and said no. Nonetheless, one day Walter Shenson and I met for lunch to "celebrate our failure." He said, "Don't know what I'll do next. There are some crazy kids from Liverpool who want me to do a picture with them, but—"

Having fallen in love with the Beatles I said, "Oh Walter, they're wonderful! Go ahead and do it."

Almost a year later, he invited us all to a screening of *A Hard Day's Night,* and that property was far more profitible for Walter. I'm glad I had even a tiny part in encouraging him to do his part for Beatlemania!

CHAPTER
·29·

Getting ready for Christmas in London was very exciting. Harrod's and other stores had window displays of fabulous toys. Some of the electrical displays of sleighs carrying Santas and elves through a sky filled with shooting stars outdid anything we'd seen at home so far and generated a feeling of wonder in all of us. Strangely enough, we found it difficult to locate a Christmas tree and finally combined two, which Brooks split and joined to give us the lush green background we wanted for the ornaments and lights we'd bought and the enticing heap of presents piled beneath.

Liza was home from Switzerland, and Pam Raffetto came from Perugia in Italy, where she'd been living with an Italian family and learning the language. We took the kids to some of the pantomimes which are "take-offs" on Cinderella and many other fairy tales. We saw the *Merry Roosters Panto,* full of laughs and wonderful musical numbers.

Duncan had been saving his money for presents for everyone and was determined that he was going shopping on his own. He knew exactly what he wanted to buy for each person, so on a drizzly afternoon, he headed toward Kings Road, several blocks away. I knew he would be all right, but he looked awfully small as he disappeared around the corner of the mews.

Several hours later he trudged back, arms full of packages, his expression triumphant. "I got everything I wanted, Mom." When I wrapped presents for the girls in our bedroom, he joined me to wrap his purchases. He had really chosen with great thought and a knowledge about everyone's preferences. I was very proud and told him so. He beamed. "Wait till you see what I got you, Mom. You'll just love it."

"I don't know if I can stand to wait," I said. I tried to imagine what my son had chosen for me, but I couldn't.

Christmas Eve is the big night of the year with us, and this one,

199

our first ever away from home, made us feel particularly close. Although for several days before, everyone had been overtired and inclined to bicker, we sat down to our turkey and cranberry sauce in a real Christmas glow.

Later, excitement grew as we opened the packages. Liza's and Pam's, of course, were mostly clothes, bits of jewelry, and a hair dryer for college. The boys were elated over their electric racing cars, which they had given up asking for as a lost cause.

Each of our kids had been asking for a guitar since they'd heard a friend's son play one in Rome. Brooks and I had discussed the pros and cons. We felt that Liza had enough to think about at college without anything to distract her from her studies. The boys were starting piano lessons at Sussex House. That left Connie, whose interest, too, had seemed the most persistent. When she opened the large box containing her guitar, she had no idea of what it held. Her screams carried, I am sure, to Cadogan Square, and continued until we shushed her vigorously. Her heartfelt thanks told us we had made a wise choice.

Brooks and I were smiling at each other when a hand tugged at my elbow. Duncan's anxious freckled face pleaded for attention. "Mom," he whispered, "can I give you my present now?"

"I'd been hoping you would," I said.

Even Connie's guitar quieted as Duncan carried his gift to my waiting hand. I read the card. "To Mom. I love ya, Duncan."

As I opened the long, flat box, I don't think he took a breath. In it lay two strands of Woolworth's finest pearls. Duncan's hands reached for them. Carefully he undid the clasp and, leaning over, he fastened them around my neck. I remembered the pictures of Queen Elizabeth at her coronation and I knew just how she felt.

Through a lump I whispered, "They're so beautiful, Dunc."

His face was full of glory. "They're the best ones they had, and the earrings are underneath there."

"Earrings, too," I gasped.

His cup ran over.

During the next few minutes, I went upstairs and came down with four flat packages that Brooks had beautifully wrapped for me. The kids looked on curiously.

"Now you'll know what I've been doing behind closed doors so many nights," I said. "These may not mean much to you now, but I'm sure in the future you'll enjoy them."

Quickly they unwrapped and opened the big albums of all the colored pictures we had taken since we left New York. There were cries of delight. "Oh, it's the Villa Valleranello—and Mauro—and the swimming pool!" "Positano!" "Portofino!" "The Ponte Vecchio." The stiff necks and aching backs Brooks and I developed while taping in and titling all those pictures were well repaid.

Liza said quietly, "Mom and Dad, I think that's the most thoughtful, wonderful gift I have ever had, outside of the trip itself."

Special hugs and kisses from the others told us they felt the same. Christmas Eve ended with everyone saying, as they always did, "This was the greatest Christmas ever!"

The Goldmans took us all to the Savoy for New Year's Eve (very *in!*), and when Sadie came back from the ladies' room, where she'd left the girls, she said brightly, "I didn't know the girls smoked." *She* didn't know!

On the boys' and Connie's Easter vacation, we decided on a trip to Rome—partly business, but mostly because we were "Rome-sick." We'd had a letter from Liza saying that she was going to Moscow with a school group. We were happy for her, and wrote her of our plans. We got a letter by return mail saying, did we mind if she left Moscow for another time? She said, "The thought of my family going to Rome without me is too much." So she arranged to meet us in Cannes.

We stopped in Montelimar on our way, at the Relais de l' Empereur, where Napoleon had visited during his cadet days at St. Cyr not too far away. They had later named the hotel in his honor and it was crowded with mementos of him. The town itself was full of the odor of nougat, my favorite candy. It's the only place it's made, and by the next day, I was unable to stand the smell!

In Cannes we had a joyous reunion with Liza. I was pretty tired from the trip and Doug seemed cranky, so the two of us stayed in our comfortable rooms while Brooks took the others out for dinner. When they came back, I asked Brooks if he noticed anything strange about Doug's profile. He said it did appear swollen. I asked the dreaded question, "Mumps?"

The next morning brought the answer. Double mumps! He looked like a chipmunk. We smuggled him out of the hotel and

took off. We whizzed through Monaco and stopped at the Italian
border for the *dogana*. I kept Doug's head in my lap, and he was
too miserable to object.

Suddenly a nearby guard strolled over to smile at Duncan. He
looked in the car and stiffened. I followed his eyes and saw Duncan's "pretend" Luger pistol on the floor. The next few minutes
were tense, as the guard lifted his gun. I picked up the Luger,
pulling it apart to show that it was a toy. The mumps went unnoticed.

Finally we hit Rome and the Villa Eva, where dear Walter Landesburgh came out to greet us. I took him aside. "You may not be
so happy to see us when I tell you that Douglas has the two-sided
mumps."

Walter saw I was near tears. He squeezed my hand. "Listen," he
laughed, "I have a couple of people in here I'd love to give 'em
to!" Then he said, "Don't worry, you'll be in your own suite.
Doug's dishes will be kept separate and no one will know he has
'em." The tears came in spite of myself.

The stay went too quickly—we revisited the villa, celebrated
Easter at St. Peter's, reunioned with John and Elaine, back with
tales of Moscow, and, it being almost one year later, I collected my
sculptured head, beautifully bronzed, and I felt like a real artist.

Liza had to leave for school early and we went home via Salzburg, where we stayed at Der Goldene Hirsch and Doug astonished us at dinner by speaking in amazing double-talk German that
had nearby diners trying to understand what he said as we laughed
with appreciation.

The only memory of our entire year and a half in Europe that
I would wish to forget was the night we were leaving for the "wrap"
party being given for the "pilot's" finish. As I started up the stairs
to get my coat, the kids were watching television, and Douglas
exclaimed, "Mom, someone just shot President Kennedy!"

"You must be mistaken, darling."

"No, Mom, and they think he's dead."

He was dead, our brave young president, and we were too
stunned to know what to do. Finally we roused ourselves enough
to go where we knew other Americans would be, at the party, which
was now a wake.

Our English friends went to a memorial at St. Paul's with the
common people and royalty of Britain and reported how they all
wept in sympathy for the Americans and the world.

For weeks we couldn't shake our depression. Finally, we took a trip to the Cotswolds and visited the fascinating tiny towns called Upper-Slaughter and Lower-Slaughter, Burton-on-the-Water, Stow-on-the-Wood, and Chipping Norton. We went to Stratford-on-Avon and saw *Henry IV* Part Two. We visited Warwick Castle and saw the Holbein portraits of Henry VIII and Elizabeth I, and the boys marveled at the suits of armor and how short the men must have been.

On our return, I received another invitation to *Night of 100 Stars.* Good Lord! Had it been a year in London already? This time, Lord Olivier (as I have to think of him now) asked me to co-host the cocktail party to help decide on the program. I answered that I'd be honored, and they sent a sketch for me to consider doing. I said it was too close for our time to leave for home to participate. I couldn't bring myself to say it was a lousy sketch!

So I greeted guests. Zsa Zsa—good heavens, was she every-where?—Luise Rainer, looking lovely but frail, Omar Sharif, and dozens of English actors I'd admired, like Kenneth More.

Not too long before, I'd had another call from Olivier's secretary, asking if I'd like two seats to *Othello.* We'd tried in vain to get seats for London—impossible—and I'd settled for four in Chichester, where Olivier would play an engagement later. So now we went to the special performance given for an orphanage, Olivier's yearly contribution, and attended by every British and American actor in town.

There is something about performing for a group of your peers that automatically raises the level of even a great performance. That night Olivier's performance inspired a fifteen-minute ovation. It was a moment in the theater to be remembered and cherished. Also it was a wonderful note on which to end our year in London.

CHAPTER
·30·

Once we'd made up our minds that it was time to go home, we decided to take the month before our ship would sail, from Algeciras, to see some of Spain and Portugal. After a week of good-byes to our English and American friends, and our darling Scottie, we climbed aboard our VW bus, with Doug sounding his battle cry: "I don't want to leave London!" We tried only to look forward to what lay ahead, ending in the word "home."

We made a stop near Chartres to get Chelsea vaccinated against rabies, since Britain won't allow even the vaccine on the island, and American law demanded that every dog be vaccinated a month before entry. We also took the opportunity to see the lovely Chartres Cathedral, with its unmatched spires, built over several centuries. Then we drove on to Bordeaux to spend the night in a hotel with great mosquito-netted beds.

We got up early to go through Biarritz and crossed the Spanish border near San Sebastián, because we planned to spend a few days in Santander and soak up some sun.

Most of the British holiday in Spain to get the sun they crave at lower prices than on the Riviera. The elegant old hotel that we arrived at was full of elderly English couples having tea on the terraces.

Dinner, while it looked appetizing, tasted slightly of rancid olive oil. However, what we were all yearning for was a good American breakfast of bacon, eggs, toast, and coffee.

In the morning, while the girls did their laundry in their room, I put Brooks's and the boys' shorts and socks to soak in the tub and finished them in the bidet, a great place to launder. While we waited for breakfast to arrive, I hung them all in the only place I could find where they'd dry—on the balcony over the railing.

Breakfast was horrendous. It *was* rancid olive oil, and I began to feel ill from the odor.

We had a try at the beach, but red sand made sunning rather unpleasant, so we came back to the hotel for lunch. That was when I realized that rancid olive oil was just a way of life there, and we decided to leave the next morning. Around four o'clock that afternoon I went to bring in the socks and shorts, only to discover that the wind had scattered them far and wide on the terraces below. Under the astonished eyes of the Britons enjoying their tea, I ran hither and yon, collecting here a sock, there some shorts, caught on rose bushes and under shrubs.

There is no expression to equal that on the face of an English lady as she watches an American woman picking her underwear off bushes. I smiled brightly, and felt like a fool. So I was glad when we got into the car the next morning.

We had a reservation awaiting us in Nazarre, Portugal. It was a town I'd always wanted to see. The fishermen who lived there wore some kind of bloomers and top of unmatching plaids, while the women wore mostly black overgarments, with billowing white petticoats, all marvelous for painting.

We arrived at five-thirty in the evening to find that our rooms had been handed over to earlier travelers, and the slips we held showing payment were denied. Not only that, but there wasn't one room to be had, neither in that town nor the adjoining one.

We sat, disconsolate, in the only place we could find that was serving food, and discussed our plight. We finally decided we'd have to spend the night in the VW—six of us, Chelsea, and all the luggage.

Since it would be impossible to find dinner before 10:30 P.M. at the earliest, we began to drive up a nearby hill, which became a mountain as we climbed. Around a curve in the road we found ourselves face-to-face with an entire walled city, small to be sure, but seeming to offer prospects of shelter and food. Its name, we discovered, was Obidos (pronounced Obidoosh). It was a treasure of tiny cobbled streets and ancient houses, and at the far end was a castle, transformed by the Portuguese Government into a *pousada,* known in Spain as a *parador.*

Divine Intervention, I was sure, as I waited to speak to the busy young man in charge. Brooks kept an eye on the boys, as they traversed the entire walled town on a narrow ledge dotted with fortifications.

Meanwhile the young man had asked me peremptorily what I wanted, and dashed my hopes with "no rooms at all."

I made a discovery then, which held good for all of Portugal: It was filled with angry young men. I realized later when we reached Lisbon that they were frustrated young men, since "freedom" was an unknown quantity under the dictator Salazar, then still very much alive.

At that moment, though, I was determined to be patient and pleasant in the hope of finding shelter for the family, so I waited as he received phone calls that were irritating him more and more. Finally he stopped and looked at me. I tried another smile. He indicated that he might have a room, since someone wasn't showing up. I said that would be wonderful. Then he had someone lead us to not one, but three adjoining rooms, each with twin beds having carved Victorian headboards quilted with lovely fabrics, with curtains to match. Patience had paid off! Far from having to spend the night in the car, we were housed in splendor, fed, and with a charming town to explore before dark. We hated to leave so early in the morning, but Lisbon was a long pull and we had reservations there.

In Lisbon the next night, while Brooks walked Chelsea below, Doug and I witnessed an episode from our balcony that may have explained the pervasive atmosphere of doom in Portugal.

A tall, very attractive young man, walking down the street, turned suddenly and ran from a group of uniformed men who sprang from a side street. They captured him within a block, peeled his dark jacket back to pin his arms, and shoved him into a waiting car and drove off. While this was happening, people gathered and seemed to be muttering curses at his captors, then they all disappeared down alleyways. It was like a menacing film scene, and started my dislike for Portugal.

The next day we had lunch at a Ritz Hotel atop a hill. It was lovely, but the mood returned as we toured the poorest section, called the Alfambra, which outdid the slums of Naples. That night we drove by cabs to a distant nightclub to hear the Fada sung. This is the Portuguese "blues," sadder than any songs I've ever heard. Returning, as we neared our hotel, our two cabs were pulled over and searched, and we were inspected with steely eyes.

I think the atmosphere affected all of us, and I became literally ill, for the first time in the year and a half of our travels. As we neared the Spanish border I began to pull myself together, and when I gratefully crawled into bed at the Alfonso XIII in Seville,

I had almost shaken off the malaise of Portugal. To be fair, I'm sure it has all changed now, without Salazar.

On our last night in Seville the girls came into our room late and sat on our bed to express their thanks for the time we'd had in Europe. As we talked, Doug's voice rose from the hallway. "Can't we cancel the trip?" he cried. "I don't want to leave Europe!" When *The Constitution* docked in Algeciras, we were amazed to see some of the crew we had left a year and a half before, hanging over the rail waving at us. We heard them call, "Hi, Wests! Glad to see you again." "Hello, Connie and Liza." "Hi, boys." We realized they had known we'd be on board.

The final touch to our welcome came as our luggage was brought aboard and Brooks told the men carrying it that we were on M Deck, in the same rooms we'd had before. We were told, "No, you're on Sun Deck." Brooks attempted to argue, but no one listened. We were conducted to two suites with tiny glassed-in lanais, where we were deposited, next to the girls, with the boys behind us in a large stateroom. Chelsea was deposited in the kennel, but was allowed to visit us often. We were really flabbergasted at the kindness of "management," which made our homecoming as special as the trip over had been. As we sailed into New York Harbor, past the Lady with the Lamp, the boys were hanging on the rail to see the skyline of New York. I couldn't locate my girls and went back to their stateroom, where I found them both crying at the thought that our idyll was over.

Liza said, "Mom, I'm going back just as soon as I can." A prophetic remark? Well, I, at least, was glad to be home. We spent a weekend at the Amsters' farm. Unfortunately, Stanley had had a heart attack while we were away. He was recovering nicely, but we worried about him, as it was impossible to keep him from working around the farm. Ann was her serene self, sure in her faith that he'd be fine.

In New York we were given a welcome-back party by Dottie Leffler, a CBS publicist who had become a good friend while doing publicity for "Miss Brooks." That evening I was miserable with what I thought might be the flu. I insisted that Brooks and the kids go on ahead. They did, but, impatient, I got out of bed ten minutes later and took a cab. I was determined to meet one of the guests, someone I'd always admired and wanted to know. When I arrived, I still felt awful, so Dottie took me to the guest room to relax awhile. I was feeling pretty sorry for myself when suddenly Dottie appeared in the door saying, "Here's some company for you," and in walked Walter and Mrs. Cronkite and their daughter Kathy.

As we talked I began to feel better and better. He's always had that effect on me, whether on TV or the few times we happened to meet him on the street. He makes me believe in the difference that one man can make in this world.

Liza had persuaded us to let her try being on her own in New York. Since she had the Amsters and other friends to look after her (and one with a very attractive nephew who'd already asked for a date), and had had a job offered her in a prestigious shop, we felt she could hardly be launched under better circumstances. We boarded the *Twentieth Century* and waved at her disappearing figure surrounded by a clump of comforting friends. Brooks and I turned and followed the rest of our family as they headed for the dining room. A year and a half of our lives had gone by, and had proved to mean even more than I had hoped for.

CHAPTER
· 31 ·

It was wonderful to be home again, and our farm looked in good shape under Earl's care. The kids adjusted well to school. In fact, the boys were skipped a grade. So much for the doom-and-gloomers about the effect our long stay in Europe would have on them.

I was the only question mark. But Glenn had an offer waiting for me to do *Wonderful Town* at a new theater in the San Fernando Valley. They had been successfully doing big musicals there. With only two weeks' rehearsal in which to learn the songs and dance steps, I was immersed in my profession again, and realized how much I loved it—hard work, long hours, and all.

The theater was in Woodland Hills, less than half an hour from the farm. As I drove in to do a matinee one day, I saw Connie riding toward me on Stepin', and I could tell something was wrong.

She tried to pass the car with a wave of her hand, but I'd seen tears in her eyes and insisted she stop. Stepin' had bolted with her and run out of control for some reason. She'd turned him into the lane leading to Dick Widmark's farm and finally pulled him up, but he'd thrown his head back as he'd stopped and hit her forehead a terrific crack. Making her promise to tell her father, I continued to the theater. After the matinee, Brooks came to meet me with the news that Con was in the hospital with a concussion. Crises always seemed to be concurrent with work! By the time I had finished the run, though, she was fine again.

Work picked up. I did a picture called *The Lady Wants Mink,* in which I wore the mink that my neighbor, Ruth Hussey, coveted, a nice switch. I also did some TV, like Ben Gazzara's "Run for Your Life," with Bobby Darin, and "The Man from U.N.C.L.E.," with Robert Vaughn.

The following summer, Brooks and I did a tour with *Beekman*

Place, then made plans to build the house we'd always wanted at the farm, double-gabled and painted green with white trim. A bit of Connecticut in Hidden Valley. It had an entrance gallery for all our paintings and a spiral staircase leading up to a studio for Brooks.

I was in my element with this, when an offer came from David Merrick to come to Chicago and replace Carol Channing in *Hello, Dolly!* as she was going on the road. When I was in London, there'd been some conversations about meeting Gower Champion in Paris to talk about a London production. This I would have adored doing. Now I was tempted, more by the rising building costs we were encountering, than the thought of Chicago in June. Since the boys wouldn't be out of school for a few weeks, and Brooks was finishing the contracting on the house, I went ahead to begin rehearsals. I refused to see the show, as I didn't want my performance to be affected by any impressions of Carol's.

I met the cast at a big publicity party, at which Carol turned over the reins, so to speak. Gower flew out from New York and it was all very impressive.

The next day, my first day of rehearsal, I was wearing thin, high heels to get used to working in them on the stairs and the ramp. My right heel slipped through a hole in the floor, my knee doubled back, and I heard a thud as it went out of its socket. It was exceedingly painful, and the knee began to swell. Someone took me to a chiropractor Carol had used, and I got it taped up.

The following day I started therapy at a nearby hospital, but rehearsals continued. Marge Henderson, a friend, had come out to be with me until Brooks would arrive. I can remember waking up, unable to open my eyes, as I thought, I can't, I just can't! Then Marge would bring me orange juice and a cup of coffee, and the brain would say, "I must, I really must," and by the time I dressed, I had willed myself into the little train that said, "I can, I can," and did.

At any rate, that first week of rehearsal was a grind of limping through steps (my knee stayed the size of a football for six weeks), memorizing lyrics and lines, and looking forward to rendering myself unconscious as soon as possible each night. If it hadn't been for Marge force-feeding me and a nightly phone chat with Brooks, I could never had made it. But at the beginning of the second week, I was able to laugh when I stumbled over a difficult step, or forgot a lyric or a line.

I will never forget Gower Champion's face when he arrived, as promised, to rehearse my second week, and watched me stumbling around stage, forgetting lines and laughing! Gower was a serious-minded director. However, things improved daily, and both of us began to feel more hopeful. But our dress rehearsal was one of those awful trials by fire when all the other actors in town are invited to attend.

In the eating scene, with a mouth and two hands full of food, my shoulder strap broke and disaster seemed imminent. Summoning the head waiter, I said, "Pierre, a safety pin, please." When it arrived, he had to do the pinning since I was busy with food and lines.

From then on, it was rewarding to play *Dolly* and our houses were great, until the night that Richard Speck murdered eight nurses in a nearby hospital. Theaters stayed almost empty for a few weeks, then gradually audiences built up again.

Just after our opening, Brooks arrived with the boys, and a couple of days later took them to camp in Maine, and stayed a night or two nearby. Duncan adjusted well, but Doug, who was okay in the daytime, wanted *out* when darkness fell. I will never know how he persuaded the Chicago operator to give him the backstage number of the Shubert Theater, but as I was thinking through the lyrics of my opening number, I was called to the phone to hear a hysterical Doug saying, "Mom, you've got to come and get me, I can't stand it here!"

As I would try to calm him and explain that I couldn't possibly come and get him, and that the music was starting for my entrance, his voice would rise dramatically and he'd plead, "Don't hang up! Don't hang up, Mother!" Somehow I managed to replace the receiver and step aboard the trolley car that took me onstage.

A few nights of this, and some calls to the camp counselor, and we decided it was a lost cause and brought him back. Duncan, perfectly happy, elected to stay. Thereafter, Douglas accompanied me to the theater most nights, where the cast and crew enjoyed him. When he was in an environment he liked, he was a very self-contained and happy young man.

He learned much that summer, as the crew explained everything he was interested in, particularly the lighting engineer, who even allowed him to help with the changing of lights. Chelsea, our Westie, who was also with us, insisted on spending her time in my dressing room. She'd learned that there were leftovers from the chicken or turkey I used in the eating scene, which the dancers would beg for her.

Our traumas were not over, though. We suddenly got word that Connie had gone directly from school into the hospital with virulent hepatitis and was very ill indeed. Brooks flew home immediately and stayed a week, until he was sure she was on the road to recovery. He came back with the news that she'd be in the hospital another month or so, and we made arrangements for her to be flown to Chicago as soon as she was released. She finally arrived at the airport and scared us to death, appearing in a wheelchair long after everyone had departed, looking very frail. She recovered rapidly, though, and we finally sent her to modeling school for half a day to keep her from getting too bored.

A letter was forwarded from Rome, from an American friend of our gondolier, Gianni Giovanni, telling us that he was coming to America to appear with a singing group of gondoliers at the opening of a new department store in Minneapolis. By the time the letter reached us, he was due to open the next day. I called and was able to locate Gianni and, with the help of an interpreter, arranged for him to come to Chicago on his day off. The interpreter, whose home was in Chicago, came with him, and they saw the show that night.

The cast all wanted to peek at Gianni's reaction to his first American musical. Gianni, who only knew me as Mrs. West, mother of four, seemed stunned by the extravagant costumes and colorful scenery, the music and the lights.

Backstage in my dressing room, he strode over to me and, kissing my hand, murmured, *"Formidabile, formidabile!"* He spent the night in the boys' apartment adjoining ours, and the next day we gave him a tour of Chicago before putting him on his plane.

I was enjoying the role of *Dolly* by now in spite of all the traumas and my swollen knee. I loved the cast, who had rallied around every time I felt I might not be able to make it, so I was reluctant to leave them, but I had insisted I could only stay three and a half months, since we had to be back to get the boys in school and finish up the interior of our new house.

When I'd speak to Mr. Merrick's assistant about a replacement for me, he'd smile tolerantly and say, "We're working on it." I finally realized that quitting Mr. Merrick was somewhat like a jester giving notice to the king. Unless the king beheaded you, you were not expected to leave while the box office was still jingling. Finally I convinced them that I was really leaving, and there was panic. When I knew they were actually looking, I agreed to give them an extra week. Then I heard that my replacement would be Betty Grable, who was playing *Dolly* in Las Vegas. I thought this was a wonderful idea, and it helped me not to feel guilty for leaving all my "gypsies."

Betty opened, and we left the next day by train. I later learned that she took sick the second day and was in the hospital for a week or so, while her understudy did the show. Then she recovered and finished the run.

Liza had come to Chicago to see *Dolly* and was wanting to quit her job. "The New York women seem so rude and difficult to deal with, and I've really decided I don't want to be a buyer of women's clothes anyway."

We saw a chance to get her back into school.

"Well, Liza, you probably won't be able to get any job but a very inferior one without more education. If you quit your job, you'll be entirely on your own. However, if you'd like to go to secretarial school we'll help you, but only if you work hard and get good grades."

She agreed, and it was arranged that Connie would live with her in New York and also attend the school, until she, too, knew where she was headed. So now we were left in our new house with just the boys.

Soon after I was asked to do the Coast company of *Butterflies Are Free,* and went to New York to rehearse it there. The small cast was excellent, and I was happy to be in New York again.

We were planning to go out to the Amsters' farm on our second weekend off, when on Saturday morning Ann called us to tell us that Stanley had passed away the morning before. Knowing I had a rehearsal, she had stayed with him alone all day, until his body was taken away for the immediate cremation he had requested.

We drove out to Connecticut for the day and brought Ann and her tiny dachshund back to Beekman Place, where we had an extra bedroom. She stayed with us through rehearsals and promised that she and her ninety-year-old mother would spend the winter in our guest house at the farm.

The management suddenly announced that we would give a

performance the next day, which was a Monday, for any actors who might care to attend, but without costumes or props. (The prop men had a day off too.)

This was a shock, but fortunately our fellow actors rallied around and enough of them gave up their day off and were a typically generous audience. We did have the ready-made set, and I loved the Booth Theater, where I'd done *Two for the Show.*

In Hollywood, shortly after, we played the Huntington Hartford, an ideal theater for this kind of show, intimate and very New York in feeling.

Desi Arnaz came to me with the idea for a new pilot, to be called "The Mothers-in-Law." It was a fairly fresh concept, and he had the original "Lucy" writers, Madelyn Davis and Bob Carroll, under contract. He wanted to get Kaye Ballard for the other mother-in-law. She would play an explosive Italian against my would-be elegant mother.

The pilot was pretty funny, with the two mothers opposing the wedding, Kaye's son, Jerry Fogel, eloping with my daughter, Deborah Walley, and Kaye and I, left in the midst of the big outdoor wedding we'd planned, fighting in the rain. When we'd finished the pilot, Brooks and I went to Atlanta to do *Barefoot in the Park,* then played it in Phoenix, where I got a call from Lucille Ball, saying how much she'd liked the pilot, and telling me that it had been sold to NBC. When I got home, we started filming the series with an audience, as I had my other series, and life settled into a pleasant routine again.

I think the plot I remember with the most amusement was the one that had Kaye and Eve, the "mothers-in-law" (we used our own first names) trying out for the lead in a local production of Wagner's *Valkyrie,* a funny idea to begin with. Of course we lost out to a real singer, Marni Nixon. Then we competed to see which of us would get to ride the only horse available and we split the vote, so both of us elected to ride.

Onstage, on a background of huge rocks, stood an unlikely group of women—tall, short, skinny, fat, and one with horn-rimmed glasses—in Valkyrie costume, but all of them had great voices trained in opera.

Offstage, Kay and I, in helmets and tunics, I in long blond braids and Kaye with crazy curving horns, mounted our charger, a swaybacked white nag, already unhappy with his part. Only when Kaye, seated behind me, grabbed my waist in a stranglehold and confessed that she had never been astride a horse before, did I learn that important fact. As we rode onstage to the stirring strains of Wagner and shrill voices raised in song, our nervous steed almost unseated us and I grew less sure of my horsemanship—as Kaye's clutch became more manic. Fortunately, we didn't have many lines —most of the rest of the program consisted of our riding across the back of the stage behind a low fence, pursued by angry Valkyries, and then riding back again, still being pursued. Why, I don't remember, but I do remember laughing hysterically at both Kaye's terror and my own.

Glenn was generally in the audience that sat in the bleachers above us during the filming of "The Mothers-in-Law." Several times he brought his friend Sean Connery along.

When Brooks and I were living in London, Glenn had taken us to meet Sean and his wife, at that time, Australian actress Diane Cilento. They'd just bought a house outside of London and were converting it from the nunnery it had been. It was a strange place for the recent but already notorious James Bond to be living in, still very chaste and painted white with a wide stairway on which I could easily picture nuns filing down to breakfast.

I had liked Sean immediately for his complete naturalness. Now, several years later, he was a world figure and a sex symbol to boot, but he sat in the bleachers minus his Bond toupee. He usually wore either a wool lumberjack shirt or sometimes a borrowed jacket with sleeves too short. This was because he usually traveled the Atlantic with one suitcase full of records and books, with only a clean shirt or two. Nevertheless, the stir he caused in our audience was palpable. Glenn told me of women who slipped notes with telephone numbers into the pockets of his borrowed jacket, where they remained as untouched as he seemed to be with the adulation that surrounded him. But he certainly did tone up our audience.

I received word from Chicago that I'd gotten the Sarah Siddons Award for my work in *Dolly*. I was very pleased but had never expected it, since Carol had won it for the same part the previous year, and there were sixty-some actresses considered for it. I was to come to Chicago to accept it on a Friday, after shooting a segment of "The Mothers-in-Law" on Thursday.

On the Sunday night before that week's rehearsals, I bent over my husband's bed to kiss him good night, and, instead, screamed in his ear, as what I'd come to call my *Dolly* knee went out of its socket and the knee "froze" as I fell on the bed. I think it was more painful than childbirth. At any rate, to my embarrassment I had to be taken to the hospital in an ambulance, and at three that morning wound up in a cast from ankle to thigh. They put me in an intensive-care ward for lack of room, with two elderly heart patients, so Brooks brought me home at 8 A.M. for breakfast.

At ten, Desi was on the phone pleading that they couldn't rehearse without me. So with all those years of "The show must go on!" imbedded in my psyche, I gave in to his assurances of "You don' haf to walk, jes' read de lines" and sat on the set each day until Thursday night, when I removed the cast and, limping only slightly, did the show.

Friday morning, leaving the cast behind, I flew to Chicago with Brooks and Glenn, brooding over an acceptance speech on the way, checked into the Ambassador East, had a quick rehearsal with the band for a parody of *Dolly,* dressed, and spent two hours in a reception line for the Beautiful People of Chicago. After the ceremony I danced until 4 A.M. I guess "The show must go on" has something to be said for it, after all.

On our first hiatus from "The Mothers-in-Law," the workaholic Wests accepted an offer from Miami to do a few weeks of *Cactus Flower.* Doug went with us, since Duncan was attending military school and was to fly down for a week's vacation at Easter. Doug was acting as his father's "dresser," handing him his jackets and ties between scenes. Evidently he'd been bitten by the acting bug too, as one day a boy who was doubling, or rather tripling, in three small parts, asked me if Doug could play the delivery boy. He said, "It would really help me, as I can't even step on stage, because they'd recognize me as the hippie in the bookstore scene."

I said I wasn't sure it would be a good idea, and who would rehearse him? Also, the stage manager would have to give permission.

He said that had all been taken care of, and Doug had already been rehearsed.

I could see a bit of collusion there. So that night a tall twelve-year-old with a delivery man's cap sitting on his ears appeared in the door of the set saying, "Mrs. Winston?"

In an unsteady voice I answered, "Yes."

He handed me a package saying, "For you," and was gone. Our son's debut!

The next night he arrived, saying, "Are you Mrs. Winston?"

"Yes."

"This package, I believe, is for you."

Already padding his part! When on the following night I got, "You are Mrs. Winston, I presume? If so, this package is most certainly for you," I put my foot down. Lines were to read as written. He never neglected his job as a dresser, though, and after his scene would come running around the corner, out of breath, saying, "Here's your jacket and tie, Dad." But he got to be a bit of a pain in the car going home each night, as he'd give us his critique on the audience and how well we played our scenes: "That was really a rotten audience. Not nearly as good as last night." Or: "You know why I think you didn't get your laugh tonight?" Ye gods! A critic in the house we didn't need!

The second season of "The Mothers-in-Law" went well. The ratings were good, and since I'd just appeared on "Laugh-In," we gave a big party and invited the "Laugh-In" group, our cast, and other friends to a celebration of what we were sure would be our third season on "The Mothers-in-Law."

Suddenly we were shocked to find out that "The Mothers-in-Law" had been canceled. It seemed that Desi owned so much of the show that the network decided what they had left wouldn't make it worth their while. We'd planned an extensive trip to Europe with the boys, including Greece, which we'd been very anxious to see, and ending with Scotland, Wales, and Ireland. We also wanted to visit Spain, where Liza was now living with Pam Raffetto. On a vacation visit to Europe she became so intrigued with Spain that she had decided to get herself a job there and stay awhile. What we didn't realize was that her life would finally center in Spain.

I sat by our pool one day in May, wondering if we should go on such an extensive trip, or if Brooks and I should take the summer tour offered us and make money, rather than spend a lot. But Liza was looking forward to seeing us in Spain and the boys had already been planning the trip.

I should explain a facet of my nature, which bewildered, amazed, and occasionally enraged my husband. I have a childlike faith that what is meant to be, will be, or, as the song puts it, "Que será, será." It seems to produce miraculous results, and the manifestations are sometimes downright spooky! This was a case in point.

Having turned my problem over to Heaven with confidence, I went indoors to answer the phone. It was my manager, Glenn.

"Are you sitting down?" he asked.

"No, but I can fix that," I said.

I was sure that this was divine, not dire, news.

"You have just been invited on a junket to Greece by Olympic Airlines," he said. "Not only you, but Brooks and the boys too."

I drew a deep breath.

"Well, you wanted to go to Greece, didn't you? And a lot of people you know will be going along. Donald and Gloria O'Connor, Ross and Olavee Martin, Lloyd Bridges, Barry Sullivan, and a lot of others."

Surprised? Not someone whose life has been rife with coincidences and wish-fulfillment.

When Brooks came home, he took the news with only a slight nervous tic and a sigh, which meant, "She's done it again!"

So on the first week in June, we were almost ready to leave when I got a call from one of the organizers of the trip, asking me if I knew an attractive young girl to "dress up" the under-thirty department.

Sometimes, my wish-fulfiller overcompensates!

I had been wishing that Connie, just out of the American Academy of Dramatic Arts in New York, could be with us, but I did have the restraint and good taste not to ask if she could go along. Now, however, I was forced to say that the only one I knew in that department lived in New York.

"Good," said the organizer. "We leave from Boston, so she'll meet us there!" Connie joined us in Boston.

This led to a trip that started in Greece and three of the islands. Then we left the group, and went to Turkey (it was *so* near!). Then to Rome, where we had a reunion with Liza and the villa where we'd lived. After that, Connie went back to New York to look for a job, and Liza, on vacation, continued with us to Luxembourg, Garmisch-Partenkirchen in Germany, and Paris, where she left us for Spain. All in all, we visited thirteen countries.

While we were in Paris, in a hotel with no television, the boys walked to a nearby Peugeot dealer who had several sets in his window, and there, with dozens of excited Frenchmen, they watched the takeoff of Armstrong, Aldrin, and Collins for the first trip to the moon. Eight days later, as we were leaving Mont-Saint-Michel, we stopped in the dining room of our hotel, the Mère Poulard, for *pamplemousse* (grapefruit to us) and one of their famous omelets, and in the most exciting breakfast of our lives watched our astronauts splash down. Television has indeed made it a small world.

CHAPTER
· 32 ·

Liza came home to spend Christmas in 1970. She'd been living and working in Spain as an executive secretary to the Spanish representative for Northrop, and then for a year as a tour guide, "to do something adventurous," she said.

Now she surprised us with the news that she was going to marry Antonio Azcona, a Spaniard who lived on the island of Mallorca. "Surprised" because the previous year she'd announced her engagement to a jai alai player of the Madrid fronton!

She had come first to break the news to us, but Antonio was determined to follow and live up to Spanish protocol by asking us for her hand in marriage.

By the time he got his passport and visa, a vaccination and a shot for cholera, demanded that year, we found that Liza's ticket would have only a week left by the time he got there. It seemed a shame for Antonio to see Liza's country for only a short time. Also, since he had not only parents but two brothers and a sister, numerous aunts and uncles and five small nephews and two young nieces, it seemed fairer that Brooks and I and the two boys should go there for the wedding. Connie, unfortunately, would be on tour with a Shakespeare company.

So Liza and I picked out her wedding gown and ordered her veil of Belgian lace, and it was arranged that the wedding would be on April 7.

Brooks and I went to Seattle to play a four-week engagement of *Under Papa's Picture* and they held us over for eleven weeks, barely giving us time to get home and pack for the wedding.

Ann Amster and her mother, Ida E., ninety-one years old, had spent the winter in our guest house. Ann had longed for years to see Europe, but Stanley hated traveling and loved his farm, and she wouldn't leave him. Now at last she was going to Switzerland, her

220

mother's birthplace. She said, "I hate to miss Liza's wedding, but I want to be in Switzerland in May when all the flowers are in bloom. Besides, it will take me that long to find someone who can stay here with Mother."

I watched her exquisite white-haired mother, daintily putting away a breakfast that would have done justice to a truck driver, and I said, "Why don't we just take her with us? The boys adore her, there'll be five of us to take care of her, and she can see her brother in Switzerland. Liza would love to have you both at her wedding."

So six of us left on the second of April to spend a couple of days in London on the way.

It was an unbelievably strenuous departure, with delays of our flight and problems with luggage. Also, I was carrying Liza's organza-and-lace wedding gown and veil in an airy see-through bag. As I was about to request the stewardess to be extremely careful with it, she grabbed our coats, then tore the delicate organza creation from my arms and, rolling them all together, stuffed them into the luggage holder over our seats. The scream in my throat stayed there as she added some strange coats on top of ours, and the damage was done.

Dinner was served shortly after takeoff, and then six tired travelers fell asleep immediately.

I woke to the sound of a stewardess announcing that breakfast would be served in ten minutes. My neck had a kink that barely allowed me to look to my left, where Ann was still deep in sleep. A few more creaks of my neck showed me Douglas to my right, sprawled over his window seat with no signs of life. In back of him Duncan, freckled face pressed against the glass, snored lightly. Brooks in the middle had obviously heard nothing.

Fearfully, I turned my head to look at our ninety-one-year-old on the aisle. She was sitting upright—every gleaming hair in place and eyes glittering in anticipation of breakfast.

We didn't arrive at the Duke's Hotel in London until ten o'clock that night after sorting out a problem with missing luggage.

I tapped gently on Ann's door at nine the next day. We knew she wanted to see the changing of the guards at the Palace, and we thought Ida E. would sleep until noon at least, but she opened the door, ready to go with us, and after the ceremony she walked through the Halls of Harrod's, enjoyed lunch at the Guinea, drove through Hyde Park, had a brief nap, dinner, saw an English variety show, and finally got to bed after midnight! From that moment on we ceased to worry about her. Another day of the sights of London, and we flew to Palma, Mallorca.

Liza had taken rooms for Ann and her mother and Ann's younger daughter Mary, in an ancient *palacio* converted into a hotel. Mary had been staying in the Canary Islands, and was delighted to visit her mother and grandmother, and to attend Liza's wedding.

Then Liza drove us to our hotel. It was Easter, Mallorca was full of tourists, and it was impossible to get seven of us in the same place.

We hadn't yet met our son-in-law-to-be, and Liza had brought his apologies. Antonio, his father, and one of his brothers owned a *fabrica,* where they made built-in furniture, tables and chairs for hotels and condominiums. That day Antonio had to meet the boat from Barcelona bringing workers he'd hired. This was not an easy job, as the men and their wives had to inspect the living quarters he'd found for them in town. Liza laughed, and said that the women were the ones he had to please with his selections. Antonio, when he appeared later, was not only tall, dark, and exceptionally handsome, but had a wonderful sense of humor. It translated through his eyes and his ready laugh, although he spoke not a word of English. Liza, translating, said that he apologized for having to get back to work immediately, but that the following day he would spend with us and the family.

After he'd gone, Liza explained to us that she had arranged for the chapel and a reception for eighty-five people, in a beautiful old *palacio,* along with the food, champagne, and wines and the wedding cake—everything that the bride's parents would ordinarily do if they were present.

The only thing that remained for us to do was to give a luncheon for the immediate family. She'd found a charming country inn outside of Palma and had reserved it for the next day, if that was all right with us. It certainly was! We were so proud of how efficient our daughter had become in her few years away from home.

The next day we met at the lovely inn she'd chosen and were introduced to the close members of the family: Mama and Papa Azcona, the beloved and respected heads of the clan; Leo, the eldest of the four junior members, handsome enough to be mistaken for a movie star, and his lovely wife Marisa, mother of their four sons. They had come from Madrid for the wedding. The next eldest was Juaquin, known as Quinito. He and his wife Elvira were parents of the flower girl, Estefania, and her baby sister, Letitia, called Letty. The second-youngest of the Azcona family, the only girl, known to the family as La Niña, had been nicknamed as a baby after a character in a Spanish play, and was known thereafter as Cuqui. Adored by all the family, she quickly captured the hearts of the four Wests, Duncan and Douglas being particularly entranced. A year or so younger than she was Antonio, the groom-to-be, the solemn, polite young man we'd met the day before. Today, surrounded by his family and his bride-to-be, he was full of fun and charm.

The only others at the luncheon were Tía Vicenta, younger sister of Mama Azcona and a very *simpática* woman, with the same charm as Cuqui. The cast of characters ended with Antonio's best friend, another Antonio named Ramos.

It was an unusual experience to fall in love with all those strangers without understanding a word they said. Our radiant daughter translated as we enjoyed our lunch. We felt complete rapport with this close-knit family and thought Liza very lucky to have been accepted with such warmth by her new family-to-be.

On the wedding morning, Liza arrived at our hotel to have an early lunch with us. I took her wedding gown from the closet where I'd hung it, and sent it down to be pressed. It had completely recovered from the manhandling on the plane, and the organza barely needed an iron. By the time it returned from the valet, Liza was bathed and ready to dress, and we had just time to take pictures of her in the lush hotel garden, where there were two live pink flamingos who worked their way into several shots.

When we all assembled in the round chapel with its stained-glass windows, I felt as if I were in the midst of a Renaissance wedding.

Ann murmured, "Oh, I'm so glad we didn't miss this."

Brooks, proud of his beautiful daughter, led her past us to the altar where Antonio and brother Leo waited.

Cuqui and a cousin who looked like her twin were two Goya paintings, in navy velvet dresses, white-collared, their hair in knots at the nape of each neck, and holding calla lilies in their arms as they sat near the altar. Next to them, Estefania, a seven-year-old beauty in navy velvet, held the bride's bouquet, and young Leito, Leo's son, held the pillow bearing the ring. As the priest performed the ceremony, the bride, beautiful as I'd ever seen her, and her handsome groom, looked extremely serious.

After the ceremony the families gathered in the courtyard of the chapel, where we met some aunts and uncles and nephews and nieces, and there was much kissing on both cheeks, and laughing as Liza and Antonio drove off to the *palacio* in a Bentley, rented as a gag by Antonio's best friend, Antonio.

Dinner was a joyous celebration, and we marveled at how smoothly everything went, with eighty-five guests spread through two large rooms of the ancient *palacio,* and we watched our happy bride and Antonio cut the wedding cake. Ann and Ida E. enjoyed it all as much as we did.

We spent the day after the wedding with the Azconas. Then, because Ann had been so anxious to see Positano, we decided to fly to Rome, rent a car, and drive her there.

Meanwhile, Ida E. was to stay in Palma and visit with Mary, her granddaughter, who would put her on the plane in time to meet us when we got back to Rome. What we didn't count on was that it happened to be Easter week. As we drove to Sorrento, we passed through small towns where we were stopped by processions of ghostlike white-clad figures having to do with Christ's resurrection.

In Sorrento we found our delightful little hotel, but from dinnertime until midnight dozens of black-clad figures, bearing candles, walked by, carrying a carving of Christ borne in a coffin. It was as spooky as our own Halloween.

The next day we took a hydrofoil to Capri. It was crowded, and to me one of the least attractive, though famous, Italian resorts. Still, Positano made up for everything, and Ann's delight in it was a joy to see.

We returned to Rome to find a telegram from Mary, saying that because of the Easter rush, she was unable to get off the Island with Ida E., but that several airlines had promised to get Ida E. to Rome.

I was frantic, feeling responsible for bringing her on the trip, so I phoned every airline in Barcelona, where she'd change planes, and threatened them all to watch out for a tiny, white-haired, ninety-one-year-old. I hung up not knowing when, how, or if she would arrive the next day.

In the morning, we drove the boys to the Rome Airport and put them on a 747, as they were due back for school. We waved them off, then had lunch in the airport café.

From then on we met any plane from Barcelona—Italian, Swiss, even Greek, I think. Finally, at 6:30 P.M., we waited for the last plane from Spain. Ann was losing her cool, and I was close to a nervous breakdown under a falsely gay exterior.

As we watched the people arriving on that plane dwindle down to a precious few and no Ida E., Ann began to shake. Suddenly, from a side exit, two men carried a litter, the figure on it covered with a sheet. Ann's desperate eyes looked at me.

"Don't even think it!" I yelled.

It was at that moment we spotted a tiny white-haired lady, accompanied by a young man carrying her luggage. Ida E. had arrived, as we should have known she would.

As we drove into Rome, she told us of having been deposited in the Barcelona lounge by a stewardess who said she'd be right back, and was not seen again! Never daunted, and with the supreme faith she had, she left her luggage on the bench and went to lunch. Then, at the end of the afternoon, she heard Rome announced, and got on board with all her luggage!

The next morning she was ready with Ann for a bus tour of Rome.

That morning, I answered a call at our hotel, and it was Liza.

"Where are you?" I asked.

"China," she said, and laughed. "We're here in Rome, Mother."

So Brooks and I spent a wonderful honeymoon with the young Azconas.

Ann and Ida E. went on to Switzerland, where Ida E. had a reunion with her younger brother, and Ann saw all the Swiss flowers she'd longed to see.

CHAPTER
· 33 ·

We decided to put Westhaven on the market while we looked for a house in town. We had started to suffer from the empty-nest syndrome, with Liza in Spain, Connie traveling with the Shakespeare company, Duncan in the army, and Doug in college. It was time to find a home for just the two of us that wasn't forty miles from town.

After we'd looked at many houses, Kaye Ballard called one day to say that she was selling one of the houses she'd bought during the run of "The Mothers-in-Law." We went to see it again, and this time I realized that the location and the view were perfect for us. The fact that Kaye hadn't had it long enough to do much to it offered me the chance I needed to create a home for us that would ease the undeniable pain of giving up the farm we'd loved so. We told Kaye we'd take it and made the down payment.

By the end of the next year, I was well into papering and painting, and rebuilding the fireplace to my satisfaction.

I was meeting with the workmen when I got a call from Susan, Ann's eldest girl and my godchild. She was in tears, unable to talk.

"What's wrong, dear? Is it Ida E.?"

"No," she cried. "It's Mother."

My heart sank. Ann had been on her way to stay with us, but had stopped in Idaho to spend Christmas with Sue and settle Ida E. in a Christian Science home where Ida E. had a close friend, and felt her last years would be made more comfortable.

Sue got herself under control, and explained that Ann had developed a very bad cough and had gone, at Susan's request, to see a doctor. The diagnosis had been cancer, well advanced. He'd removed water from her lungs, but insisted she should go where she'd get proper care.

My dear friend Ann. I asked Susan, "Is she able to travel?"

"Yes, and I've called Dr. Hallauer. You remember my friend? He's now a cancer expert. If you can possibly meet her, Aunt Eve, he will arrange to begin treatment in the hospital over the weekend. I'll be able to get away the first of next week."

I assured her that we would meet Ann and have her spend the night in our new home with us, and drive her to the hospital the next day. After the weekend, we'd take her to the farm, where we still spent most of our nights.

Unfortunately, I had signed a contract to do six weeks of *Butterflies Are Free* in New Jersey, and it was too late to cancel, as we were due to leave the following week. I explained this to Sue, and she said she and Ann's other daughter, Mary, would both be there by then.

I hung up and went upstairs with a heavy heart. I looked at the guest room that I had furnished with Ann in mind, and thought of the years we'd been friends, the summers we'd spent in Connecticut, the winters they'd spent in our guest house, and the happiness and sadness we'd shared, and I cried.

That evening I broke the news to Brooks, who loved her too, and the following day we met her at the airport. I held her tight and we talked about how happy we were to have her there. She looked well, and was joyful to see the new house and her room.

The next morning I drove her to the hospital, helped her get settled, and stayed until the doctor came. He said I could pick her up on Monday.

Brooks and I spent a worried weekend, trying to reassure ourselves. We brought her to the farm Monday afternoon. She felt nauseated and couldn't eat much dinner, but seemed to pick up later. When she was ready for bed, she sat and looked at the pictures we'd taken on our previous summers in Connecticut. She chatted happily, but suddenly her voice slurred and she seemed to be semiconscious.

We got her to bed, and after smiling at us, she slept. The next morning, after I got her to eat some breakfast, I was encouraged enough to drive into town and keep a hair appointment, knowing I would have to leave for New York in two days.

When I reached the beauty salon, I got a call from Brooks telling me that Annie had collapsed, that he'd called the doctor, who'd immediately sent an ambulance to bring her back to the hospital.

We talked to the doctor that evening. He told us she'd had a stroke, and that the cancer had spread to the brain. He said I could come to see her the next day, and that she didn't realize what had happened. Her daughters had arrived that afternoon.

When I saw her she was amazingly bright and anxious to talk. The only indication of her stroke was a drooping cheek and a slight slur in her speech.

The girls found it difficult to talk, so Ann and I chatted away, she about her plans to live in California where her girls could visit her, and I recalled every funny story about our summers in Connecticut, and things the children had said and done.

Finally I had to leave. I kissed her good-bye, and she said, "I'll see you tomorrow, dear."

Then came the hardest speech I've ever had to make. As the girls stared numbly at me, I summoned a laugh from somewhere and said, "Darling, you forgot that I'm leaving for New York tomorrow to rehearse for *Butterflies*, but I'll call you from there, and I'll be seeing you in a few weeks."

"That's right." She smiled. "Have a good show, dear." We hugged and I left.

I started rehearsals on the twenty-fifth of January, and on the twenty-eighth my darling Ann passed away. Fortunately, the New Jersey engagement was an easy one. I was able to stay in New York, and played only four nights, from Thursday through Sunday. A limousine picked us up every evening, and brought us back after the show. Without Brooks's comforting presence and love, and the discipline of responding to a new audience each night, it might have been too difficult.

We got a call from Sue and Mary to say that they were in Connecticut at the farm, and could we please come out and help them dispose of some of Ann's things. A few days later we came prepared to spend the night, and found that the real problem was that they had brought the urn containing Ann's ashes, and had been shocked to find the one containing Stanley's on the mantelpiece in the master bedroom. What should they do with them?

Brooks and I talked it over, and suggested that since the farm had meant so much to them both, that was where they should rest. So the next morning, Brooks prepared a place under the largest and most beautiful dogwood tree, where they'd never be disturbed.

Along with Mary's baby girl, the four of us held hands, and each of us silently said our own prayer. Then we hugged and cried a little, and when Brooks was finished, I took the burlap bag of seeds that Annie always kept for her precious birds, and emptied it around the tree. Somehow, I think we all felt happier, as if we knew the Amsters were content.

But life seemed to take with one hand and give with another. This time it was going to give us a grandchild in midsummer. We made plans to be with Liza for the big event, and started Spanish lessons three days a week in New York.

Armed with some sixty hours of Spanish lessons, Brooks and I arrived in Mallorca, afraid that Liza might already have given birth.

However, through the glass doors of the airport we saw our daughter, still extremely pregnant but glowing and pretty in a red pant suit, with Antonio standing by her waving us a welcome.

After ten minutes of hugging and kissing and laughing, Antonio stowed our luggage in the Seat, the Spanish model of the Fiat, and we were driving past all the windmills along the coast, away from all the other Seats.

As we'd planned, Brooks and I refrained from any Spanish greetings. It was only when we had bypassed Palma and were on the Carretera de Valdemossa on our way to La Cabaña that Brooks and I started our conversation in the back seat.

I said, "*Tenemos que ir a la ciudad tan pronto como posible, comprar cosas por el niño, no?*"

Brooks replied casually, "*Sí, necesito también comprar hojas de afeitar yo mismo.*" (A little small talk about buying things for ourselves and the baby-to-be.)

The necks in front of us grew rigid and then turned two unbelieving faces toward us with total disregard for the traffic and our safety. There was a rush of overlapping questions and answers, and delighted bursts of laughter when we explained about the lessons.

Then Liza said seriously: "Mom and Dad, I can't tell you what you've done for this man." She patted Antonio's shoulder lovingly and continued, "He was so worried about trying to communicate with you and felt awful about not being able to learn more English. He did start a class at Berlitz right after we were married, but his business hours are so long that when he went to class right after work, he'd fall asleep, so I made him quit. Now you've lifted a weight off his shoulders and I think it was wonderful of you!" Her eyes were moist as she added, "Thank you, Mom and Dad."

The smile on Antonio's face was added proof that our struggle with those "damned verb endings" had been worthwhile.

Shortly after, we drove up to some enormous wooden gates set in a wall of native stone, and Antonio got out to open them.

Since they had bought an almond grove and built La Cabaña a year or so before, we were amazed to see how much they had accomplished. La Cabaña, eventually to be their guest house, sat on the right with a paved area for parking. The entire property was completely surrounded by a thick white stucco wall, its six feet topped by a sturdy green wire mesh. The wall had square recesses every ten feet or so to break the monotony, and these were planted with climbing roses, jasmine, and bougainvillea. From the gate to the rear of the property, where the main house would eventually sit, a road passed under two huge carob trees, which cast pools of shade.

There was another structure close to La Cabaña, which seemed to contain several rooms and had in front of it a tiled floor covered with a handsome latticed roof. Liza explained that it contained the men's and women's showers for the not-yet-built pool and tennis court. It was putting the cart ahead of the horse, it seemed to me, but it made a lovely place to have breakfast out of doors.

Beyond the terrace was a large vegetable garden, for which we'd provided the seeds for special tomatoes Liza had requested— along with corn, which on Mallorca is only fed to hogs, being an inferior strain.

Several almond trees from the original orchard dotted the grounds, and oleanders and other shrubs completed the land- scape.

The lushness of the planting reminded me of Westhaven. Brooks, with the ESP we have for each other's thoughts, said qui- etly, "Just like her mother," referring to my tendency to overplant.

La Cabaña was spacious and attractive but, as a guest house, confined to two bedrooms. Despite our protests, we were in- stalled in the master bedroom with its queen-size bed—a rarity at that time in Mallorca. Later, when we realized that pregnant Liza and six-foot-two Antonio would be sleeping in single beds, we protested again, knowing that each of them would overhang the bed in one direction or another. Spanish pride and hospitality silenced us.

In the kitchen we met Isabel, cook-housekeeper and, at the moment, the bane of Liza's existence, as she spent most of her time redoing what Isabel had just completed.

The first night we went through a trial by fire, as we were initiated into a couple of facets of Spanish life that are perhaps the most difficult for Americans to adjust to—the lateness of the dinner hour, and the unpredictability of callers.

To begin with, we were having dinner early (ten-thirty!) out of deference to our jet lag. As we finished eating, the sound of a motor was heard. Liza and Antonio looked questioningly at each other. Antonio's family had been warned about jet lag, and were planning a large gathering the following evening.

The late arrivals turned out to be Julio and Maria, an attractive couple we remembered from the wedding. After the customary greeting of a kiss on each cheek from each of them, returned by each of us, we sat again at the table while they were proffered cheese and nuts and brandy.

The conversation began when Liza informed them with pride of our new proficiency in their language, a fatal mistake, as she neglected to warn us of Julio's machine-gun delivery. With this, he proceeded to mow us down and leave us gasping. Not one word could we salvage. It was useless for Antonio to point out that even among his peers Julio was noted for never taking a breath, the damage was done!

I credit that devastating encounter with undermining our confidence, linguistically, for the rest of our stay. From then on I couldn't recall the simplest of verb endings, and while Brooks, the grammarian, could conjugate any verb, his conversation was riddled with Italian words, American slang, and body language.

By now the Wests had jet lag in spades and our smiles were frozen under Julio's barrage.

We were learning a lesson in Spanish etiquette. Under no circumstances do you indicate, as you might with friends at home: "Hey, fellas, we're knocked out. So go on home, will ya?" No Spaniard would be so gross. So, until the guest's exuberance, stimulated by brandy, is spent and he indicates he's ready to leave, the Spanish host and hostess grin and bear it.

I think it was when my eyes closed involuntarily five or six times that Julio and Maria apologized profusely and left at 2 A.M.

The weeks that followed were filled with visits to and from the Spanish relatives, and every Friday a visit to Dr. Lizarbe, Liza's obstetrician. When she was dismissed until the following week, our overly pregnant daughter immediately planned a trip to another section of the island.

I was concerned about her driving at this late date, and when, on being told to "come back Friday" for the third week, I protested, she said she felt marvelous, and that Antonio would drive and we must not miss Formentor. So I reluctantly agreed, but this time, as a precaution, I carried some large beach towels, scissors, and string, in case labor began. Where I would "boil water," I hadn't figured out yet.

The drive to Formentor was winding and precipitous, but beautiful. We had lunch on the hotel terrace, surrounded by flower beds in a riot of color. Liza, as usual, survived the trip well, although we thought we noticed a slowing of her pace and a definite shelf in her body profile where formerly all was round.

For several days Brooks and I had sensed Antonio's growing concern about Liza. He joined us on the terrace at breakfast the next morning while she slept. In his few English phrases, combined with slow and distinct Spanish, he began: "You no speaking to Laisa!" he warned, and went on to inform us that there was a problem connected with the baby's delivery.

He said that Dr. Lizarbe didn't want to alarm us, but Antonio thought we should be prepared. It had to do with a small obstruction in the neck of the womb that had grown as the baby grew, and was now interfering with its descent into the birth canal.

The doctor had assured Antonio that both Liza and the baby were in perfect condition, and that he was in control of the situation, and, when the time was right, he'd decide whether she could deliver naturally, or he'd need to perform a cesarean.

The thought of anything going wrong was a shock to us, but we had such belief in Liza's strength of body and spirit, and the vigor and well-being of the baby, that we were able to dissemble. But we did wonder how much longer it could possibly take. A day or two later, Liza and Antonio visited a friend who'd been very ill, while we tried desperately to make conversation with two Spanish friends who dropped in.

Finally we had dinner at ten-thirty and noticed that Liza was very tired.

At one-thirty I woke and heard Liza moving around, and again an hour later, but she called to reassure me and told me to go back to sleep. When, however, I heard her calling Antonio at three-thirty, I went in to see what was happening. I found her lying in bed, looking at her watch. There was a large broom on the floor at her side. She started to giggle at my expression. To my horror she said, "The pains are six minutes apart, Mom. Antonio was afraid I wouldn't be able to wake him, so he left me this broom to hit him with, but it hasn't done any good." She laughed again. "What a character!"

I looked at poor Antonio, worn out by work, worry, fiestas, and visiting in-laws, and regretted what had to be done.

"Antonio"—shake—"Antonio, wake up! Antonio, Liza's going to have the baby soon," I shouted.

His eyes cracked open, but stared uncomprehendingly. I repeated my assertion and he sat up, head in hands. So far, so good.

Liza, with time out for a contraction, gave him a run-down, in Spanish, of course, on the closeness of the pains. *"Claro?"* she asked.

I was suddenly thinking, "No phone!" Spanish bureaucracy had refused to extend phone lines this far for another six months, a woman's pregnancy notwithstanding.

Antonio, thoroughly alarmed by now, was struggling into a pair of pants. He decided to drive to the nearest *pueblo,* where there was a public phone, to call Aurora the midwife.

"Tell her to send an ambulance—*ambulancio,"* I tried. He nodded and went off buttoning his shirt.

Liza was checking contractions. "Five minutes apart," she said calmly.

Antonio's trip was fast and productive. Liza translated, "Aurora said to bring me to the *clínica* and call her from there. No ambulance."

At 4:30 A.M., accompanied by a groggy Brooks and with Liza distributed over the front seat and floor, Antonio drove us through the black night. Brooks checked Liza's pains, which now swung erratically from six minutes to four and back again.

Unlike an American hospital, where you could have the baby before you could answer all their questions, at the Policlínica Mirimar, Liza was admitted, in bed, and examined in minutes. Aurora arrived soon after to "control" for Dr. Lizarbe. The midwife calls the doctor to the hospital only when the baby is imminent.

Antonio's sister Cuqui came to be with Liza and instruct her in a method of breathing very much like the Lamaze method. She told us that Aurora said it would be several hours before the doctor would be needed.

I persuaded Brooks that he would be more help at La Cabaña, informing a bewildered Isabel why she'd awakened to an empty house, and then getting some sleep himself until we called him.

I got out some needlepoint and sat in the little sitting room. Liza's *dolores* were pretty steady at four minutes now and it was difficult to listen to her suffering, although the only sounds she made were the soft hissings of her breath during contractions. As the day wore on, she began low murmurings, hard to understand, until I realized that our very American girl was swearing in Spanish!

"*Aiee,*" she moaned, "*aiee,*" but never once did she utter a *grito* (scream), although several were heard from another part of the maternity ward.

Dr. Lizarbe arrived and, according to Cuqui, said that the baby was fine and in the right position, but refusing to move downward.

Not until five in the afternoon did Dr. Lizarbe finally inform us that Liza was being prepared for delivery and, if necessary, cesarean section.

Brooks, who had returned at noon, was looking pale, and we were relieved to know that her suffering was almost over.

She was wheeled into the delivery room at ten minutes of six. A drained Antonio sat near the door, with Cuqui, who had been a nurse, giving him encouragement.

Brooks and I, too nervous to sit quietly, told Antonio that we'd be waiting in the garden at the rear of the hospital. We paced there for about ten minutes, then found a bench under a tree.

Suddenly I saw Antonio rush from the hospital door and look frantically around for us. My heart constricted, and I prayed a little harder. Brooks called to him and Antonio ran toward us and I heard him shout: "*Es un niño y Laisa está vale!*"

He threw himself at me and broke into great wracking sobs. Fortunately, I had learned that the word *vale* (pronounced "bali") meant okay.

The long day was over. Antonio had his *niño*, we had a *nieto*, and our Liza was *vale!*

Laughing and crying as we ran, we joined a joyous Cuqui, and then, since it would be some time before we could see Liza, we rushed up a ramp to the maternity-nursery to watch for Antonio, Jr. To our amazement he was already there being bathed. He was kicking vigorously and we could hear his cries of protest at having his head washed.

A moment later he was draped in a blanket, and the nurse brought him to the window. We looked at what appeared to be a three-month-old child but with the pearl-pink skin of a newborn. His tiny nose wrinkled as he opened almond-shaped eyes and looked directly at us with a steady gaze.

A group of Spaniards, there to see several other new babies, moved closer to see the recent arrival. There were murmurs of *"guapo," "guapísimo"* and *"es un rubio!"*

There was a sudden rush in the corridor as we were joined by Mama and Papa Azcona, Quinito, Elvira, and Tía Vicenta. There began another chorus of *"guapo," "guapísimo,"* and *"cara de Laisa"* (face of Liza), but I was watching Papa Azcona. This sturdy man, who resembled a more handsome Ari Onassis, stood looking at his eighth grandchild with wonder. Then, with a smile that lit the corridor, he turned and, shaking the tears from his eyes, threw his arms around his son and kissed him on both cheeks. It was unself-conscious joy at its most beautiful, and very Spanish. Then everyone kissed everyone else, and again I bumped my nose, starting on the wrong side.

When Liza was finally wheeled out, she was still unconscious, very pale with dark circles under her eyes. To my surprise, we were all permitted a quick kiss on her cheek before she was taken back to her room.

Dr. Lizarbe came forth and modestly parried our congratulations, and told us of his hope for Liza to deliver naturally, and his final decision on a cesarean when the baby's position didn't improve quickly enough, and he was unwilling to subject Liza to more suffering.

All of us went down to the restaurant and drank toasts of champagne to the new arrival, while Antonio rushed back and forth making and receiving phone calls.

When we returned to the *clínica* in the morning, we found Toñete (nickname for Antonio) already with his mother, and learned another fact of life in Spanish hospitals that would have given the Cedars of Sinai a real jolt. In the nursery each newborn was bathed, wrapped, put in a plastic cart, and turned over to its father. He then wheeled it away to Mama's room, usually with one or two siblings hanging on the side, tenderly kissing the new brother or sister. Certainly a no-no in most American hospitals.

Antonio greeted us with a happy smile. Liza, though still exhausted, was happy to see us and hear us rave about her son, who looked more than ever like a big beautiful doll in his "trolley."

I noticed that Liza looked at him with the puzzled expression of many new mothers. She was trying to relate to him as her son, and wondering why she didn't immediately feel the strong bond of motherhood, even though she was thrilled by his perfection as a baby.

In his sleep, Toñete popped his thumb into his mouth with expertise. Liza looked worried. Above her was suspended the bottle of glucose, containing the antibiotics being fed into her veins because of the cesarean. She knew she couldn't nurse Toñete while taking them and she felt guilty. He slept peacefully, and for several days lived off the fat of his ample nine pounds.

Toñete's first full day of life found the sitting room of the suite crowded with relatives and friends, and what space was left was filled with flowers—roses, carnations, gladiolas, daisies, and orchids.

As the day wore on, more people and flowers arrived, but not many seemed to leave. As parents, we were concerned that Liza wasn't getting any rest. We waited for one of the nurses to order everyone out, including us. Although several of them wandered through to check blood pressure and the antibiotics, they left with no more than a nod or smile to the crowd. We attempted to cover our agitation with greetings to each arrival, and the air was filled with shouts of *"Encantado"* and *"Con mucho gusto."* And, every few minutes, Toñete's chubby limbs were unwrapped and kissed by aunts and uncles and countless small cousins. It was an agonizing period for two very new American grandparents.

Liza had been watching us, and when she could claim our attention, said quietly, "Cool it, Mom and Dad. It's *la costumbre.* There's nothing you can do about it!" It was a custom I found hard to adjust to.

We had overstayed our tickets by several weeks, so we added another ten days for Toñete's christening in a tiny nearby church, and a celebration dinner on the lawn of La Cabaña, with seventy-five grown-ups at small candlelit tables, and twenty-five children at a long table on the terrace.

Two exhausted people left for home the following morning.

CHAPTER
· 34 ·

In the next two years we played Canada and the Midwest, where Brooks and I fell in love with the marvelous barns, which were beginning to disappear from the landscape. So Brooks began a series of barn paintings.

We added *Beekman Place, Goodbye, Charlie,* and *Under Papa's Picture,* also a new play or two to our repertoire. Then I was offered a lecture series. They lined up an immediate triple engagement for me in Michigan at Grosse Pointe, Detroit, and Pontiac. I found them fun to do until I learned that I'd have to commit myself to a tour a year in advance. This made it too difficult, since I realized that Brooks, after five years of sobriety, was still having a struggle with alcohol. He had gone into the Chemical Dependency Unit in St. John's Hospital in Santa Monica. It seemed like an easy victory after a couple of weeks there, and everyone in the unit adored him as he was so helpful to the others there.

I'd learned, however, not to underestimate what I'd come to know was indeed a disease to be reckoned with.

The inevitable recurring stresses of our profession could so easily lead to its return. Still, with everything we had to be grateful for in our lives, and the love we felt for each other, I was sure we'd be able to handle it.

Right after Toñete's second birthday, we looked for an excuse to see our grandchild, and invited Liza and Antonio to spend a couple of weeks with us in Switzerland, including Toñete in the invitation. On their acceptance we flew via London to Palma to pick them up.

It was a nervous time in London, as the Hilton had been bombed by terrorists not too long before. The taxi taking us to our hotel seemed to be going well out of its way. I mentioned it to Brooks audibly so the driver would know that we were familiar with London. He answered the challenge immediately.

"I'm sorry, madam, to be taking you out of your way, but the police have cordoned off a part of Knightsbridge. Some hostages have been taken in the Spaghetti House Restaurant, and the police are waiting for them to be released."

We learned later how well the London police had dealt with the situation. It took ten days of patient waiting, and then all of the hostages were freed without a shot being fired.

We arrived in Palma eager to see our grandchild, only to find him in the throes of "the terrible twos." He refused to have anything to do with perfect strangers whose Spanish had eroded to a few phrases. So we bided our time and adored him from afar.

During the week we spent in Palma before leaving for Switzerland, Glenn called to tell me that Brooks and I had an offer to play *Applause* in Australia in September. My immediate reaction was "Dammit, why couldn't this have happened a few years earlier?"

Then Glenn called again and said that the offer from a young Englishman had been urgently repeated, and the terms were very good indeed, and to please think it over seriously. After two more calls, the Scarlett O'Hara in me spoke up. "Oh, say yes, and get on with Switzerland. You'll have three months to worry about it."

So we all flew to Zurich, rented a Volkswagen bus, and drove to a tiny town called Vitznau on the edge of Lake Lucerne. Antonio's sister Cuqui and Charles, her Swiss husband, drove up from Lausanne to spend a few days with us at the Hotel Vitznauerhof.

At dinner that night our table sounded like a United Nations Committee at work, as Cuqui tried to explain to me in French that Toñete's tantrum over his dinner being late was because little Spanish boys were permitted to express themselves freely. This was to allow *la force* to grow within until it became the "macho" of a Spanish man. Fortunately, my French wasn't fluent enough to express my reaction to this idea.

Meanwhile, Liza calmed Toñete in Spanish, as Antonio chatted with the waiters in Italian and German, and Charles spoke perfect English to us. I envied the Swiss their facility with languages. Charles had learned fluent Spanish in six months in order to court Cuqui.

We paid a visit to one of my favorite landmarks, the "Lion of Lucerne" a day or so later, and then Cuqui and Charles returned to Lausanne, while we continued our tour with a drive up a steep mountain to Grindelwald, a German-Swiss town facing the Eiger and two other mountain peaks, and having an actual glacier encroaching on the far side of the main street.

We had presented Toñete with a stroller padded in red patent leather, which we hoped would keep him under control on the steep slopes of Switzerland. He was delighted, but insisted on pushing it himself in all directions, which kept the four of us in a constant state of alarm.

The Swiss chalets on the hillside surrounding us were ablaze with window boxes full of geraniums. We lunched on a restaurant balcony under the still snow-covered Alps, but when we looked over the geraniums surrounding us, the green mountains swooped so far down beneath us that the chalets on it looked like tiny toys.

Our hotel would have been a pleasure, but our little balcony overhung that same sweep of green, and was so tempting to Toñete that we had to lock the French doors. Then he went into our bathroom, locked that door, and ignored my pounding and pleading. Liza came from their room and said, "Just leave him alone, Mother. He'll come out eventually. I've hidden the key to ours." So we took the risk of being interrupted in the tub and hid ours too, and thought about *la force*.

I was relieved when, a couple of mornings later, we drove down the mountain and by noon were in the French-Swiss town of Gruyères. It was more relaxing there. The entire town is a narrow cobblestoned street, leading up to a château. No cars were allowed on the cobblestones. The street was lined with charming shops and restaurants. At one of these we had a much needed glass of *vin ordinaire* and a delicious lunch of *poulet et pommes frites*.

Toñete joined two little girls at the community fountain where they splashed happily, while we looked at the charming French architecture of the shops and restaurants and the ubiquitous window boxes with bright geraniums.

A few days later Antonio flew home with his son, insisting that Liza needed time alone with her parents. It was thoughtful of our son-in-law, and we decided to take Liza to Coppet, a town on the edge of Lake Geneva that a friend had told us about. It was our good fortune to arrive on the day Coppet was celebrating its first fête in a hundred years or more. People were in costume, bands played, there was dancing in the street, all the shop windows were decorated, and flower stalls were everywhere. We visited the château on the hill where Madame de Staël had lived. Before dinner we fed the swans on the lake, then dined outdoors on the terrace of the Hotel du Lac.

All too soon the time came to drive Liza to Geneva and see her off to Palma, where Antonio and their adorable terrible two were waiting. We caught the plane for London.

Home again, there were many phone conversations with the nice-sounding Englishman who was producing *Applause;* also contacts with the Australian consul in Los Angeles, who had not received our permits or visas yet. Until these arrived, I gathered, nothing else would happen. There were reassuring calls from the Englishman in Sydney and then suddenly tickets arrived, and everything was "go."

We went to the airport, where Doug and his girl Carole were to see us off. We were paged, to be told by Doug that Carole had been hit by a car as she was about to get into theirs. Doug assured us that she wasn't badly hurt, and we were not to worry. We returned to the VIP lounge, a little shaken, though, and sat down.

I became aware of a man standing a few yards away, staring at me with a disdainful expression. I smiled and started to wave, but thought better of it. I turned to Brooks and said, "Doesn't that man look like Deke?" (Richard Deacon from "The Mothers-in-Law.")

Brooks looked and said, "It is."

I looked back, but if anything, his expression was even meaner. Then I saw the woman next to him, who was glaring at me too, and recognized Deke's friend Jane Dulo. I started to laugh. They'd come to see us off, of course, but pretended not to recognize us.

They spent an hour telling us jokes and dispelling our "blues." They'd brought us books and magazines and candy, and when our plane was called we left them in high spirits, grateful for their efforts.

We were still laughing as we buckled on our seat belts, only to sit from 8 P.M. takeoff time until midnight, when a necessary piece of radar equipment arrived and we were finally allowed to leave.

We changed planes in Hawaii somewhere around 3 A.M. and were happy that we'd decided on an extra-night stopover in Fiji. Sometime before we reached Fiji, we crossed both the equator and the International Date Line.

Arriving at the Nandi Airport the next day, we waited an hour in steaming humidity until half of our luggage was delivered, and another hour until we were told that the rest of it was still on the plane on the way to New Zealand!

A cab took us through unattractive countryside, but deposited us at a stunning new hotel. Separate buildings, all with thatched roofs, connected by bridges and stairs, were at once primitive and elegant in feeling.

The Fiji men were very large and handsome. The one who carried our luggage was typical. From his Afro-style haircut to his waist, he was bare except for native necklaces and bracelets. As I remember, without having stared too hard, he wore a short-skirt thingamajig above massively beautiful legs. Bare feet completed his ensemble. I do remember lots of bronze skin.

We phoned our producer in Sydney and informed him about our luggage now in New Zealand, and he promised to have it for us when we arrived.

The trip from Nandi to Sydney was long. We got there after dark, and were met by our attractive, thirty-ish producer and his pretty secretary. We were ushered to a limousine and a fur lap robe was thrown over our knees, while the luggage from Nandi and New Zealand was stowed in the trunk.

As we drove up a hill to an apartment overlooking Elizabeth Bay, we were advised to sleep late, since there would be a cocktail party in the afternoon for us to meet the press and our cast.

The only problem with sleeping in our five-room apartment was that none of the draperies had arrived, and we lay staring at the lights on several war ships in the harbor. Then, when our excitement became exhaustion, our drooping eyes were snapped open by the sounds of martial music being played on the deck of one of the ships. This, we discovered, was a naval practice at 6 A.M. every single morning. We gave up and, prowling in the kitchen, found the cupboards and refrigerator, considerately stocked with everything we might need. So we had breakfast to the tune of "Waltzing Matilda," courtesy of the band below.

By that afternoon we had unpacked and met our second producer, a young Australian. A limousine took us to a reception set up in private rooms of a new hotel, where we met members of the press. Someone handed us drinks, and we were introduced to our cast. I had never heard so many Australian accents at once, and it was quite a shock.

The girl who was to play Eve was most attractive, accent and all, and I was told she had a terrific voice.

I had a greater shock when I was introduced to my leading man. I remembered that, in a long-distance conversation with our producer, I had mentioned being fairly tall. I now gazed at the man who was to play Bill and wished I'd kept my big mouth shut. They had overcompensated with a tall, dark, and handsome six-foot-seven! This could be a problem. (It was!)

I decided not to be judgmental and just to enjoy meeting everyone. I'd sort them out later.

We went back to the apartment in a nice glow at the warmth of our reception. The draperies hadn't arrived yet, but jet lag knocked us out and we slept.

The next morning we were taken to the rehearsal hall, and when we walked through the door, the chorus and cast burst into a spirited rendition of "Applause." It was very exciting.

The next couple of weeks were busy ones. We rehearsed dance numbers in the mornings, the book in the afternoons, and in the evenings we drove across a bridge to the home of the musical director to work on the songs.

When we had time, we had the cast come to our apartment to work on various scenes, as several of them hadn't done much stage work. Also a few were anxious to tone down their broad accents. They were long and exhausting days, but we were full of enthusiasm and they were all so anxious to do their best.

We had a little time when the choreographer was concentrating on chorus numbers, so Brooks and I took off in the car they'd provided for our use, to see some of Sydney.

About the only landmark we recognized was the famous Opera House that looked like a ship in full sail. I remembered that it had been greeted with ridicule when first built, even by Australians, but it was now admitted to be beautiful. I loved it, and we hoped to attend an opera or ballet there soon. I had begun to do TV and radio interviews. I appeared on the Australian version of "Hollywood Squares," and they presented me with a lovely blue-and-purple opal. But the day that remains the most vivid in my memory is one I was dreading—an appearance on TV with a man who had started as a real film buff and had developed his own popular program about film and film stars.

I had never seen too many of my pictures, because I couldn't be objective about myself, and I had no idea what agony I might be put through on his show. However, I not only watched clip after clip of my movies, along with stills from ones he hadn't been able to find clips for, but I sat astonished as one by one they rolled by and I enjoyed them, even *me*, thoroughly. We discussed each of them between clips, and memories of my co-workers and the films' directors poured forth.

What this man knew about movies put me to shame. He had a neat gimmick to make it more interesting. He'd say, "Now in this next scene, after Eve's line to Jack Carson, the door will open! See if you know the actor who enters." In scene after scene he would point out a bit player who became a star, or two players who later married or divorced, or a star who'd been the center of a scandal. I was as enthralled as his viewers. It was an afternoon that finally convinced me that I had contributed enough to the screen to justify the scripts that still called roles "an Eve Arden part."

One day our producer took me to see the scenery he'd designed that was now in production. Margo's apartment had an entry hall with a circular staircase of Lucite leading to her study above. This was a single unit on wheels, to be moved by pulleys. Her living room, also on casters, had a Lucite-and-chrome sofa with lush cushions of beige. Another section—a glittering bar—moved into center stage. Even in its incomplete state it was impressive. Since I was playing Margo (the Bette Davis part in the film *All About Eve* and Lauren Bacall's role on Broadway), I was interested to see Margo's dressing room and the night spot, patterned after Joe Allen's in New York City, where I was to dance.

I met the man who was to do my costumes, and saw sketches and chose material. The designer, Billy Gordon, had bought two small Victorian houses out of town. He'd painted them different colors with white gingerbread trim. We had our fittings out there, and I admired the houses and loved the five King Charles spaniel puppies in his backyard. The clothes he was making for me were theatrical and beautiful, and the fittings were a nice break in the day.

But I was getting worried about reaching Glenn by phone. We were nineteen hours ahead of California time, a whole day, really, and having a satisfactory business conversation, even if he could be reached, was difficult at best, and I didn't want to disturb him unnecessarily. Certain rumors were circulating among the chorus about the stability of our untried producers, and a suggestion that the "mechs" (short for mechanics and meaning stage hands) might strike. Also there was a strange hint that the producers had insured *Applause* with Lloyds of London, and would receive hundreds of thousands if the company closed. It seemed unlikely to us that Lloyds would insure anything as ephemeral as a theatrical production. But I did question the producers about the possibilities of strikes, and was laughingly told that the union was largely Communist, and because they were new producers, and in competition with the only big-time Australian producers, the "mechs" were giving them a hard time.

I thought, When Glenn arrives, he'll straighten it all out. Glenn had been assured of a round-trip ticket, and he planned to stay through Christmas with us. The ticket hadn't arrived, but there were weekly assurances that it would be there any day. There were requests from the producers for Glenn to speak to Joel Grey about doing *Cabaret* as their next production, and would Glenn please send them a couple of albums of that show.

We now moved rehearsals to the theater. It was in a newly renovated movie theater with red velvet seats, but it was a very long, narrow auditorium for a musical.

Suddenly rehearsals accelerated and unforeseen kinks developed. The gorgeous scenery on wheels proved extremely cumbersome to move. The mechs were grumbling that they needed more stage hands. Instead, the choreographer, who had whipped the chorus into difficult but effective routines, was asked to devise additional ones in which the boys would assist the hidden mechs to move the set pieces with ropes as they danced. It was now a question as to which group would strike first!

I was finding difficulty in adjusting to my leading man. As a person he was a darling, and tried desperately to please, but when he clasped me to his chest, my nose was pressed nearer his navel. I'd never felt so tiny in my life. Then, too, his forte was light opera, and these numbers were not easy for him. When he sang, his eyebrows pointed upward (he reminded me of Rudy Vallee) and gave him a pained expression.

When we started run-throughs with costumes, I remembered agreeing to some script tightening that had seemed plausible. Now, I found myself dashing offstage after "But Alive" and its strenuous dance routine, making an unusually fast change, and arriving onstage far too out of breath for my next number. Then there were problems with a drummer who had a particular niche down at stage left of the orchestra pit, which was where most of my numbers took place. He must have come from some out-of-work rock group. He was uninhibited and impossible to tone down or to move to any other spot.

I had been talked into making another mistake. The wig I had agreed to wear, out of pure vanity, was glamour personified, but made of real hair. I knew better, but they had persuaded me that my hairdresser was *the* best and would keep it in perfect condition. But at dress rehearsal, as I ran off after the first strenuous number, each lock of delicious red hair was a hank of dripping brown. The hairdresser did his best to restore it, but it never looked quite the same. I yearned for that dependable Lurex, which you could wring out night after night and which would immediately spring back into place.

I envied Brooks, because he had no numbers to sing, no wigs or drummers to worry about. He was so good in his part, and relished playing a villian for a change.

Opening night started with flowers, champagne, and good-luck kisses. The house was full of elegant people and everything went well. But when the Second Act started, there was no sign of air conditioning, and the audience was full of waving programs. Incidentally, they had spent a fortune on programs, with pictures of everyone right through the chorus members. There was a section of my movie stills, and another of "Eve's Family Album," with pictures of all of us aboard ship, Liza's wedding in Mallorca, our new grandson, and many others. I loved it, of course, but couldn't help thinking that it must be really hot in the audience to use those heavy programs as fans.

In spite of some opening-night gaffes, there were cheers and showstoppers, and after the performance we met an invited group from the audience at a large table of hors d'oeuvres and champagne onstage. There were some members of the ballet, and among them the male lead, who was the newest sensation, and who invited Brooks and me to come and see *The Merry Widow* when we had time.

The second night went much better, despite no improvement in air conditioning. The following morning the producer called and told us there would be no performance that night because the Board of Health had demanded that the air conditioning be repaired. The chorus would rehearse the new steps, which would assist the mechs to move the scenery.

So Brooks and I went to see a matinee of *The Merry Widow.* It was the most interesting ballet I'd ever seen, and even Brooks, not a ballet buff, was overwhelmed by the excitement of the production. We went backstage to thank our friend for the experience, and raved so much to our company that everyone was determined to see it.

That evening we invited the leading man out to dinner. His height and his opera training were still giving him problems and he was depressed, so we tried to make helpful suggestions over a glass or two of wine, and he cheered up.

The next day all hell broke loose. We were told by someone in the box office that all the cash being taken in for performances was being moved upstairs and locked in the producer's office. Only checks were left.

When we had inquired about our considerable salaries, we were told that the bank had forwarded the money to our bank in California. My husband astutely inquired at the Sydney bank, and found that no such large sum had gone forth from there.

When we were able to reach Glenn in the afternoon *our* time, we reached him the day *before* in the *morning!* He told us that he'd been assured by the producers that our salaries had been deposited in Sydney. This, combined with the fact that he was planning to leave daily, but still hadn't received his ticket, really alarmed him on our behalf. Like the song says, "Do nothing till you hear from me," he warned.

At the theater that night, we were told that the mechs had gone on strike and were threatening that worse was yet to come. To show how convincing our two young producers were (or how gullible we were?), even our musicians, a breed usually the last to take a chance with money, wanted to continue the show, saying they had faith in its having a long run.

While the mechs were arguing about closing the show, Brooks and I went out to talk to the waiting audience. We then introduced the cast and the chorus, and we all sang "Applause," accompanied by our loyal musicians. It was to no avail. The mechs turned out the lights on us. A disgruntled audience left, and found no box office open from which to demand their money back.

The next morning our charming producer called a rehearsal, and with the Actors Equity representative at hand, told us that problems with the theater management and the sound were forcing them to find a new theater to move us to, and that he already had a line on a better one. Then he called our attention to a

61. A portrait by the late John Engstead, my favorite photographer of the Golden Era of Films.

62. My one and only night club appearance.

63. Taken aboard the U.S.S. *Constitution* on our return from Europe.

64. With Liza on her wedding day.

65. Mr. and Mrs. Antonio Azcona cutting the cake at the wedding reception.

66. Leito

67. Estefania

68. Letty

In Mallorca waiting for the birth of our first grandchild.

70. Toñete, "La Force."

71. My son Douglas, now a writer, and daughter-in-law Carole, an executive, at Tavern on the Green in New York.

(*Left*) America, taken by Grandma.

72. Playwright Samuel Taylor provided some witty dialogue for Brooks and me in his play *Beekman Place,* but obviously actress Barbara Bergeray does think it's very funny.

73. A scene from *Beekman Place,* one of the many shows Brooks and I toured in.

74. The first episode of "The Mothers-in-Law." Kaye Ballard and I haven't enough sense to come in out of the rain.

75. A spoof on Wagner's *Valkyrie* from "The Mothers-in-Law."
The look of terror on Kaye Ballard's face is for real.

76, 77, 78. Stills from the National Company of *Hello Dolly* in Chicago 1966–67.

79. *Under the Rainbow.*

80. One of the few times I got my beloved Brooks to pose for a portrait with me.

81. On our first trip to Europe Brooks painted the Arc de
Triomphe and added our yellow Hillman Minx,
a balloon seller, an artist doing the scene, and me.

82. The lower third of the Eiffel Tower is a favorite
among Brooks's many paintings.

83. The magazine stand on the Via Veneto where we kept up daily with the news while in Italy.

84. The Queen's Band in winter.

telegram guaranteeing the mechs' salaries. Our problems seemed taken care of.

As I did my first number that night, the mike gave me trouble. I came offstage to find that the nice sound man, who had done the show in London and had been so complimentary about my performance when I needed it, had been fired because he was too expensive. So someone else was "doubling" in brass, and controlling the sound from the light booth out front!

At that moment for the first time I understood the actresses who threw tantrums and screamed offstage. But even if I'd wanted to, I couldn't reach that front booth to complain, and I also had to make my fast change.

When the show was over, we called everyone to our dressing room, and everyone came except the producers. The chorus boys complained that they couldn't dance and pull scenery as well. The mechs said, "We told you so!" and added that the reason the chorus was pulling scenery was that half the mechs had been fired. The chorus said they'd been handed pay checks postdated for after the weekend. We were told by a couple of the chorus who "knew" that a few of them wouldn't be able to eat until then. Before we left we called the "knowing" members to distribute some funds.

The next day was Armageddon. In the morning we got a call from the Fraud Squad, who asked to see us. It seemed a woman who had bought 380 or so tickets for a Red Cross benefit several weeks before had heard rumors of trouble with the production and tried to get the money refunded. She couldn't contact the producers. We told the detectives what we knew, and called a meeting at the theater with Equity. We learned that our producers, who were nowhere to be found, had persuaded the Equity agent not to demand a bond (unheard of!).

He apologized profusely and said, "They were so convincing."

Then a girl who had been acting as business manager for the pair spoke up and astonished us. She had worked for the Englishman on a production he'd done aboard a Russian boat. He'd used an alias, left the group stranded, and taken all the money. A year or so later, he'd called her to work on this project, and assured her she'd not only get back the salary he owed her, but a bonus besides. She was now holding three bad checks! We found that the costumer had been paid only for the materials he'd used, not labor.

When the meeting broke up, it was obvious that the show had closed. We sent for the theater owner, and although he, too, was owed money, he opened the dressing-room doors so that the chorus could get their things. Equity applied for union funds to pay the chorus members.

Brooks and I took only the freezer full of champagne that our generous producers had thrust on us and invited one and all to a farewell party that night.

As we left the stage door, the young girl who'd sold tickets in the box office, and who was the sister of the Australian producer, threw her arms around my neck weeping, and said, "If you can't trust your own brother, who can you trust?" I truly felt sorry for her and invited her to join the party.

When we got home we had calls from all the newspapers and TV stations. We found that the "swag men" had been indicted but were out on bail.

The entire cast and some of the crew arrived at seven, and although we had plenty of liquor and food, they all brought wine and beer and more food, and someone contributed a luscious Australian pastry called a Pavlova. It was a great party. We toasted our entrepreneurs in hilarious terms, and at 2 A.M. we pushed the last of a weeping group out the door. This was the hardest part, as we'd grown fond of them all.

Then we sat and assessed our feelings about what had happened. The money we'd been supposed to earn we hadn't lost because it was totally unreal to us. The reality was we'd had a round-trip ticket to a place we might never had seen otherwise, and six weeks in a lovely apartment. We talked of all the friends we'd made and things we'd seen. I said, "I can't go home without seeing a koala bear." So the next morning we took a ferry to the zoo and saw not only koalas, but kangaroos and a duck-billed platypus.

That afternoon a man rang our bell and asked if he could talk to us. We'd met him opening night. He was one of the backers and just couldn't understand how this could happen. He said they'd asked him for more money, so we figured they'd been underfunded from the beginning. He seemed so disappointed in them, said they'd been such "nice young fellas."

We packed, then went to see about our tickets. Brooks said, "Do you know, it would only cost us five hundred more to go home by Hong Kong, Japan, and Hawaii." What a marvelous idea! We left Sydney the next day, and there at the airport was our cast bearing gifts: beautiful books of the Australian myths, which everyone had signed. One boy, who I knew could ill afford it, gave us a book in gorgeous color of the Australian forests and birds.

The press arrived along with lights and TV cameras. We submitted to an interview or two but hoped they'd all go away so we could be with our cast. I went to the lounge, but no one left, and I pulled myself together and came out to shoo the cameras away so we could say good-bye to all of them—Judi Conelli, who sang "Eve" with such a thrilling voice—Jon, my tall leading man—Dolores Ernst, the head "gypsy" who stopped the show with "Applause" —even some of the mechs and musicians.

Ron Challinor, who was so funny as Duane, Margo's hairdresser, came up to us and said, "I finally went to see *The Merry Widow* last night, and it was terrific—but guess what. In the entr'acte my friend said, 'Well, look who's here!' I turned around and there, arm and arm with their secretary, were our newly indicted producers. Can you believe it?" I could!

They all walked us to the aircraft gate. We were sad to leave them, but what an experience. A first for us!

CHAPTER
· 35 ·

After doing a segment of "Maude" in early 1977, Brooks and I went east to try out a new play for a couple of weeks at The Little Theater on the Square in Illinois.

When we got back I found that I'd been cast, in the newspapers at least, in a movie called *Grease.* Neither my manager nor I had heard anything about it, and since I'd seen the musical in New York, I knew that there was no part that Eve Arden could play. However, Allen Carr, who was producing it, insisted that there would be. He and the director and casting director came to see me in a few days, but with only one idea. I would play a principal called Miss McGee (shades of "Miss Brooks"!). But as we talked, a few ideas popped up, and it sounded like fun. At least it was a promotion!

They had John Travolta, whom I'd seen in *The Boy in the Bubble* and *Saturday Night Fever,* who was both talented and sexy; Olivia Newton-John, a charming Australian, who went from sweet to sexy in the script; and Stockard Channing, whom I'd thought a very talented comedienne in *The Fortune,* with Warren Beatty and Jack Nicholson. It augured well for the picture, so I decided to take a chance with Miss McGee.

Grease was a wild and wonderful experience and I was sure the picture would be a hit—but how could I know that it would become the top-grossing musical of all time!

During the making of *Grease* I left the house early each day for the location, a school south of Los Angeles, and usually returned after seven each night. I could tell after a few weeks that Brooks had begun to drink again, but even though I asked him to drink in front of me, he refused. I knew through his anger that it was serious.

This time I was inspired to ask someone for help whom I'd known for years, but who had recently admitted in print that she'd overcome a drinking problem in AA. Jan Lerner had lost a beautiful young daughter in a senseless car accident many years before. Her retreat into alcohol had led to an addiction. Jan was very helpful and encouraged me to take several steps, so a week later I got ready to leave the house after dinner, telling Brooks that I'd be back in a couple of hours. Startled, Brooks looked up from a crossword puzzle and asked where I was going. I told him I was going to attend an Alanon Meeting.

The meeting was fascinating and the people even more so. All of them related in some way to a person having a problem with alcohol. As I listened to others' experiences with the results of this really deadly disease, I could only be grateful for what we'd escaped so far. Alanon convinced me that I needed to change my protective attitude toward Brooks and even our children and to turn my attention to my own problems.

It had only taken two evenings of my attendance to convince Brooks that he must need help. Then we attended an AA meeting together and heard one of our loveliest actresses tell a harrowing story of her fight against alcohol. That afternoon we made arrangements for Brooks to enter the Glendale Memorial Hospital three days later. We agreed on that day since he wanted us to spend our anniversary together the night before.

Although Brooks had attended the Science of Mind Church with me several times and seemed to enjoy the service (I think mostly because he was so intrigued by its informality, and by hearing laughter in a church) he was still resisting AA. But he and I did attend the meetings in the hospital.

On the night we had an invitation to a party at Olivia Newton-John's ranch in the Malibu hills, Brooks insisted that I go, as we were both very fond of Olivia. So I made an excuse for his absence and took our friend Marge. It was a beautiful party, and when I saw all the animals that Olivia had in the hills surrounding her home, I felt a terrible pang for Westhaven, and the thought of Brooks alone in the hospital was even harder to bear. I wished then, for the first time, that we could turn back the years and use the knowledge we'd gained to handle our problems better.

We had a contract pending to do our new play, *The Most Marvelous News,* in October. We hoped to be with Liza in Spain for the birth of her second child in December. I was worried about Brooks's recovery, but he was making fast progress and was, as usual, adored by the unit and nurses alike. I thought about what a great doctor he would have made. He always seemed to inject those around him with such hope and even a sense of fun with their struggle. Now, with a play to look forward to, a trip to Spain and a new baby in the family, he was eager to be on his way.

We picked up our script for *The Most Marvelous News,* and agreed to play four weeks only. After the problem of Toñete's birth we wanted to be there for this baby, too.

Then I got word that Columbia Broadcasting System was celebrating its fiftieth birthday and my presence was requested on December 1. On December 5 I finished a number with Dick Crenna and Gale Gordon, and rushed home to call Liza and tell her that we were flying to London and then Palma to be with her.

The number rang in Palma and an unfamiliar, high-pitched voice answered. I inquired for Liza Azcona and the voice broke into such a torrent of Spanish that I couldn't grasp a word. The Palma operator, trying to be helpful, only complicated matters with her Spanish, and then admitted she was Italian. So I tried again. I then heard *"enferma"* (ill).

"Liza es en hospital?" I asked.

Suddenly, breakthrough. *"Usted es su madre?"*

"Sí," I gasped, *"Por favor, el nombre de hospital?"*

I got one number, but my helpful operator got a different one, and she was stubborn. She tried her number first. Only after a male voice denied any connection with the hospital did she call mine. The voice that answered gave the name of the hospital. The only problem was that the name "Azcona" meant nothing to the nun in charge.

"Momento." And I was left alone on the wire for minutes that seemed like hours. Suddenly, she was back. *"Perdone, pero no Laisa Azcona."* Then, as I was going under for the third time, I heard a tentative *"Laisa Owest?"*

*"Oui—sí—*yes!" I shouted, and Brooks joined me on the kitchen extension.

"Of course," he yelled. "I remember from the last time that mothers are always registered under their maiden name." We held our breaths until the *teléfono* rang in the distance.

"Dígame," said a sleepy voice, recognizable as Antonio's. Our Spanish had deserted us completely, and in our anxiety we interrupted each other.

"Antonio, is Liza all right?"

"Is she in labor?"

"What is happening?"

It was nine hours later in Palma, about one-thirty in the morning, and understandably Antonio reverted to his native tongue. *"Laisa está vale."*

We breathed easier, and then realized what he meant.

"She's had the baby already?"

"Sí."

"And how's the baby?" we yelled.

"Está bien," he said and added, *"es una niña."*

A girl! Our secret hope fulfilled.

"What's her name?"

Liza had begged us to help with boys' names. "Carlos," we'd suggested. "Eduardo." "Marco." But she'd declined any ideas for a girl's name. We felt it was because she'd really wanted a girl and was perhaps a little superstitious.

Antonio didn't answer my question, but his English returned.

"Jost wan meenute," he said.

A groggy voice asked, "Mom? Dad?" The greetings over with, I asked:

"When did you have the baby?"

There was an aggrieved tone in her voice as she replied, "I don't know, Mom. I just woke up!"

It isn't often a mother gets to tell her daughter: "You've had a baby girl, dear."

She seemed stunned.

"Go back to sleep, honey, and we'll call you day after tomorrow from London."

But a thrilled grandmother couldn't hang up without asking that important question: "What's her name?"

A slight hesitation, then she answered proudly, "America." And with a tired sigh she hung up.

Our first reaction was disbelief. As we recovered from our surprise, however, we remembered Liza's constant questions about her country. She loved Spain and her life there, and Antonio's family who'd accepted her with such warmth; but as her exploration and consequent appreciation of Spain grew, so did her interest in her own country and what was going on there. It was hard to understand riots and drugs, and Nixon and Watergate.

"Mom and Dad, I have to know how I can explain these things to my Spanish friends!"

We tried to help by keeping her informed with *Time* and *Newsweek,* and bolstered her pride with questions.

"Can you think of any other countries where these things would be allowed to be printed or broadcast? Do you think Spain (then under Franco) and Russia don't have scandals as bad or worse?"

As she listened to the Watergate hearings, her head rose higher.

A couple of years later, she'd brought her son to Texas, where we were doing a play, and Brooks's family in Austin celebrated Thanksgiving with us. Antonio then joined us for Christmas at home and she'd had the joy of showing him her own country, at least from Los Angeles to San Francisco, with a bit of Las Vegas and the San Diego Zoo and, of course, Disneyland. Then at Christmas, with the whole family gathered, she'd confided to me in a quiet moment: "I love my country so much!"

So here we were with a new granddaughter named America, a tribute to her mother's love for the land of her birth.

Soon we were on our way to New York with two thrills ahead. We were flying to London on the Concorde, and when we got on board we were on our way to see "America"!

Since I first set eyes on that elegant bird called the Concorde, I knew I had to fly in her. This from a gal who had entrained her whole family countless times across country on the *Chief* and *Super Chief,* and always went by ship to Europe until she overcame her fear of flying.

As we waited in the British Special Lounge for the Concorde flight, we were told we would board two by two. Not until we walked down a ramp past a window did we see her. What a surprise! In the distance were the great 747s taxiing by, and below us sat our delicate bird, so little! No wonder we had to enter two by two.

I thought about the claustrophobia I still occasionally felt, but now there was no apprehension, only excitement. To think we'd be reaching London in an unbelievable three and a half hours! We bent low to enter the plane. Our British attendants welcomed us aboard and aimed us down the narrow aisle to our seats mid-plane.

When I saw the tiny porthole-like windows, I had a bad moment, but once installed in our comfortable seats with hand luggage stowed and coats wisked away by an affable Englishman, I began to relax.

The narrowness of the aisle fostered a convivial atmosphere, and as the steward passed champagne, caviar, pâté, and other hors d'oeuvres, the friendly conversation started. It stopped suddenly when the flight attendant carried in a huge stuffed dog, sat it in the window seat ahead of me, and placed a guitar on its lap. He assured the startled seat-mate on the aisle that "its" fare had been paid. There was laughter and speculation. We figured only a rock star or an oil sheikh could afford a special delivery like that.

We were silenced with the revving of the motors. Seat belts were fastened, including the dog's. As we took off, I remembered the sight on TV of the Concorde's steep upsweep, and was surprised to feel much less of an angle than I expected.

In no time we were being served an elegant dinner. We watched the mach meter on the wall, which already registered mach 1 (meaning we were doing about 670 miles an hour). It crept up to mach 1.5 (1,000 miles an hour).

At an altitude between 50,000 and 60,000 feet, with only a slight jolt at our backs, we reached mach 2 (1,310 miles an hour). The only difference Brooks noticed was that it was noisier than the 747.

Just after dark, the head flight attendant came to me and asked if we'd like to visit the flight deck. Evidently this was a little VIP attention our travel agent had arranged. We followed him down the narrow aisle and entered the tri-cornered room covered with banks of lights. Three men, obviously pilots and navigator, looked up and nodded pleasantly at our introduction.

My claustrophobia gave a gasp in this small space, as I looked frantically for windows. I could find only two small, black eyes by the corner of what obviously was the bird's beak. We were happy to return to our seats.

We reached London exactly as scheduled in three and a half hours. However, we had lost five hours difference in time, so it was 9:30 P.M. in England. On our return flight we left London at noon and arrived in New York at 10:30 A.M.—*before we left!*

When we called Liza from London the next morning, she told us that in spite of the difficulty of Toñete's birth, ending in a cesarean, America's had been a quick and easy natural birth. Spain was several years ahead of the United States, which was still proceeding on the theory of once a cesarean, always a cesarean.

Liza said she'd be going home in a couple of days, but suggested we enjoy them in London, as she was breaking in a new maid (the one with the high, squeaky voice) and wanted us to meet our new grandchild in an orderly house.

Four days was all we could wait to cuddle an adorable America and a four-year-old handsome Toñete.

We had planned to stay with Liza and her family through Christmas, but America's christening was to follow, and I was her godmother, as Brooks was Toñete's godfather, so we extended our stay.

Liza told me that America had to have her ears pierced before the christening. I was so horrified that Liza dropped the subject until the event was only two days away. Then she said nervously, "Mom, all little Spanish girls have their ears pierced this young." I agreed to drive them to the hospital and furnish the first gold studs, but absolutely would not watch the deed done! Aurora, Liza's midwife, who had again assisted Dr. Lizarbe, laughed at my expression as she took the baby from my arms, and I fled to the farthest end of the hall. There a workman was breaking open a wall with a sledgehammer. That's good, I thought. I can't hear anything with that racket. Two minutes later he took a break. That was when America yelled.

She happily recovered, and at her christening received a tiny pair of diamond earrings from her godfather, Uncle Leo, and from others, a wardrobe of earrings: pearl, diamond, and gold.

In her proud godmother's arms she dazzled the guests at the christening and God blessed America.

In January Brooks started lithographs of two of his paintings. The studio where he was to learn the process was in San Francisco, so we spent two weeks in Berkeley with the Raffettos, and while I was doing some writing Brooks commuted back and forth.

In February I started a play by the English playwright Alan Ayckbourn. While living in London, we'd seen most of his plays and I'd written him my one and only fan letter. I was delighted, therefore, when the Ahmanson Theater in Los Angeles asked me to do eight weeks of his *Absurd Person Singular*. The cast was excellent, including John McMartin, whom I greatly admired, to play my husband, and Stockard Channing from *Grease*, who played an hilarious cockney lady who cleaned everyone else's kitchens.

On opening night I arrived to find my newly decorated dressing room filled with flowers, and a tall Benjamina Ficus tree in a basket. I was thrilled, and read the card: "Love from Allen Carr," producer of *Grease*, of course! Then I read above it: "Stockard Channing." So I reluctantly dragged the whopping tree down the hall to Stockard's dressing room. In her room was a twin tree and this one said: "For Eve. Love, Allen Carr." So down the hall I happily dragged my own gorgeous tree.

I had always hoped for an eight-week engagement at the Ahmanson. The only trouble with this one was that Los Angeles was having "unusual weather," and this was more like a monsoon. I drove through downpours each night and finally a mudslide covered half of the freeway. The detour I had to take home was in an unfamiliar part of town where I constantly got lost. But I did enjoy the play, the cast, and having my family and friends out front and visiting me backstage.

During one of these visits, Brooks and I learned that Douglas, our youngest (could he possibly be twenty-four?), and Carole Coates were going to be married on April 15. They had met in college, where she had played Desdemona to Doug's Othello, with this result. Her family planned to have a large reception at the Bel Air Hotel. The bride and groom wanted a quiet family wedding first, at our home. We were delighted! Duncan had been married in the Fort Ord Chapel and Liza in Spain. This one would be in front of our fireplace.

The ordained minister was a woman, a friend of Doug's and Carole's. The bride's two sisters, almost as beautiful as she was, were bridesmaids. Doug's sister Connie, another bridesmaid, read one of Shakespeare's sonnets, and the fourth bridesmaid had arrived the day before from Mallorca, carrying in a basket four-and-a-half-month-old America! "She wasn't going to miss her uncle's wedding," said Liza firmly.

The wedding was what every mother imagines for her child, and, as I heard the vows, I realized that in a short span of time I had become a grandmother, a godmother, and a mother-in-law.

In November I was asked to do *Critic's Choice* in a large new theater in Long Beach. The play, by New York critic Walter Kerr, was a good one and the cast was excellent, with Ed Nelson, Eleanor Ackerman, Rue McLanahan, and others. During the eight weeks I commuted to do the show, we were building a new room and bath on the house. Now that we had a new grandchild, we needed more room for visits from Spain.

In the spring I received a script for a "Love Boat." It was a good one and when I accepted I found it was one to be done on board the Princess Line as it sailed down to Acapulco. The cast, besides regulars, included Loni Anderson, Rich Little, Slim Pickens, and Donny Osmond, and all the husbands and wives of the cast were invited to go along. It was a pleasant experience and prepared us for a cruise we'd already signed up for with the L.A. Museum.

Then in June we flew to Venice and introduced our cruise companions to Gianni Giovanni, our favorite gondolier. Two days later we boarded a Greek ship and sailed to Dubrovnik, the fabulous fortress in Yugoslavia. It was a trip that touched at Corfu in Greece, Tunis in Africa, the island of Malta, until recently an English possession, Elba, Napoleon's first exile, then Portofino in Italy, and Monaco. I made a quick TV appearance with Mike Douglas at a Princess Grace Tennis Tournament, where Sean Connery was playing, along with Princess Caroline and Prince Albert. That was the formal end of our trip, but as usual, Brooks and I added a side trip to see our grandchildren in Palma and a week in Paris to be alone.

In 1980 I was invited to appear on the Antoinette Perry Awards, informally known as the Tonys in New York City. Even though it had been years since I was tempted to do a play on Broadway, I was delighted to be asked. The Tonys is always such a well-produced show that I welcomed the chance to appear and also to see some theater while I was there. This time Douglas and his wife went with us. Carole had never seen New York, so her excitement was added to ours.

Our daughter Connie, who'd become an extraordinary designer, with her clothes admired by Edith Head, Jean Louis, and Bob Mackie, created a beautiful costume for me to wear, from an ancient Japanese obi combined with beige Alix jersey. So I was a proud mother indeed when, later on, even people on the street asked me, "Who did that beautiful outfit you were wearing?"

The theme of the Tonys that year was "Understudies." Carol Channing, who'd been my understudy in *Let's Face It*, told of going on for me in a matinee (the only performance I had ever missed in the theater) and being fired immediately because she did a "scat" version of my duet with Danny Kaye. I was back in the show that evening because Danny objected to her mimicry of him. Then she introduced me, saying that I had taken over for her in *Hello, Dolly!* when she left Chicago. I was amazed to receive a very warm ovation from the audience. It made me feel a part of Broadway again. I told of understudying Fanny Brice, playing Baby Snooks on Fanny's only missed performance.

Evita was the big winner of the Tonys that year. I personally was happy to see Dinah Manoff, who'd been in *Grease* with me, win a Tony for her first Broadway appearance in *I Ought to Be In Pictures*. It was a wonderful trip for us, and ended for me with a Dick Cavett interview.

In June, Brooks and I joined Donald O'Connor in the musical *Little Me* in Dallas. Brooks played Patrick Dennis, the author of *Auntie Mame* and *Little Me*, interviewing Belle Poitrine (me) about her life, while the young Belle (Sandy Bernard) enacted her romances, with Donald playing seven diverse roles. It was a tour de force for Donald. We had a wonderful young company of singers and dancers and were directed by the talented Lucia Victor. We rehearsed in Dallas, and played there for two weeks—in 114-degree temperature every day! Fortunately the theater was thoroughly air-conditioned.

From there we flew to St. Louis the morning after closing in Dallas. We had to open that same night at the St. Louis Municipal Opera, an enormous outdoor theater.

The stage there is so huge that we knew we'd have to adjust to larger strides between entrances and exits—and a fifty-yard dash backstage for quick changes. But our hope for an afternoon rehearsal was squelched by a thunderstorm and driving rain, so we gathered in a covered rehearsal room for a run-through of music cues for the orchestra, then went back to our hotel to unpack and grab a sandwich to sustain us.

We went back to the theater, expecting to be dismissed, as a heavy sprinkle was still falling. To our astonishment, we found an almost full parking lot, with people walking toward the amphitheater wearing yellow slickers and mackintoshes and carrying cushions and umbrellas. We were told that the audiences in St. Louis were so used to weather that nothing as simple as rain could keep them away.

At eight o'clock the rain had stopped, and we opened with no rehearsal to over twelve thousand people, all of us nervously praying that we'd find the right entrances and exits.

Brooks, looking very elegant in his dark suit, was the only casualty. A quart or two of water suddenly descended on him from some moving scenery as he was about to make the first entrance of the show. The cold water was a shock, but his suit just looked a little darker than usual. For the rest of the week there was no rain, but very high humidity, and every night a full moon beamed down on full audiences. We moved to Orlando, where we were told about a race riot only blocks from the theater, but were not aware of it. Then to Atlanta for our final week, where everything was comparatively calm, and where we ended our run with a gala closing-night party, and the usual regrets at parting.

Brooks and I had signed to do six weeks of a new play in October, but I was sent a script for a movie in preparation. It was very funny and intrigued me, so we took advantage of a cancellation clause in the play and I agreed to become the Duchess of Luchow in the movie of *Under the Rainbow*.

I had an eight-week guarantee on the picture starting in October, so when the management of the Earl Holliman Theater in San Antonio, Texas, wanted to reschedule our play, *A Single Indiscretion*, for February, this time with no cancellation clause, we felt perfectly free to agree. The movie was to star Chevy Chase and Carrie Fisher, and Joe Mahar, a Tony-winning New York actor, was to be my Duke of Luchow. There were also 150 adorable "little people" in the movie.

We started filming in late October, with Joe and me, as the Duke and Duchess, arriving in New York aboard the *Queen Mary*, being met by a young FBI man, Chevy Chase, who was to be our bodyguard on the train trip to Los Angeles. We shot the scene in the actual Royal Suite of the *Queen Mary* (now permanently docked in Long Beach).

As I finished my first scene, Steve Rash, our director, said, "While you are waiting for the next setup, go and relax in either one of the bedroom suites."

Something seemed to guide me to the suite on the left, and when I entered it, I was stricken with a powerful sense of déjà vu. It was the same suite Brooks and I had had on our first trip to Europe aboard the *Queen Mary* in 1953! I suppose, since royalty didn't travel that often by sea, the bedroom suites were "let" now and then. It was one of the pleasantest engagements I'd ever had, and eventually one of the longest.

In December, having little remaining to do, I gave a party for the group. In January I was still waiting to do a few lines here and there.

Then the company moved to the Columbia Ranch to do outdoor scenes while the weather was good. I was getting very nervous, as I was due in San Antonio on February 4 for rehearsals. They finally quieted my protests by saying that I'd be able to fly up on my first Monday off after the opening of my show on February 20.

But in the middle of rehearsals, my manager was told that since they'd never taken me off salary, I was obliged to finish the picture when they needed me, and that they would need me two days in a row for a few weeks. I was now in the twentieth week of *Under the Rainbow*.

I had never had to cancel a performance in the theater, but Earl Holliman and his partner, Pat Bauldauf, understood the situation I was in and arranged to cancel three Tuesday performances, for which I reimbursed them. Fortunately the play was doing good business.

Brooks and I opened on Friday the twentieth, played two shows on Saturday and one on Sunday. On Monday morning I took a seven o'clock plane to Los Angeles, arriving at nine-thirty. Terry, my studio driver, picked me up and drove me to the studio and I was ready to work by eleven and worked until eight-thirty that night. I spent that night in my own home, oh bliss! I worked all day Tuesday, and then took the plane to San Antonio, where Brooks picked me up around eleven in the evening.

Wednesday was our matinee day. I'd been experiencing a strange phenomenon in my right eye for several days. Silver circles appeared and disappeared. It was only disconcerting when it happened on stage and it wasn't painful, but we decided I should have it examined. We found a well-recommended opthalmologist, Dr. Braverman, in San Antonio. On Thursday morning I went to see him in his hospital office. Dr. Braverman, charming and solicitous, asked me to lie down on one of those high black leather tables. Then he put a black glove on his hand and stood above me. Suddenly I was in the middle of a horror film. The glove had a steel hook on the forefinger. The hook descended and picked up my eyelid. The doctor stared into my eye with some kind of magnifying device, and now I felt the hook lifting my eyeball!

When I am confronted with sheer terror, my impulse is to laugh. As I tried to control myself, I was aware that the doctor, in the midst of his gruesome task, was quietly humming a happy little tune.

Fortunately he ceased his probing and its musical accompaniment before I broke into hysterical laughter. A few minutes later I was completely sobered by his words. He said he'd hoped to have good news for me, but that he'd found two tiny holes in the retina of my right eye, plus a small tear on the edge from which the jellylike lining was threatening to escape.

Nervously I asked what should be done and when. He answered that it should be done as soon as possible, that he would treat the tiny holes with a laser beam, and since the tear could not be reached with the straight laser, it would need to be frozen.

I saw no sense in putting it off, so, moving into his operating room next door, I now found myself sitting in a chair with my head in a metal frame that clamped my forehead against a leather cushion and rested my chin on a leather cup from which there was no escape.

I had heard that laser beams were not painful, so I was relieved when four white flashes left me with no sensation. The fifth one would have sent me through the ceiling if I hadn't been strapped in.

"What was that?!" I demanded, shaken.

The doctor explained that "it" had hit a nerve. It was too late to back out, so for the next endless hour or so, "nerves" seemed to predominate.

The freezing I don't remember, it was such a relief when the laser zaps stopped.

We went back to our apartment, and I rested until it was time to leave for the theater. When I looked into the mirror, instead of my right eye I saw a glistening cherry tomato! At the theater I put on my makeup and an extra-heavy pair of eyelashes, and the consensus was that I could get by with it. Evidently I did, since no one demanded his money back, and the show got just as many laughs. But the eye stayed a brilliant red through my next pilgrimage to the studio. The director, realizing that the color might show on screen, put me as far from the camera as possible, while we all waved good-bye to a character who was driving away.

When I left for San Antonio Tuesday night, I was told that they would now need me on Thursday after my matinee day, but would try to finish my role by that night. I was furious at all that meant in the way of rearrangements for the theater—rescheduling the canceled Tuesday performance and canceling a sold-out Thursday show.

I said they'd bloody well better finish me Thursday night, as I was not about to cancel a Friday performance, which was always sold out. When I flew up and started work on Thursday I was pretty tense, as shooting seemed to move very slowly. So when Chevy Chase came on the set and said, "Hey, did you hear about some guy taking hostages on a Continental plane? I think that was the plane you came in on, Eve," I laughed and said, a bit testily, "Enough, Chevy. I'm in no mood for jokes today!" Chevy, a tease as well as a comedian, looked hurt and said, "I'm not kidding!" Then, as the director's wife, Maggie Rash, came on the set, he said, "Maggie will tell you. She was watching the TV too."

Maggie said that a man had stepped into the first-class section on the Continental plane and taken the stewardess hostage. Then, since there was no one else in that section, he'd taken the entire economy class hostage as well. Sure enough, it was the plane from San Antonio. Since I'd been the only passenger in first class that morning, I'd obviously stepped off just before he'd stepped on!

All day we listened to reports on the hostage situation, until eight o'clock that night, when I finished my last line on *Rainbow* and heard the hostages being interviewed on radio as I was driven back to our house.

Friday morning I boarded the San Antonio plane and gave a sigh of relief. I still had a red eye, but it seemed as if my problems were over. Three hours later we hadn't taken off yet, and I was told that since they couldn't fix something on the plane, they would put me on a plane to Houston. Houston! From there they'd get me on a plane for San Antonio.

In Houston I was paged and answered a call from Brooks. He was concerned about how I felt. How was my eye? he asked.

"Just pink now," I said, adding that if I could ward off a nervous breakdown, and if they could get me on a Texas International plane, I would arrive about seven.

He said not to worry, that Pat would hold the curtain, and he would be at the airport at seven. At last I got on an extremely crowded plane that *did* arrive at seven and the curtain rose on time.

From then on, our last weeks in San Antonio were relaxed and pleasurable, with one experience that made up for a lot of the difficulties. We were taken to meet the owners and the young trainer of Cass Ole, the black stallion from the movie of that name.

As far as I was concerned, it was the best picture of that year, and I jumped at the chance to meet its hero. In the field stood this beautiful, ebony animal. His young blond trainer had learned to control him with a flick of her whip, and he came trotting up to meet us.

This was breeding time for the owner's stable, and Cass Ole was "at stud" for seven mares, yet he was gentle enough to let all of us stroke him and have pictures taken with him.

He loved to tease his trainer, and occasionally would seem to say, "Enough of this," and run kicking down the field, but would docilely return and kneel when she asked him.

We hated to leave him, but were offered the pleasure of seeing about six of his colts, all black except for the youngest. He was tan. He was also the friskiest. While the rest of our cast moved on to the next stall, I waited with my hand out as he skittered away, then, to my delight, put his trembling chin into my cupped hand. He ran away again, kicking up his heels. When he returned he once more put his chin in my hand and stood looking at me trustfully for a minute. I felt as if I'd been knighted.

CHAPTER
·36·

In 1981, Liza, Antonio, and our grandchildren arrived to help celebrate our thirtieth anniversary. Toñete, now dark-haired and very handsome, and seven years old, and America, an adorable three and a half, were excited, but the visit began traumatically as our Spanish had disappeared and the kids refused to speak English. The obligatory trip to Disneyland followed, and when we got back Liza took a sentimental trip out to Westhaven alone. We had almost repossessed our farm several times and had recently been informed that a buyer had been found and we would be receiving cash for the first mortgage we still held, but no one was to know the buyer's name.

Secrets are hard to keep, however, and we learned who it was from another real estate man on the very day Liza drove out there. Meeting the caretaker at the gate, she asked if she could just walk through and see it once more, as she'd grown up there. He gallantly said of course and added, "I guess you know that it now belongs to Sophia Loren and Carlo Ponti?"

It was fascinating to think of it going from a hideaway for English Ronald Colman to a farmhouse that nourished our American family, and now a place of discovery for Sophia's two young Italian boys.

Brooks and I celebrated our thirtieth wedding anniversary with Liza and Antonio, Doug and Carole and Connie. On the Azconas' return to Spain, I began to reprise Miss McGee in *Grease II*. This time the director was Pat Burch, who'd been choreographer on the first *Grease,* and I was delighted for her. I missed John Travolta and Olivia Newton-John, but the new young cast was very good, and I was reunited with Dodie Goodman and Sid Caesar who were both in the first *Grease.* Sid told us that he became literally a new man after giving up drinking.

During two weeks off I had at Christmas, Brooks and I decided to take a Caribbean cruise. It was pleasant enough, but what really excited us was seeing a film in the ship's theater of Isaac Stern's trip to China called *From Mao to Mozart*. It had won an award, but we had never happened to see it.

I had met Isaac Stern years before at a party at Arthur Rubinstein's and thought him charming, but this film of his trip through China, meeting the young musicians of China, playing for them, hearing them play, and communicating through his warmth and his genius, was a revelation. It not only made us lifetime fans of his, but started us thinking of a trip to China.

Brooks and I had just finished our "Garden Project," which had grown from a simple lath house to a splendid creation of pergolas with patterns of white lath. A red brick floor with open spaces held plantings of impatiens, and completing its glory were hanging baskets of fuchsias and ferns.

When we'd finished lighting the garden and its new additions, we decided it was time to give that special party we'd wanted to have for a long time. We invited everyone available from the casts of "Our Miss Brooks" and "The Mothers-in-Law," and that evening there was Walter Denton in the person of Dick Crenna, with his wife Penni, and Mr. Boynton, whose real name is Robert Rockwell, with his wife Betts.

Missing was our famous principal, Mr. Conklin, as the wonderful Gale Gordon was appearing in a play in Toronto. But Gloria McMillan, the girl who played Harriet Conklin, his daughter, was with us, and so was Miss Enright, my rival for Mr. Boynton. She was Mary Jane Croft, and her husband Elliot Lewis, who had directed "The Mothers-in-Law," stood nearby talking to motion-picture director Hy Averback and his wife Dorothy.

Richard Deacon, previously in the "Dick Van Dyke Show" and then in "The Mothers-in-Law" as Kaye Ballard's husband, brought actress Jane Dulo, who had now and then appeared in both my series. Kaye Ballard was at that time appearing in New York in *The Pirates of Penzance,* so wasn't able to be with us. The writers of "The Mothers-in-Law," Madelyn Davis and Bob Carroll, who had also done all the "Lucy" shows and were now executive producers of "Alice" and "Private Benjamin," were ordering drinks in the pergola with Madelyn's husband, Dr. Dick Davis.

All of the guests were friends of long standing, including Larry

Gelbart and his wife Pat, who were living in London when we spent a year there. Larry, of course, is best known as the writer of the more than popular "M*A*S*H" TV series.

Rounding out the reunion were Herb Rudley, my husband from "The Mothers-in-Law," his real-life wife Marilyn, and Maurice Marsac with his wife Melanie. Maurice had played the French teacher that Miss Brooks had used to make Mr. Boynton jealous, and he had very recently done a play with us in San Antonio.

The weather was glorious. The city formed a glittering carpet below us and the guests held drinks and talked animatedly. I walked across the lawn to chat with Penni Crenna, delighted that this was one of those happy evenings when everyone knew one another and was glad to renew old friendships.

As I reached Penni, the view of the city below us began to whirl, the lights became a blur, and I fainted for the first time in my life! I came to with Dr. Davis taking my pulse and saying, "Stay right where you are," as I struggled to sit up. "I couldn't get any pulse at all," Dr. Davis said.

My son Doug was holding my other hand as Brooks brought me an icy cloth. I felt fine, just silly, as Dr. Davis finally allowed me to sit up, and Dick Crenna behind me said, "I make a fine back rest."

The party, which had come to a screeching halt, gradually regained momentum as the hostess seemed to recover. Only Dr. Davis wasn't satisfied, but he permitted me to sit at one of the round party tables on the terrace as dinner was served. He sat beside me and asked, "Is it true that you and Brooks are leaving on a trip to China in less than two weeks?" I said that it was. Dick said, "Don't you dare leave before your doctor gives you all the tests she thinks necessary."

I laughed and said, "Dick, I'm sure that this was nothing more than pure euphoria at having so many dear friends all together." But I assured him that I'd go to my doctor, Elsie Giorgi, the next week. I enjoyed the rest of my party enormously as I think the guests did too.

After Dr. Giorgi's tests she said, "I can't find a damn thing wrong." However, she sent me to an otolaryngologist (whew!) to test my ears. This took two days and ended with warm and then cold water running in and out of them.

When I went back for the results, Dr. Hutcherson looked at me accusingly and said, "You hear better than I do!" He told me that there was nothing wrong with me and that I should forget about it. Should I take along pills for vertigo? I asked. His advice was, "Don't take anything. It will never happen again." He agreed with me that it was probably "pure euphoria."

A week later we flew to San Francisco and the next day took off for China. China is worthy of a whole book on its own. Suffice it to say that I came through the fabulous three-week trip with flying colors, although losing twenty-odd pounds because I couldn't eat the constant banquets they served us.

Soon after our return from China I received two offers from New York. One was from the distinguished director George Abbott. It was for a revival of *On Your Toes.* I was sure it would be a success with him at the helm, but the part was so "on the nose" for Eve Arden twenty years ago that it was no challenge.

The second offer was for a comedy-mystery. It was wild and different, and Glenn and Brooks both felt it was the kind of thing that might be a hit on today's Broadway. I believed that with enough rewriting, it might work, and allowed myself to be tempted by "starring above the title" and by the charming and persuasive producer and director who flew out and took us to dinner to clinch the deal. The writer, whom I met later, I was more dubious about. It was his first "baby," and I sensed a reluctance to make any changes. What I didn't realize was that since my last appearance on Broadway, the Writers Guild had passed a ruling that the writer must have complete autonomy over the script, and not a word could be changed without his consent. Also he could be, and was, present at every rehearsal.

Meanwhile, before I left for New York, I had a personal call from George Abbott. He said, "I know I'm not going to change your mind, but I was curious to know why you turned down a part you're so perfect for."

I said that perhaps that was the trouble, and then mentioned that I'd always wanted to do a show for him and finished with, "Maybe we can work together sometime in the future."

George replied, "You'd better hurry up, honey, I'm ninety-five!" What a man!

When rehearsal started I still had hopes that what turned out to be the disaster of Broadway's '83 season, called *Moose Murders,* could be rescued by one of those Broadway wonder men who step into a show, know what is wrong, and fix it immediately. But as rehearsals got longer but no better, I began to feel we were doomed. It became a question of what or who went down the drain first. I won and was "allowed" to withdraw—and a very nice younger actress was hired to struggle through the unchanging rehearsals and step into the void of opening night, which was unfortunately also closing night.

Actually I got the best notices, as one of the critics claimed I was the lucky one not to have been there.

On my return home I got a call asking me to replace the actress in the now great hit *On Your Toes* while she took her vacation. But I'd had my fill of Broadway for a while.

However, as I was considering a TV movie, I got another offer for the Public Broadcasting movie of *Alice in Wonderland,* in which I was offered the part of the Queen of Hearts. When I saw the cast list I accepted immediately.

Kate Burton, Richard's daughter, would play Alice, and Richard Burton would play the White Knight. Maureen Stapleton and Colleen Dewhurst were cast as the White Queen and the Red Queen. The King of Hearts was Jimmy Coco, and my dear friend Donald O'Connor was to play the Mock Turtle. Kaye Ballard, my partner from "The Mothers-in-Law," was the Duchess, Austin Pendleton the White Rabbit, and André Gregory—the actor from the movie *My Dinner with André*—was the Mad Hatter. Fritz Weaver was the Caterpillar, Swen Swenson the Griffon, and Geoffrey Holder the Cheshire Cat. Who could resist that cast?

We had left New York shortly after the blizzard of '83 in February. We took a five-day Hawaiian vacation in Kauai, recently battered by a hurricane, and on our return I found that my book (this one) had been sold. We were back in New York to begin rehearsals for *Alice* in June.

It was good to see Colleen Dewhurst, to whom I'd presented the Sarah Siddons Award in Chicago, the year after I'd won mine. Maureen Stapleton, whom I'd always admired, greeted me with "I have a TL for you. Oh, you've probably heard this before." When I protested that I hadn't heard a real Trade Last (compliment) in years, she astounded me by saying that I was Woody Allen's favorite comedienne. Nothing could have surprised me more! The cast was filled out with dancers and singers from *On Your Toes* and *Brighton Beach Memoirs,* Neil Simon's newest play, which Brooks and I had enjoyed tremendously.

On my nights off we sampled some of New York's great restaurants, and Mary Jane Maricle, who'd been my "standby" in *Dolly* and whom we'd taken on tour in *Cactus Flower* and other plays, gave a party to which she'd invited our old friends from Auntie Mame, Isabelle Price and Dorothy Blackburn.

It was three weeks of pure enjoyment, and atoned for those endless rehearsals of the still talked-about *Moose Murders*.

CHAPTER
· 37 ·

The experience of *Moose Murders* had been even more traumatic for Brooks than for me. Unable to use his directorial skills to help, he was frustrated and generally stayed away from rehearsals. Then, with an exhausted, discouraged wife, who hadn't the energy to go out to dinner, he'd patiently fix us some food and then cue me before an early bed time. I worried about him, knowing the effect this kind of stress could have on his disease. But I was unable to detect it when he finally did take the first drink.

Before we went back to New York in June to film *Alice in Wonderland,* however, Doug, who'd been aware of his dad's problem for several years, took Brooks to lunch. After some small talk Doug said, "Dad, I know you've been drinking, and I want you to stop!" Doug's direct attack gave him the courage for his new battle against his old enemy.

He was making plans to enter the Riverside Hospital Alcoholic Unit on the advice of our family psychologist and friend, Dick Knowles, but he wanted to wait for the two weeks it would take me to film, in order to accompany me. Doug offered to take his place so that he could go into the hospital sooner. But Brooks feared that I would be upset, and that my concern might cause me to turn the project down. Doug agreed to wait for the two weeks.

On our return Brooks entered the hospital in the Valley, and, after a rocky start in which he said to his counselor, Barbara Likens, "I'm here to quit drinking but I don't want to hear about AA," he suddenly accepted the spiritual side completely. When he finished his stay in detox he continued to read his AA book, *One Day at a Time,* faithfully each morning. He attended the weekly meeting of his unit with the other men and women who'd gone through it with him. He also went to one of the many AA meetings held in Los Angeles, Beverly Hills, or the Valley each week. I accompanied him to this whenever he requested.

On Monday nights we went to the couples' meetings conducted by his counselor Barbara, which we both found fascinating and informative.

One day Brooks announced that he was going to do two paintings of London for me that I always hoped he'd do: the Queen's Band marching out of the gates in front of Buckingham Palace, and the Queen's Household Guard, parading behind Whitehall. He finished them both in an unusually short time.

I received an offer from Woody Allen to do a movie. I was surprised and delighted, and thought that perhaps Maureen Stapleton had been right. It was Brooks who suggested this time that we go to New York early and spend Christmas there, just the two of us, before I was due to start filming in early January. He finally admitted the reason he'd always dreaded the big fuss I'd made each year over Christmas. It was because it had contrasted so with the ones his family had had in the years after his father lost his business. Then the token gifts, given out of necessity, never matched the ones his peers took such pride in. Why had he never mentioned this before? I agreed that Christmas alone together this year would be wonderful.

He seemed so confident in his sobriety now and I joined enthusiastically in his plans. He wanted to celebrate perhaps in the snows of New England, an area we both loved. We studied the *New Yorker* to see what interesting plays were in New York theaters, and talked of old friends we'd see and places we'd go.

In the midst of this I discovered that Brooks was concerned about the possibility of a prostate operation. He decided to have the preliminary testing done before we left for New England and make arrangements for hospitalization when we returned from New York. After the testing was done he felt miserable and I postponed our trip for a couple of weeks.

I spoke with Jeff Kurland, the designer for Woody's picture, on the phone, and we agreed on colors and ideas. He decided he would get my measurements through Western Costume so he could start work. He said that Paul Huntley would be making my wig and could send someone to fit a wig cap so that he could begin too. By the end of the two weeks our plans were made again and we took the kids to dinner to say good-bye. It was a lovely evening, but Brooks complained of dizziness when he stood up to leave. We knew he hadn't had a drink, so I was concerned that the effects of the testing hadn't worn off; however, he seemed to recover quickly.

The morning before we were to leave for our vacation Brooks and I started out to do last-minute Christmas shopping. Suddenly he felt dizzy and ill. I made him sit at an outdoor table in a shopping plaza while I found a drugstore with some Bonine. In the huge underground garage he waited again while I searched frantically for the tiny new Prelude he'd just bought me. It took what seemed like hours to find it, and when Brooks said, "You drive, darling," I became really frightened. I adjusted the seat so that he was lying back comfortably and then said, "Brooks, I'm driving you to Dr. Giorgi's office—it's only two blocks away and I want her to see you." Brooks protested that she'd just put him in the hospital, but I told him I didn't care. After she'd made a few tests, Elsie said, "I need more information, and I want you to take him to the emergency entrance at Cedars of Sinai, where I can get results faster."

There Brooks was put in a wheelchair and I went to phone home and tell our housekeeper Ana what had happened. When I came back, Brooks was no longer where I'd left him and the nurse reported that he was taking a test, that the emergency area was filled, and it was impossible for me to be with my husband during the rest of the tests.

By the time I got Elsie's office on the phone and she called them back, at least an hour had gone by. I felt so helpless not knowing what was happening to him. When at last I found him he was extremely uncomfortable and cold. I called a nurse and asked for a warm blanket. My poor darling promptly threw up all over it. I got another and covered him, then went to see how long it would take to complete the tests and get a hospital room where he could be made comfortable. It was after 5 P.M. by the time he was in bed and Elsie had arranged for a night nurse from the registry.

During that night Brooks had a small stroke. It seemed to have affected his throat, so that he swallowed with difficulty, and one side of his mouth pulled down slightly. But he was feeling better, for which I was very grateful. Elsie had put a neurosurgeon on the case and they were to take a CAT scan a little later. The special day nurse, Edith, came on duty and struck up a great rapport with her patient and his family. Doug and Connie and I were with Brooks most of the day except when he slept. He seemed to make daily gains and later in the week he was doing crossword puzzles aloud with Doug and was beginning to complain (a good sign) about the orange-flavored

Jell-O, which was all he was allowed to swallow. We brought the Christmas cards that were arriving daily and tacked them on the wall where he could see them. I did manage to get the Jell-O changed to raspberry, which he regarded as an improvement. He also received his second chip from AA, which indicated six months of sobriety and which meant a great deal to him.

I received a message from Woody Allen's company asking if I could come back for only three days to fit my costume, now ready. I would then have time before they actually needed me for filming. I was torn between dreading to leave my husband for a moment and guilt over causing Woody any more delay. Brooks now took charge and insisted I must go and take Doug with me. He ordered that Doug must take the heavy tweed coat Brooks had bought in London and wool sweaters and mufflers because it was so cold now in New York.

Not until Dr. Giorgi and the neurosurgeon concurred that Brooks was doing very well and that I should go, certainly for the three days, did Doug make our plans.

We left on Monday, after telling Brooks that we'd be talking to him on our arrival at the Wyndham. Doug and I tried to keep each other's spirits up during the trip, but neither of us felt easy about leaving Brooks, in spite of his improvement.

When we had unpacked I put in a call to the hospital. Connie answered the phone. "Mom," she said, "there's been a little problem with Dad's swallowing and they think he may have pneumonia." I thought, Thank God he's in a hospital, where they always say they can't cure the common cold but can easily cure pneumonia.

Connie said, "Dad's reaching for the phone." My love was trying to tell me something, but I couldn't understand a word.

I said, "We'll be back tomorrow, darling, just rest and don't worry about anything but getting better." I talked to Connie once more, who said she would stay at the hospital with him, and then she said, "Dad wants the phone again." He was trying desperately to say something, but not a word could I understand. The frustration I felt then I hoped I would never feel again.

That night neither Doug nor I slept much. When I heard the phone ring in his room I would wait for him to give me any news, but if I asked he would reassure me that it was just a conversation with Carole, his wife.

In the morning I had my fittings with Jeff Kurland, and Paul Huntley, who had made the lovely wig. I was unable to confide my fears to the costumers, who were jubilant that everything was beautiful and fit perfectly, and told me how happy Woody would be and that he was already adding lines for me. I felt uneasily guilty, although I was praying for good news when I got back to the hotel.

Doug put in the call and it was then we learned that Dad was now in a coma. I was stunned. Not until much later did I learn that those late-night calls to Doug had been from Connie saying that she and the nurse were trying to keep Brooks awake, as he seemed to be slipping into the void of the coma.

I think Doug and I ate more out of concern for each other than any appetite and we packed our bags automatically. I asked my manager Glenn, who was in town on other business, to please arrange a meeting with Woody, who was unaware of our real problems. Woody was on location in Harlem and I got word that he would send a car to bring us there at five-thirty.

The hours dragged endlessly but finally the car arrived and drove us to a small church in a deserted area of Harlem. It was filled with technicians. The church was softly lit and the architecture beautiful and we knew what the camera would see. The altar was hidden from us for the moment by the camera and I could hear Mia's voice speaking lines. In a few minutes Woody came out to greet us and asked if we'd mind waiting until this shot was finished and he'd have time to talk to us while they moved the camera to another area. I said of course and he went back to finish the close-up of another actor. Mia came over to say hello and that she was so happy I'd be with them. I couldn't explain until finally Woody came back and I told him of the serious turn Brooks's illness had taken.

Woody said that he was so sorry and not to worry, that they were flexible and could wait, but I interrupted him. "Woody, it would be unfair of me to ask you to wait. I'm afraid you'll have to replace me. This is a marriage of thirty-five years, and there's no way I could turn my back and leave him now."

Woody was so understanding, and Doug and I left, grateful that we'd been able to explain personally. We had our reservations for the morning. Glenn called and said, "You won't be getting any more calls from the hospital tonight, so I've gotten you tickets for the theater to try to occupy your minds for a while at least. So Doug and I went to see a musical that we might have enjoyed under other circumstances, but we were too exhausted to keep our eyes open for more than moments at at time.

Doug told me later that in one of these periods of sleep he'd had a vivid dream in which his dad came to him, surrounded by light, and said, "Good-bye, Doug, I love you. Take care of Mom."

After a night of very little rest Doug got some sleep on the plane. The stewardesses, although not knowing what caused his exhaustion, refused to wake him, and kept his dinner warm.

We took our luggage home and left for the hospital, where Brooks was in intensive care, words that struck terror in my heart, and a reality even harder to face. In one of the small rooms that opened on a large central room where nurses sat monitoring the patients, I found my darling. There was a respirator in his mouth, his eyes were taped closed to keep dust out. There were IVs in his veins, and red and green lights flashed signals to someone, but he looked peaceful, as he did when he slept. Edith, his special nurse, was with him. She wasn't able to tell us much. I put my arm around him, between the tubes, and spoke into his ear. I told him that Doug and I were there and we were sure he was going to be all right, that Doug had talked to Liza in Spain and she'd sent her love and prayers for his recovery. Then Doug spoke in his ear all the things we were trying desperately to believe. It seemed so strange to get no response or even movement from our vital, active Brooks.

Leaving reluctantly, we found Connie in the hall, where she'd spent the two nights since we'd left, on a couch nearby. Then Dr. Giorgi found us and told us what she could, and mentioned more CAT scans and tests to be taken. That night Liza arrived from Spain. Doug was trying to contact Duncan through the Red Cross. I'd had a letter from him with papers for me to sign, saying, "At last I'm going to war," and I knew that his unit was due to replace the Marines in the bombed headquarters at Beirut. Our days revolved around our morning and afternoon visits to Brooks. And Liza, Connie, Doug, and I had our own moments to tell him of our love and need for him, to hold his hands and talk to his nurse of responses we thought we noted and how sure we were that he heard us. Elsie Giorgi, too, was seeing him morning and night, and, afterward, we always conferred with her. But daily the news was less encouraging. Christmas came and went unnoticed. Duncan arrived from Beirut and was shocked, I'm sure, in spite of recent familiarity with death, to see his father lying so helpless.

I thought of a remark I'd made to Doug a month or so before, right after I'd sold this book. "Life is full of miracles, Doug, but they're not always the ones we pray for." Now I thought, It is a miracle, the whole family together after all these years. But it wasn't the miracle we were praying for.

The days went by. Duncan went back to Beirut and the shooting. I tried to persuade Liza to return to Spain, where Toñete and America waited with Antonio. Like me, she was waiting for that miracle, but finally she left.

A time came when Brooks moved his head and his feet and I frantically called Elsie's office to report. She said, "Now don't get too excited. Let me speak to the floor nurse," and my heart sank. Later she explained he'd been given a drug to see if it would stimulate action.

Doug said, "Mom, I can't bear to see your spirits constantly rise and fall again like that. Let's go to Elsie's office and look at that last CAT scan." So we made an appointment. Elsie explained that the area that had been flooded with blood during the stroke covered the entire brain stem, which controlled all his motor responses. Even if he should recover, he would never be the Brooks we knew, she said. "Keep your wonderful memories of him," she urged. I'd lost many pounds so far, and she was beginning to worry about her other patient.

That afternoon at the hospital I held Brooks's hand for three hours. His eyes were uncovered and the yellow-green pools with their black fringes were bottomless and empty, and I knew the spirit I loved was no longer there. I also knew that Elsie was right when she said, "Keep your memories."

I thought of Brooks's attempt only a few months before to make a living will, not then legal in California, and saying, "I don't ever want to be a vegetable." A life like that was not for my Brooks. So now I kissed him good-bye and whispered my release into those deaf ears and I went home to wait.

But Brooks was stronger than either of us had known. His heart had the strength of a lion and he lived on. Each day I came out on our lawn and saw the garden and pergola we'd created and then my eyes would be drawn inexorably down to the hospital building where he lay, subjected to indignities I could no longer stand to know, and I would go back into the house and call Edith and ask, "Any change?"

"None, Mrs. West."

She told me how doctors came from other parts of the hospital, not able to believe that Brooks had gone from intensive care to a private room, and after the respirator had been removed had gone on breathing room air. He was absorbing very little food, but his skin showed no deterioration. No one understood why.

At night I called the male nurse who shaved and bathed him and trimmed his hair. After each session on the phone I cried out my grief. I went to bed each night at eight o'clock and read until my eyes couldn't stay open. I'd wake around three or four to cry a little more and then sleep until five or six. During the whole time I never took as much as an aspirin or a sleeping pill. Doug and Connie had to go back to work but called me every day, and I talked to Liza in Spain.

I received a letter from Woody Allen:

> Dear Eve—
>
> I hope everything is not going too badly for you and your family. Naturally we were all wrecked that 1) you had this sudden problem 2) you couldn't be in the movie.
>
> Every time I mentioned to anyone that you were in the film their eyes lit up, from the actors, to the crew, to the studio heads. People (like Mia) going around muttering, "I'm going to be in a movie with Eve Arden." All this with disbelief. Perhaps one day it will happen. At least I had the chance to meet you—you've made me laugh so many times—and in the best way. Oh well, best with your troubles and let's hope the future will lighten up. Regards to your son.
>
> Best again—
>
> Woody—(Mia too)

Woody's letter, arriving in the darkest days of my life, lifted my spirits with its loving warmth. I awakened myself from my apathy and began a search to find a small Westie, which Brooks and I had planned to get as a replacement for our Chelsea. She was fifteen when she left us. Now I felt the need for a warm little friend with a loving disposition to let me know I was still living. Glenn located a West Highland breeder with four-month-old pups, and we went out to Malibu, where Angus, as I called him, picked me. It was as if he was meant to be a comfort. He was a happy, playful pup who housebroke himself, played with his toys on the lawn like a kitten, and was never heard from after being put to bed.

It was now February, and one day I said to Edith, "I can't stand it any longer, I'm coming down this afternoon to see him." Edith asked me to please wait.

"Today for the first time I sense a change in him. Tomorrow, if there is nothing else, come down."

On the following day, February 7, he left us. I had prayed so much in two different directions. Now one prayer had been answered, and all I could feel was numbness.

My daughter-in-law helped. She said, "Whatever you decide to do, do it right away or it will all become more difficult." I thought of how Brooks and I had talked about people celebrating lives, rather than deaths, so I roused myself and began to call friends. "Please come to a celebration of Brooks's life—and no tears or flowers," I asked.

From 1 P.M. to 8:30 P.M. almost ninety people arrived. There was a buffet and people shared memories of Brooks: his love of words and puns, jokes he'd told, and funny things they remembered.

Upstairs in his studio, there were over fifty of his paintings. Most of the unit I'd invited from the hospital were surprised to learn he'd painted. Outside on the lawn, Angus romped and was petted and admired. It was a day that I knew Brooks would have loved.

Then Brooks's AA sponsor John, a man he'd greatly admired, took me aside and said, "You know, Mrs. West, Brooks's unit had been praying for his recovery at every meeting since he became ill. Last Tuesday night at seven forty-five we all joined hands and prayed for his quick release. Five minutes later he died." A miracle? I believe it.

The next day I called Brooks's family in Austin and told them about the celebration. I said, "I know it would comfort you to have a church ceremony for Brooks, and I'm sure if you keep it one he would enjoy, he'd be happy to be remembered by his Austin friends, and above all his family." His older brother Guy said he would make the plans whenever I wished. Doug said, "Mom, don't push yourself too much," so I said to give me a week, but instead of resting I flew to Berkeley to be with my friend Connie Raffetto, who'd been through a small operation, and I stayed five days.

On my return I picked my daughter Connie up and we flew to Austin for the ceremony. Doug had to work and couldn't go with us, and I was sorry he missed it. The church was full of people who'd known and loved Brooks. One woman shared a letter with me he'd written her when her husband died suddenly while she and Brooks were appearing in a local show together. It had been such a dear letter that she had kept it all these years. A friend of Guy's, now an Austin critic, said he'd always admired Brooks, who was younger than he, because Brooks had the gumption not to wear a tie and wore, instead, an ascot. Laughter filled the church several times during the ceremony, and I thought how Brooks would have loved that. Later Guy and Martha's home was full of young nieces and nephews and many of their beautiful children. They talked about how they'd adored Uncle Brooks and wished their own children could have known him. I watched the whole family enfold Connie in love and make her their own. It was a wonderfully healing night for both of us.

Now I faced the hardest part that lay ahead—missing every day the warmth of his physical presence and his reassuring love. But I had my children and friends to help me find my way, and the wonderful memories of the full life we'd shared.

I hoped I'd find meaningful work to do when I felt ready. I even had a letter from Woody saying that he felt I "owed them one," how kind! I don't understand everything that has happened in my life, but I am grateful for the many miracles and even, I suppose, will someday be grateful for the pain. At least I will better understand others' pain and perhaps be able to contribute something worthwhile to this sad and wonderful world.

INDEX

Abbott, George, 268
Absurd Person Singular, 256–257
Ackerman, Eleanor, 257
Ackerman, Harry, 72, 197
Aherne, Brian, 189
Albert, Prince of Monaco, 258
Alda, Alan, 71
Alda, Robert, 71
Aldrich, Richard, 54
Aldrin, Edwin "Buzz," 219
Alexander the Great, Eve's sculpture
    of, 177–178
Alice, Princess of England, 191
Alice in Wonderland, 269, 271
All About Eve, 243
Allen, Joe, 243
Allen, Woody, 272, 273–274, 278
Amster, Ann, 122, 170
    death of, 226–229
    Eve's friendship with, 31, 83–85,
        208, 213
    Eve's travels with, 220–225
    family visits to, 72, 83–85, 142,
        207
Amster, Mary, 222, 227–229
Amster, Stanley, 170, 220
    death of, 213
    Eve's friendship with, 31, 37,
        83–85, 208
    family visits to, 72, 83–85, 142,
        207
Amster, Susan, 226–229
Ana (housekeeper), 273
Anatomy of a Murder, 132
Anderson, Loni, 258
Angel (servant), 141

Applause, 238, 240–248
April Love, 116
Arden, Elizabeth, 26
Arden, Eve (Eunice Quedens):
    antiques collected by, 46, 125, 188
    articles written by, 55–57
    Bergen's marriage to, 45–46
    childhood acting experiences of, 2,
        8, 11
    critics' reviews of, 27, 134–135
    early acting career of, in California,
        12–22
    early acting career of, in New
        York, 22–36
    father rejected by, 2
    Foster Parents children of, 64, 88,
        148
    health problems of, 261–262,
        267–268
    home life of, 92–124
    houses of, 45–46, 48, 90–99,
        110–111, 124, 158, 187–188,
        210, 227
    mother's death and, 37–39, 44
    movie career of, 39–44, 48–50,
        52–54, 60–62, 65–66, 68–70, 72,
        113, 132, 260–263, 265, 274–275
    overseas travels of, 87–88,
        119–120, 140–207, 218–219, 268
    pets and farm animals of, 42,
        92–95, 101–102, 104, 105–106,
        107–110, 113–114, 122–124,
        129–130, 194, 278
    pregnancy and chiildbearing of, 90,
        96–98
    press agents of, 75

281

Arden, Eve (continued)
  psychoanalysis of, 63–64
  return to theater of, 124–131,
    209–210, 220, 240–248, 251, 259
  romances of, 20, 30–31, 34, 39, 45
  romantic involvement feared by,
    39, 45, 67, 77, 78
  Sarah Siddons Award of, 215–216
  school days of, 3–11
  sculpting as interest of, 177–178,
    179
  as stage name, 26
  television career of, 78–80, 89–90,
    101, 121, 209, 214–217, 250,
    257, 269
  theater as love of, 2, 8, 54, 65, 75
  West's marriage to, 83–87
Armstrong, Neil, 219
Arnaz, Desi, 42, 214, 216, 217
Arnstein, Nicky, 32
Auerbach, Oscar, 90, 96
Auntie Mame, 127, 259
Aurora (midwife), 233–235, 256
Averback, Dorothy, 266
Averback, Hy, 266
Ayckbourn, Alan, 256
Azcona, America, 257, 265
  birth of, 252–253, 255
  christening of, 256
Azcona, Antonio, 265
  Liza's marriage to, 220–224
Azcona, Antonio, Jr. (Toñete), 265
  birth of, 229–236, 252
  childhood of, 237–239
Azcona, Cuqui, 223, 233–234, 238
Azcona, Elvira, 222–223, 235
Azcona, Estefania, 223
Azcona, Juaquin, 222–223, 235
Azcona, Leito, 223
Azcona, Leo, 222, 256
Azcona, Letitia, 223
Azcona, Liza West, see West, Liza
Azcona, Mama and Papa, 222, 235
Azcona, Marisa, 222, 256

Bacall, Lauren, 243
Bacon, Lloyd, 50
Balanchine, George, 26

Ball, Lucille, 41, 42, 44, 214
Ballard, Kay, 214–215, 226, 266, 269
Bandbox Repertory Company, 22
Bankhead, Tallulah, 58
Banton, Travis, 46
Barefoot in the Park, 167, 214
Barry, Gene, 121
Barton, Earl, 134
Bauldauf, Pat, 261, 263
Beatles, 198
Beatty, Warren, 250
Bedtime Story, 53
Beekman Place, 124, 209, 237
Behrman, Sam, 65
Benchley, Nat, 59
Benchley, Robert, 27
  acting career of, 60–61
  Eve's friendship with, 54, 59,
    68–69
Bennett, Joan, 53, 197
Bergen, Edward (Ned):
  Eve's divorce from, 71
  Eve's marriage to, 45–46
  military service of, 59
Bergman, Ingrid, 76
Berle, Milton, 35
Bernard, Sandy, 259
Billie Burke's Ziegfeld Follies, 22, 27–33,
    35–36
Biography, 65
Birdwell, Russell, 75
Blackburn, Dorothy, 270
Blitzstein, Mark, 34
Blythe, Ann, 65
Boone, Pat, 116
Borden, Dr., 114
Born Yesterday, 121
Bowes, Major, 29
Boy in the Bubble, The, 250
Braverman, Dr., 261–262
Brian, David, 67
Brice, Fanny, 26, 28, 32–33, 35, 39,
    259
Bridges, Lloyd, 218
Brighton Beach Memoirs, 269
Brisson, Freddie, 127
Brown, John Mason, 54
Brynner, Yul, 76

Buchanan, Alice, 16–19, 29, 37, 38, 45, 84
Buck (caretaker), 94, 101, 109
Burch, Pat, 265
Burke, Billie, 22
Burton, Kate, 269
Burton, Richard, 188, 269
Burton-on-the-Water, England, Eve's trip to, 203
Butterflies Are Free, 213, 227

Cabaret, 244
Cactus Flower, 216, 270
Caesar, Sid, 265
Cannes, France, Eve's trip to, 201
Canova, Judy, 29
Carnarvon, George Herbert, Lord, 196
Carnarvon, Tilli Losch, Lady, 196, 197
Caroline, Princess of Monaco, 258
Carr, Allen, 250, 256–257
Carroll, Bob, 214, 266
Carson, Jack, 41, 65, 243
Cavett, Dick, 259
Challinor, Ron, 249
Champion, Gower, 210, 211
Chandler, Jeff, 72, 78
Channing, Carol, 42, 134, 210, 215, 258
Channing, Stockard, 250, 256–257
Charles (Cuqui Azcona's husband), 238
Chartres, France, Eve's trip to, 204
Chase, Chevy, 260, 263
Cherry Orchard, The, 190
Child Is Born, A, 49
China, Eve's trip to, 268
Chipping Norton, England, Eve's trip to, 203
Cilento, Diane, 215
Cino (sculptor), 177–178, 179
Clift, Montgomery, 76
Coates, Carole, 257
Cobra, 13
Coco, Jimmy, 269
Cohn, Harry, 61
Collins, Michael, 219

Colman, Ronald, 40, 91, 265
Columbia Broadcasting System (CBS), 71, 72, 122, 124, 207, 252
Columbia Studios, 61
Comrade X, 17, 52
Conelli, Judi, 249
Connery, Sean, 184, 215, 258
Conway, Tom, 67
Cooper, Leo, 1
Coppet, Switzerland, Eve's trip to, 239–240
Corey, Wendell, 70
Cover Girl, 61
Cradle Snatchers, The, 54
Crawford, Christina, 66
Crawford, Christopher, 66
Crawford, Joan, 77, 125
    Academy Award won by, 65
    children adopted by, 60, 66
Crenna, Penni, 266, 267
Crenna, Richard, 72, 79, 121, 252, 266, 267
Critic's Choice, 257
Croft, Mary Jane, 72, 266
Cronkite, Kathy, 208
Cronkite, Mr. and Mrs. Walter, 208
Crosby, Bing, 130
Crouse, Russel, 35
Cummings, Constance, 189
Curtiz, Michael, 65

Daily Variety, 135
Darin, Bobby, 209
Davis, Bette, 68, 119, 134–135, 243
Davis, Dick, 266, 267
Davis, Madelyn, 214, 266
Davis, Roger, 32–33, 38
Day, Doris, 72
Day at the Circus, A, 48
Deacon, Richard, 240, 266
de Costa, Morton, 127
de Havilland, Olivia, 68
Denton, Walter, 72
Dewhurst, Colleen, 269
Dietrich, Marlene, 53, 135
Dinner With André, 269
di Spinola, Marchese, 157–161, 183
Doughgirls, 62

Douglas, Melvyn, 54
Douglas, Mike, 258
Duff, Howard, 67
Duffy, Henry, 15, 17, 49, 72
Duke, Vernon, 35
Dulcy, 11–12, 77
Dulo, Jane, 240, 266
Dumont, Margaret, 48
Duntley family, 100

Earl (gardener), 118, 209
Ebsen, Buddy, 26
Ebsen, Vilma, 26
Edith (nurse), 273, 276
Ellington, Duke, 133
Elsie (Eve's aunt), 5–7, 9, 23, 31
Emery, John, 197
Emmy Award, 89
Ernst, Dolores, 249
"Eve Arden Show, The," 122, 124

Fabray, Nanette, 54
Fabulous Las Vegas, 135
Farrow, John, 49
Ferrer, Mel, 65
Fielding, Jerry, 134
Fields, Dorothy, 54
Fields, Herb, 54
Fiji, Eve's trip to, 240–241
Fisher, Carrie, 260
Flamingo Road, 66
Florence, Italy, Eve's trip to, 184–185
Fogel, Jerry, 214
Fontaine, Joan, 189
Fontanne, Lynn, 11, 76–77
Formentor, Spain, Eve's trip to, 232
Fortune, The, 250
Francis, Kay, 49
Franco, Francisco, 254
French, Eleanor, 107–108
Freund, Papa, 98
Froman, Jane, 26
From Mao to Mozart, 266

Gable, Clark, 16–17, 52
Gabor, Zsa Zsa, 53, 135, 203
Garbo, Greta, 58
Gardner, Ava, 67–68

Garland, Judy, 52–53
Garmisch-Partenkirchen, Germany,
  Eve's trip to, 218
Gazzara, Ben, 132, 209
Gelbart, Larry, 267
Gelbart, Pat, 267
General Foods, 197
George (gardener), 94, 111, 118
George, Gladys, 49–50
Georgy Girl, 190
Gershwin, Ira, 35
Gertrude (cook), 43
Giampiero (gardener), 176, 178, 184
Giorgi, Elsie, 267, 273, 276, 278
Giovanni, Gianni, 185–186, 212, 258
Golden Arrow, 189
Goldman, Harold, 190–191, 201
Goldman, Sadie, 190–191, 201
Goldwyn, Sam, 68
Goodbye Charlie, 237
Goodbye My Fancy, 77, 125
Goodman, Dodie, 265
Gordon, Billy, 243
Gordon, Gale, 72, 79, 91, 252, 266
Gordon, Max, 47
Gordon, Ruth, 126
Grable, Betty, 213
Grade, Lew, 191
Graham, Sheilah, 190
Grant, Cary, 69
Grease, 250, 259
Grease II, 265
Great Sebastian, The, 76
Greece, Eve's trip to, 218
Gregory, Andre, 269
Grey, Joel, 244
Grindelwald, Switzerland, Eve's trip
  to, 239
Gruyères, Switzerland, Eve's trip to,
  239

Hallauer, Dr., 227–228
Hamilton, Lady Emma, 146
Hamilton, Murray, 132
Hammerstein, Oscar, 46–47
Hammond, Percy, 27
Hard Day's Night, A, 198
Harlow, Jean, 42–43

Harper's Bazaar, 58
Harrison, Rex, 125
Harvey, Laurence, 190
Having a Wonderful Time, 44
Hayworth, Rita, 61
Head, Edith, 258
Hellinger, Mark, 62
Hello Dolly!, 42, 210–213, 215, 258
Henderson, Marge, 210, 251
Henry IV, 203
Hepburn, Katharine, 41
Here Today, 71, 85, 125, 126
Hirschfeld, Al, 55
Holder, Geoffrey, 269
Holliday, Judy, 121
Holliman, Earl, 261
Hollywood Reporter, 135
Holm, Eleanor, 32
Hope, Bob, 35, 36, 59, 130
Hopper, Hedda, 75
Horton, Edward Everett, 39, 43
House Beautiful, 46
Howard, Eugene, 26
Howard, Willie, 26
Howe, Dorothy, 84
Hoyt, John, 65
Huntley, Paul, 272, 273
Hussey, Ruth, 209
Hutcherson, Dr., 267

Ida E. (Ann Amster's mother), 220–225
Ile de France, 88, 89
"I Love Lucy," 42
I Ought to Be In Pictures, 259
Isabel (housekeeper), 231, 234
"It Gives Me Great Pleasure," 122

"Jack Paar Show," 139
Joan of Lorraine, 76
John Paul Jones, 119
John XXIII, Pope, Eve's audience with, 178
Jones, Jennifer, 67
Josefina (servant), 141
Josephine, Empress of France, 146
Julio (Liza's friend), 231

Kaiser Aluminum, 197
Kaltenborn, H. V., 58
Kanin, Fay, 184
Kanin, Garson, 126
Kanin, Mike, 184
Kaufman, Harry, 25, 30
Kaye, Danny, 54, 58–59, 66, 68, 258
Keeler, Christine, 190
Kelly, Gene, 61
Kennedy, Jacqueline, 135
Kennedy, John F., 202–203
Kern, Jerome, 46–47
Kerr, Walter, 257
Kid from Brooklyn, The, 68
Kimbrough, Emily, 122
Knowles, Dick, 271
Knox, Alexander, 197
Kruger, Otto, 61
Kurland, Jeff, 272, 273

La Cava, Gregory, 41–42
Ladd, Alan, 100
Ladd, Sue, 100
Lady Takes a Sailor, The, 72
Lady Wants Mink, The, 209
Lamarr, Hedy, 52
Landesburgh, Walter, 154–155, 161, 202
Last of the Duanes, 53
Lawrence, Gertrude, 47, 54, 124–125
Lawrence of Arabia, 188
Leeds, Andrea, 41–42
Leffler, Dottie, 207–208
Lerner, Jan, 251
Let's Face It! (movie), 59
Let's Face It! (play), 54–55, 58–59, 258
Lewis, Al, 72, 113
Lewis, Cathy, 87
Lewis, Elliot, 266
Liberace, 113
Likens, Barbara, 271–272
Lillie, Bea, 28–29
Lindsay, Howard, 35
Lisbon, Portugal, Eve's trip to, 206
Little, Rich, 258
Little Me, 259–260
Lizarbe, Dr., 231–235, 256

Lo and Behold, 22
London, England, Eve's trips to, 187–204, 221, 237–238
Loren, Sophia, 265
Los Angeles Herald Examiner, 135
Losch, Tilli, Lady Carnavon, 196, 197
Louis, Jean, 68, 258
"Love Boat," 257
Lower-Slaughter, England, Eve's trip to, 203
Lubitsch, Ernst, 54
Luce, Clare Booth, 45
Luden, Allen, 196
Luft, Joey, 53
Luft, Lorna, 53
Luft, Sid, 53
Luisa (cook), 169
Lunt, Alfred, 76–77
Lurie, Lou, 128–129
Luxembourg, Eve's trip to, 218

McCann, Bill, 90–91, 101
McClellan, Dad, 11
McGuire, Dorothy, 65
Mackie, Bob, 258
MacLaine, Shirley, 134
McLanahan, Rue, 257
McMartin, John, 256
McMillan, Gloria, 72, 79, 266
McMurray, Fred, 44
McRae, Gordon, 139
McRae, Sheila, 139
Mahar, Joe, 260
"Man from U.N.C.L.E., The," 209
Manoff, Dinah, 259
Manpower, 53
March, Fredric, 53
Margaret, Princess of England, 191
Maria (Liza's friend), 231
Maricle, Mary Jane, 270
Marriage-Go-Round, 124
Marsac, Maurice, 72, 267
Marsac, Melanie, 267
Marshall, Everett, 26
Marshall, Herbert, 40
Martin, Mary, 47
Martin, Olavee, 218

Martin, Ross, 218
Marx, Groucho, 48–49
Marx, Harpo, 49
Marx Brothers, 48–49
Mary Mary, 190
"M*A*S*H," 267
"Maude," 250
Maxwell, Elsa, 28
Mearns, Ted, 159
Melcher, Marty, 72
Menjou, Adolphe, 41
Mercouri, Merlina, 135
Merrick, David, 210, 212–213
Merry Roosters Panto, 199
Merry Widow, The, 245, 249
Mildred Pierce, 65, 68
Milland, Ray, 192
Miller, Ann, 41, 42, 43, 44
Miller, Sid, 134, 135
Mills, Hayley, 189
Mills, Juliet, 189
Minelli, Liza, 53
Minelli, Vincente, 35, 52
Montelimar, France, Eve's trip to, 201
Montgomery, George, 53
Moose Murders, 268, 270, 271
More, Kenneth, 203
Morgan, Dennis, 72
Morgan, James, 121
Morgan, Jane, 72, 79–80
Mori, Dr., 185
Morrell, Barbara, 172, 179
Moses, Anna Mary (Grandma), 85, 86
Most Marvelous News, The, 251–252
"Mothers-in-Law, The," 214–217
Murphy, Audie, 130
Murrow, Edward R., 58, 74–75
My Dream Is Yours, 72
My Fair Lady, 125
"My Friend Irma," 87
My Reputation, 61–62

Naples, Italy, Eve's trip to, 144–150
Napoleon I, Emperor of France, 146
National Education Association (NEA), 79
National Geographic, 87

National Velvet, 66
Natural Ingredients, 124
Nazarre, Portugal, Eve's trip to, 205
Nelson, Ed, 257
Nelson, Lord Horatio, 146
Nesbitt, Kathleen, 125
Newsweek, 254
Newton-John, Olivia, 250, 251
New Yorker, 27, 85, 272
New York Herald Tribune, 55
Nicholson, Jack, 250
Night and Day, 69
Night of 100 Stars, 188, 203
Niven, David, 46
Nixon, Marni, 214
Nixon, Richard M., 253

Oberon, Merle, 40, 54
Obidos, Portugal, Eve's trip to,
    205–206
Obliging Young Lady, 53
O'Brien, Eddie, 53
O'Connell, Arthur, 132
O'Connor, Donald, 218, 259, 269
O'Connor, Gloria, 218
Oh! Doctor, 39
Olivier, Lord Laurence, 188, 189,
    190, 203
Olympic Airlines, 218
Onassis, Aristotle, 235
One Day at a Time, 271
One for the Book, 70
One Man's Family, 62
One Touch of Venus, 67
On Your Toes, 268, 269
Osmond, Donny, 258
Othello, 203
O'Toole, Peter, 188
Our Miss Brooks (movie), 113
"Our Miss Brooks" (radio show), 72,
    78
"Our Miss Brooks" (television show),
    42, 97, 121–122, 207
    cast of, 78–80, 121
    Emmy award won by, 89–90
    shooting schedule for, 101
    syndication of, 121
Over Twenty-One, 76, 77, 126

Paglia, Iole, 159, 178
Paley, William, 71
Palma, Mallorca:
    Eve's trips to, 229–236, 238
    Liza's wedding in, 222–224
Pan-Americana, 60
Parade, 34
Paramount Studios, 44
Paris, France, Eve's trip to, 218
Parker, Cubby, 20–21
Parker, Dorothy, 27
Parker, Eleanor, 70
Patrick, Gail, 41
Peck, Gregory, 65, 66
Peck, Greta, 65, 66
Pendleton, Austin, 269
Pickens, Slim, 258
Piera (teacher), 169
Pirates of Penzance, The, 266
Pisa, Italy, Eve's trip to, 181
Pitts, ZaSu, 59
Pius XII, Pope, 178
Pompeii, Italy, Eve's trip to, 147
Ponti, Carlo, 265
Porter, Cole, 54–55, 69
Porter, Don, 113
Portofino, Italy, Eve's trip to,
    181–183
Positano, Italy, Eve's trips to,
    172–176, 224
Preminger, Otto, 132, 133
Price, Isabelle, 270

Quedens, Eunice, *see* Arden,
    Eve
Quedens, Lucille:
    acting career of, 1
    business career of, 1–2
    death of, 37–39
    Eve's relationship with, 1–6, 9–10,
        20, 23, 33–34
Quillen, Al, 72

Raffetto, Connie, 119
    Eve's correspondence with,
        167–170
    Eve's friendship with, 62, 71, 256,
        279

Raffetto, Mike, 119
Eve's friendship with, 62, 256
Raffetto, Pam, 199, 217
Rainer, Luise, 203
Ramos, Antonio, 223
Rapallo, Italy, Eve's trip to, 181,
182
Rash, Maggie, 263
Rash, Steve, 260
Reagan, Ronald, 70
Redgrave, Lynn, 190
Redgrave, Sir Michael, 190
Redgrave, Vanessa, 190
Remick, Lee, 132, 133
Revere, Anne, 65–66
Rice-Davies, Mandy, 190
RKO studios, 41, 44, 60–61
Roache, Viola, 84, 125–126
Road to Rome, The, 70, 75
Robert (cook), 43
Robinson, Hubbell, 72
Rockwell, Betts, 266
Rockwell, Robert, 78, 121, 266
Rogers, Ginger, 41, 42, 43, 44
Roman Spring of Mrs. Stone, The, 153
Rome, Italy, Eve's trip to, 150–184
Rose, Billy, 32
Rose, David, 52
Rose, Glenn:
as Eve's friend, 75, 104, 215, 275,
278
as Eve's manager, 75, 134, 209,
215, 218, 238, 243, 246, 275
Rashomon, 184
Rosie (nurse), 193
Rudley, Herb, 267
Rudley, Marilyn, 267
Ruman, Sig, 65
"Run for Your Life," 209
Russell, Jane, 102
Russell, Rosalind, 99, 127
Rutherford, Dame Margaret, 190,
197

Salzburg, Austria, Eve's trip to, 202
San Francisco Examiner, 16
San Frutuoso, Italy, 182–183

Santa Margherita, Italy, Eve's trip to,
181
Santander, Spain, Eve's trip to,
204
Saturday Night Fever, 250
Savo, Jimmy, 34
Schweitzer, Albert, 177
Scott, George, 132
Scott, Zachary, 65, 69, 196
Scottie (nurse), 193–194
Seagull, The, 190
Sellers, Peter, 197
Selznick, David, 67
Seville, Spain, Eve's trip to, 206–
207
Sharif, Omar, 203
She Knew All the Answers, 53
Shenson, Walter, 197–198
Sheridan, Ann, 62, 69, 78
Sherwood, Robert, 70, 76
Shubert, Lee, 22, 26, 32, 34
Shurr, Louis, 26
Sarah Siddons Award, 215–216
Sillman, Leonard, 22
Simon, Neil, 167, 269
Sinatra, Frank, 68
Single Indiscretion, A, 260–263
Smith, Alexis, 62, 69
Smith, C. Aubrey, 46
Smith, Len, 72
Smith, Maggie, 190
Smith, Rex, 16, 18, 29
Soldatenkov, Principessa, 153, 154,
160, 161
Speck, Richard, 211
Stage Door, 41–42, 49
Stanton, Frank, 72
Stanwyck, Barbara, 61
Stapleton, Maureen, 269, 272
Steinbeck, Elaine, 124, 172, 196–197,
202
Steinbeck, John, 124, 172, 196–197,
202
Stern, Isaac, 266
Stewart, Jimmy, 132, 133
Stow-on-the-Wood, England, Eve's
trip to, 203

Sullivan, Barry, 65, 75, 218
Swenson, Helen, 99, 103, 111, 112, 131, 141, 170
Swenson, Swen, 269
Sydney, Australia, Eve's trip to, 241–249

Talley family, 100
Taming of the Shrew, The, 76
Taylor, Elizabeth, 66, 188, 189
Tea for Two, 72
Tempi Duri (boatman), 182
Terry, Phil, 60
Tex (foreman), 100, 101
Theater Guild, 34
There Shall Be No Night, 76
Thorn, Bert, 125–126
Three Husbands, 77
Time, 254
Tone, Franchot, 53
Tony Awards, 258
Travolta, John, 250
Turkey, Eve's trip to, 218
Two for the Show, 214

Uncle Vanya, 190
Under Papa's Picture, 220, 237
Under the Rainbow, 260–263
Unfaithful, The, 69
Universal Studios, 39, 40, 44, 196
Upper-Slaughter, England, Eve's trip to, 203

Valkyrie, The, 214–215
Vallee, Rudy, 244
Vance, Vivien, 54
Vaughn, Robert, 209
Venice, Italy, Eve's trips to, 185–186, 258
Very Cold for October (formerly *Very Warm for May*), 46–47
Vicenta, Tía, 223, 235
Victoria, Queen of England, 191
Villa Eva, Rome, 154–161, 202
Vitznau, Switzerland, Eve's trip to, 238
Voice of the Turtle, 70

Wald, Jerry, 69
Walker, Robert, 67
Walley, Deborah, 214
Ward, George, 91–92
Warner, Jack, 62, 69
Warner Brothers, 49, 61, 62, 65, 68, 72, 113
Washington, George, 177
Weaver, Fritz, 269
Welch, Joseph, 133
Welles, Orson, 61, 180
West, Brooks:
    acting career of, 76, 124–126, 128, 132, 209–210, 216, 220, 240–249, 259
    children's relationship with, 86–87, 273–278
    drinking problem of, 106–107, 237, 250–252, 271
    Eve's first meeting with, 75–77
    Eve's marriage to, 83–87
    illness and death of, 272–279
    paintings by, 175, 184, 188, 237, 256, 272
West, Carole Coates, 257
West, Connie, 213, 220, 226, 257, 265
    adoption of, 71
    childhood of, 73, 84, 86, 92–95, 123, 200, 212
    as clothes designer, 258
    European tour of, 140–207
    father's relationship with, 86–87, 273–278
    horsemanship of, 116–117, 209
    trip to Greece of, 218
West, Dame Rebecca, 190
West, Douglas Brooks, 265
    birth of, 97–98
    childhood of, 106, 111–112, 211, 216
    European tour of, 140–207
    marriage of, 257
    parents' relationship with, 271, 273–278
West, Duncan Paris:
    acting debut of, 216–217

West, Duncan Paris (*continued*)
  adoption of, 88
  army career of, 226, 276–277
  childhood of, 111–112, 199–200,
    210, 216, 226
  European tour of, 140–207
  marriage of, 257
West, Guy, 279
West, Liza (Liza West Azcona), 208,
  213, 257, 276
  adoption of, 60, 62–63
  America's birth and, 252–253
  Antonio Jr.'s birth and, 229–236
  childhood of, 66, 70, 73, 83, 84,
    86, 92–95, 99, 115–118
  European tour of, 140–207
  marriage of, 220–224
  trip to Switzerland of, 239–
    240

Westhaven, Hidden Valley, Calif.,
  92–99, 110–111, 124, 210, 226,
  251, 265
West Side Story, 188
Whitney, Liz, 59
Widmark, Richard, 209
Williams, Emlyn, 77
Wilson, Marie, 87
Winters, Dale, 15
Women, The, 45
Women in the Wind, 49
Wonderful Town, 209
Wyman, Jane, 62, 72

Young, Loretta, 46, 53, 135
Young, Robert, 77

Ziegfeld Girl, 52